Aptitude for Destruction

Volume 2

Case Studies of Organizational Learning in Five Terrorist Groups

Brian A. Jackson
John C. Baker
Kim Cragin
John Parachini
Horacio R. Trujillo
Peter Chalk

Prepared for the National Institute of Justice

INFRASTRUCTURE, SAFETY,
AND ENVIRONMENT

The research described in this report was supported by Grant No. 2003-IJ-CX-1022 awarded by the National Institute of Justice, Office of Justice Programs, U.S. Department of Justice. The research was conducted within RAND Infrastructure, Safety, and Environment (ISE), a division of the RAND Corporation, for the National Institute of Justice. Points of view in this document are those of the authors and do not necessarily represent the official position or policies of the U.S. Department of Justice.

Library of Congress Cataloging-in-Publication Data

Aptitude for destruction : organizational learning in terrorist groups and its implications for combating terrorism / Brian A. Jackson ... [et al.].
   p. cm.
   "MG-331."
   Includes bibliographical references.
   ISBN 0-8330-3764-1 (pbk. : alk. paper)
   1. Terrorists. 2. Organizational learning. 3. Terrorism—Prevention—Government policy. I. Jackson, Brian A. (Brian Anthony) II.Title.

HV6431.A67 2005
303.6'25—dc22

2005003983

"MG-332."
ISBN 0-8330-3767-6

Photo courtesy of iStockphoto.com Inc. Copyright 2005 iStockphoto Inc.
Online at http://www.iStockphoto.com/Photographer: John Bohannon

The RAND Corporation is a nonprofit research organization providing objective analysis and effective solutions that address the challenges facing the public and private sectors around the world. RAND's publications do not necessarily reflect the opinions of its research clients and sponsors.

Published 2005 by the RAND Corporation
1776 Main Street, P.O. Box 2138, Santa Monica, CA 90407-2138
1200 South Hayes Street, Arlington, VA 22202-5050
201 North Craig Street, Suite 202, Pittsburgh, PA 15213-1516
RAND URL: http://www.rand.org/
To order RAND documents or to obtain additional information, contact
Distribution Services: Telephone: (310) 451-7002;
Fax: (310) 451-6915; Email: order@rand.org

Preface

Continuing conflicts between violent groups and states generate an ever-present demand for higher quality and more timely information to support operations to combat terrorism. In particular, better ways are needed to understand how terrorist and insurgent groups adapt over time into more-effective organizations and increasingly dangerous threats. To adapt, terrorist organizations must learn. A group's ability to learn determines its chance of success, since learning is the link between what the group wants to do and its ability to gather the needed information and resources to actually do it. Despite the importance of terrorist group learning, comparatively little focused research effort has been directed at understanding this process and identifying the factors that influence group learning ability. While relevant data and insights can be found in the literature on terrorism and terrorist organizations, this information has not been collected and systematically analyzed to assess its importance from the perspective of efforts to combat terrorism. This study addresses that need in an effort to both analyze current understanding and stimulate further study and research in this area.

The National Institute of Justice provided funding to the RAND Corporation to conduct an analysis of organizational learning in terrorist groups and assess its implications for efforts to combat terrorism. The work was performed between November 2003 and November 2004, a period during which the threat of international terrorism was high and concern about the capabilities of terrorist organizations and how they might change over time was a central focus of policy debate and U.S. homeland security planning. The study is described in this report and in a companion volume, *Aptitude for Destruction, Volume 1: Organizational Learning in Terrorist Groups and Its Implications for Combating Terrorism*, MG-331-NIJ, which applies the analytical framework described in the second part of this report to the practical demands of intelligence and law enforcement activities.

This report should be of interest to a wide range of audiences, including professionals with interests in terrorism, counterterrorism, emergency response planning, and homeland security. It extends RAND's ongoing research on terrorism and domestic security issues. Related RAND publications include the following:

- Brian A. Jackson et al., *Aptitude for Destruction, Volume 1: Organizational Learning in Terrorist Groups and Its Implications for Combating Terrorism*, MG-331-NIJ.
- Brian A. Jackson et al., *Protecting Emergency Responders: Lessons Learned from Terrorist Attacks*, CF-176-OSTP, 2002.
- Kim Cragin and Sara A. Daly, *The Dynamic Terrorist Threat: An Assessment of Group Motivations and Capabilities in a Changing World*, MR-1782-AF, 2004.
- Peter Chalk and William Rosenau, *Confronting the "Enemy Within": Security Intelligence, the Police, and Counterterrorism in Four Democracies*, MG-100-RC, 2004.
- Bruce Hoffman, *Insurgency and Counterinsurgency in Iraq*, OP-127-IPC/CMEPP, 2004.

This research was conducted within RAND Infrastructure, Safety, and Environment (ISE), a division of the RAND Corporation. The mission of RAND ISE is to improve the development, operation, use, and protection of society's essential built and natural assets; and to enhance the related social assets of safety and security of individuals in transit and in their workplaces and communities. The ISE research portfolio encompasses research and analysis on a broad range of policy areas including homeland security, criminal justice, public safety, occupational safety, the environment, energy, natural resources, climate, agriculture, economic development, transportation, information and telecommunications technologies, space exploration, and other aspects of science and technology policy. Inquiries regarding RAND Infrastructure, Safety, and Environment may be directed to:

Debra Knopman, Vice President and Director
RAND Infrastructure, Safety, and Environment
1200 South Hayes Street
Arlington, Virginia 22202
703-413-1100
Email: ise@rand.org
http://www.rand.org/ise

Contents

Part II: Theory and Application

CHAPTER SEVEN
Theory: Organizational Learning as a Four-Component Process

CHAPTER EIGHT
**Application: The Four Components of Organizational Learning
in the Case Study Groups**

CHAPTER NINE
Concluding Observations

Figures and Tables

Figures

Tables

Acknowledgments

The members of the research team would like to extend their thanks to the many individuals in governments, academic institutions, and other organizations around the world who gave generously of their time and expertise as the study progressed. Study workshop participants from a variety of law enforcement, homeland security, and intelligence agencies provided critical input that made the analysis possible. Because of the sensitivity of the topics involved, these outside contributors are not identified here, but the necessity of maintaining their anonymity in no way diminishes our gratitude for their participation.

We gratefully acknowledge the funding from the National Institute of Justice that supported this research. The direct assistance and support we received from Marvene O'Rourke and Sandra Woerle, who served as the NIJ grant monitors for this effort through the period of research and writing, were also invaluable in facilitating our efforts.

We also gratefully acknowledge the contributions of our reviewers, Dennis Pluchinsky and Terrence Kelly. The report benefited greatly from their thoughtful and thorough reviews and the insights and suggestions they provided.

A number of our RAND colleagues gave generously of their time and insights. We would like to acknowledge Claude Berrebi, Sara Daly, Bruce Don, David Frelinger, Scott Gerwehr, Bruce Hoffman, Angel Rabasa, Bill Rosenau, and Mike Wermuth. Susan Bohandy of RAND's Research Communications Group provided valuable assistance and input that greatly improved the report. Jeremy Roth and Merril Micelli provided administrative support for both the project workshop and the overall project. Janet DeLand also provided extremely valuable input during the final edit of the text that greatly improved the report's readability.

Finally, we would like to acknowledge Patricia Touw, Anduin Touw, Craig DeAlmeida, and Katherine DeAlmeida, who provided research and editing assistance during various phases of the study.

Abbreviations and Acronyms

ASG	Abu Sayyaf Group
Aum	Aum Shinrikyo
ELF/ALF	Earth Liberation Front/Animal Liberation Front
ETA	Basque Fatherland and Liberty
GHQ	general headquarters
IDF	Israeli Defense Forces
IPG	improvised projected grenade
JDA	Japanese Defense Agency
JI	Jemaah Islamiyah
KMM	Kumpulan Majahidin Malaysia
MILF	Moro Islamic Liberation Front
MMI	Mujahidin Council of Indonesia
NPA	National Police Agency (Japan)
PFLP-GC	Popular Front for the Liberation of Palestine-General Council
PIRA	Provisional Irish Republican Army
PRIG	projected recoilless improvised grenade
RPG	rocket-propelled grenade
SLA	Southern Lebanese Army
TOW	tube-launched, optically tracked, wire-guided (missile)

CHAPTER ONE

Introduction

Brian A. Jackson

In today's environment, the threat of terrorism[1] and insurgent violence,[2] including high-impact and unconventional attacks, is constant. The evolving nature of this threat has created the need for new ways to examine the terrorism problem and to analyze the behavior of terrorist groups. Novel approaches can provide new insights into the level of threat a group poses, expose unanticipated vulnerabilities, help anticipate how the group might change over time, and suggest potentially effective countermeasures.

One such innovative approach is to examine terrorist organizational learning. Terrorist groups are organizations that operate in volatile environments where the ability to change is the linchpin not only of effectiveness, but also of survival.[3] Change, in turn, usually requires learning. While a terrorist group may have ample motivations for change—technological developments, counterterrorism measures, shifts in people's reactions to attacks—change does not occur automatically. To be able to transform itself when needed and wanted, an organization must be able to learn. Otherwise, change is no more than good luck and far from calculated.[4]

---

[1] In this report, we adopt the convention that *terrorism* is a tactic—the systematic and premeditated use, or threatened use, of violence by nonstate groups to further political or social objectives to coerce an audience larger than those directly affected. With terrorism defined as a tactic, it follows that individual organizations are not inherently "terrorist." We use the terms "terrorist group" and "terrorist organization" as shorthand for "group that has chosen to utilize terrorism."

[2] Though many of the violent substate groups discussed in this study use tactics that are not purely terroristic in nature—for example, mixing traditional military operations against opposing security forces with terrorist bombings or assassinations—we use "terrorism," "terrorist violence," and "counterterrorism" as generic descriptors of groups' violent activities and government efforts to counter them.

[3] For a variety of discussions of change and adaptation in terrorism and terrorist group activities, see Cragin and Daly, 2004; Crenshaw, 2001; Gerwehr and Glenn, 2003, pp. 49–53; Hoffman, 2001; Jackson, 2001; Kitfield, 2001; Stern, 2003; Thomas and Casebeer, 2004, pp. 35–38. We particularly acknowledge Lutes (2001), an unpublished paper that did not come to our attention until late in the study. Lutes brings the literature on organizational learning to bear on terrorism, specifically on al Qaeda.

[4] While change in the way a group carries out its activities is frequently indicative of learning, the occurrence of change is not sufficient to indicate that organizational learning has occurred. Changes are not necessarily intentional; they can be made unintentionally or for exogenous reasons incidental to the behavior that is changed (e.g., a change may occur in one area simply as a result of a change made in another). In this study, we define learning

A terrorist group skilled at learning can find solutions to many problems, modify tactics and behaviors, systematically fulfill its needs, and advance its strategic agenda by design. Learning enables groups to adapt in response to a changing environment. This learning can range from efforts to *continuously improve* skills in activities the group already carries out, such as improving marksmanship or bomb-construction skills, or more dramatic, *discontinuous changes,* such as adopting entirely new weapons or tactical approaches. The greater a group's learning capabilities, the more threat it poses to its adversaries and the more resilient it is to the pressures exerted by law enforcement and intelligence agencies.

In the face of this sort of adaptive threat, the law enforcement and intelligence communities must try to stay one step ahead of the enemy. Understanding the process by which terrorist groups learn—i.e., organizational learning—can help provide that advantage.

The Need to Both Describe and Explain Learning

Organizational learning in a terrorist group is the acquisition of new knowledge or technologies that the group uses to make better strategic decisions, plan and design tactics more skillfully, increase morale and confidence, and conduct more-successful operations. In short, learning is change devoted to improving a group's performance.

While organizational learning requires that individual members of a group build new skills and knowledge, it is more than simply the sum of what each individual member knows or can do. An organization is a system with a "memory" greater than that of any individual member. This memory enables the organization to utilize the capabilities of individual members to achieve group goals, while at the same time reducing its reliance on any one person. When knowledge is fully *organizational,* a group has attained new or expanded capabilities in such a manner that it need not depend on particular individuals to exploit them.

To understand how a group changes to improve its performance, we must be able to describe what the group has learned (or has tried to learn) and why; discern the outcomes of its efforts; and explain how the group actually went about learning. With this knowledge, we may be able to better map out ways for counterterrorist specialists and the law enforcement community to make their strategies and operations more effective.

---

as sustained changes that involve intentional action by or within a group at some point—such as one or more of the following: intentional seeking of new knowledge or new ways or doing things; intentional evaluation of behaviors, new or old, that leads to efforts to retain valuable behaviors and discard others; and/or intentional dissemination of knowledge within a group or among groups when such knowledge is deemed useful or beneficial. Furthermore, we categorize as learning only changes that are beneficial to the terrorist group.

This study focuses on learning in terrorist groups at the tactical and operational level, specifically, the efforts terrorist groups make to

- Become more effective at applying their chosen tactics and weapons
- Adopt new, often increasingly damaging, tactics and weapons
- Alter their behavior to fend off attempts to infiltrate, undermine, and destroy them

About This Study

This research effort addresses two basic questions:

- What is known about how terrorist groups learn?
- Can that knowledge be used by law enforcement and intelligence personnel in their efforts to combat terrorism?

To answer these questions, we designed a methodology to explore why and what terrorist groups learn, to gain insights into their learning processes, and to identify ways in which the law enforcement and intelligence communities might apply those insights. The research process comprised four main tasks:

1. **Review of the literature on organizational learning.** The rich literature on learning in organizations is focused predominantly on learning in legitimate groups, particularly commercial organizations, but it provides a wealth of models and hypotheses on group learning practices that can be applied to terrorist groups. Later phases of our study were informed by ideas and concepts drawn from this literature.
2. **Review of available literature on terrorism and insurgent violence.** We reviewed the published literature and other data sources on groups that have used terrorism to assess what was already known about organizational learning activities in such groups and to assist in selecting individual groups for detailed study.
3. **Terrorist group case studies.** The research process consisted primarily of preparing and reviewing a set of case studies of organizations that have used terrorism as a component of their violent activities. We selected five organizations for these case studies:[5]

---

[5] Al Qaeda was deliberately *not* selected to be a case study group. The goal of the study was to examine organizational learning across different types of terrorist organizations to find commonalities and differences among their experiences. The rapid change occurring in al Qaeda during the study period and the volume of information available made it such a complex subject that we would not have been able to satisfactorily examine a sufficient number of other terrorist groups.

- Aum Shinrikyo
- Hizballah
- Jemaah Islamiyah (JI)
- Provisional Irish Republican Army (PIRA)
- The Radical Environmentalist Movement

These groups, having a variety of characteristics, were selected to cover the full spectrum of organizations that have used terrorism: Aum Shinrikyo is a religious cult that pursued chemical and biological weapons; Hizballah is a social and political movement with insurgent and terrorist aims and activities; JI is a smaller, better defined terrorist group linked to and influenced by the global jihadist movement; PIRA is a traditional ethnic terrorist group with a long operational history; and the radical environmentalist movement (focusing on terrorist activities claimed by organizations identified as the Earth Liberation Front and the Animal Liberation Front, among others)[6] is an example of a much less-defined terrorist "front" of a broader ideological movement. These organizations are described in more detail in Part I of this volume.

In addition, to focus the study on learning behavior, we chose terrorist groups that have a reputation for innovative activities.[7] The wide variety of group types

---

[6] It should be noted that the radical environmental movement is significantly different from the other groups examined in this study. Examining the actions claimed by organizations identifying themselves as the Earth Liberation Front (ELF), the Animal Liberation Front (ALF), and others from the perspective that they are carried out by a defined "group" is problematic as these organizations function as pieces within a broader ideological movement, rather than defined and bounded groups in a traditional sense. However, because of assumed cross-membership of individuals and cross-fertilization among many groups within the radical environmental movement, law enforcement and counterterrorism efforts frequently treat ELF, ALF, and affiliated groups as a single organization for analytical purposes, while recognizing that the organization's diversity adds a unique dynamic to such analyses. In this study we will refer to these groups as either radical environmentalists or, for shorthand purposes, ELF/ALF. Given the relevance of similar movements in modern terrorism—e.g., extremist right-wing, anti-globalization, violent anti-abortion, and global *jihad* movements—the differences between the learning processes of ELF/ALF and those of more traditional organizations are of significant interest.

[7] Throughout this report, terrorist groups that can learn effectively are contrasted with groups that are not effective learners and, as a result, pose less serious levels of threat. Because of the design of the study, specific groups that learn poorly were not examined in detail and are generally cited as a class rather than as individual groups. Terrorism-incident databases and compendia, such as the Memorial Institute for the Prevention of Terrorism's *Terrorism Knowledge Base* (http://www.tkb.org), provide a range of examples of groups that are poor learners—groups that staged only single types of attacks of limited effectiveness, communicated so poorly that their agenda and intent were difficult to discern, or were rapidly rolled up by security and law enforcement. It should be noted that even terrorist groups that one might consider poor learners overall obviously learned in some areas, but their inability to do so in the areas most critical to their effectiveness limited their impact. Such groups include the following:

- The Tupac Katari Guerrilla Army in Bolivia was active for two years. It had approximately 100 members but did not learn what was needed to maintain its activities after its leadership was captured (http://www.tkb.org/Group.jsp?groupID=4289).

selected was intentional—addressing the study's research questions required examining the relevance and utility of organizational learning theories and frameworks across a range of terrorist groups.

To provide a common approach and structure for the individual case studies, the researcher examining each terrorist group began his or her work with a common set of areas to explore, including the group's motivations for learning, the areas it chose to learn, the outcomes, and—to the extent possible—how it carried out its learning efforts. The case study process included review of available published information on each group's learning activities, supplemented by examination of other information sources and interviews with experts in the academic, intelligence, and law enforcement communities who had direct experience with the groups being studied.

4. **Project workshop.** We invited practitioners from law enforcement and the intelligence community, along with academic experts, to participate in a workshop held concurrently in RAND's Washington, DC, and Santa Monica, CA, offices on September 29, 2004. Approximately 25 individuals participated in the workshop, where discussions were held on a not-for-attribution basis. The workshop focused on practical insights into how to improve the design of policies for combating terrorism. Starting with the preliminary results of the case studies, the discussion explored how analytical approaches based on organizational learning might be relevant and applicable to combating terrorism.

About This Report

This report presents results from our review of the organizational learning and terrorism literatures and the case studies of learning in individual terrorist organizations. A companion report, *Aptitude for Destruction, Volume 1: Organizational Learning in Terrorist Groups and Its Implications for Combating Terrorism*, MG-331-NIJ, focuses on the application of these concepts to policy for combating terrorism. That report

---

- Terra Lliure in Spain disbanded after approximately 20 years, during which it never developed effective strategies to build significant support among the Catalan population it sought to champion (http://www.tkb.org/Group.jsp?groupID=4281).

- The Free Papua Movement, partially due to its goals and ideology, did not pursue technologies that would pose a significant threat (http://www.tkb.org/Group.jsp?groupID=4023).

- Black Star in Greece, which carried out attacks via two tactics—using gas canister bombs and setting cars on fire—demonstrated neither the interest nor the ability to carry out operational learning in its attack modes (http://www.tkb.org/Group.jsp?groupID=32).

A number of other terrorist groups carried out only one or a handful of attacks before disbanding, disappearing, or being arrested without any of their stated goals accomplished. Assessing such groups is difficult, however, as the "new" terrorist groups could be established organizations adopting a cover name for a few operations.

presents an abbreviated overview of the research presented here and describes the results of the project workshop.

The present volume has two main parts. Part I contains the five case studies; Part II presents insights drawn from the organizational learning literature and applies those insights to the case study groups.

References

Cragin, Kim, and Sara A. Daly, *The Dynamic Terrorist Threat: An Assessment of Group Motivations and Capabilities in a Changing World*, Santa Monica, CA: RAND Corporation, 2004.

Crenshaw, Martha, "Innovation: Decision Points in the Trajectory of Terrorism," prepared for the Conference on Trajectories of Terrorist Violence in Europe, Minda de Gunzburg Center for European Studies, Harvard University, Cambridge, MA, March 9–11, 2001.

Gerwehr, Scott, and Russell W. Glenn, *Unweaving the Web: Deception and Adaptation in Future Urban Operations*, Santa Monica, CA: RAND Corporation, 2003.

Hoffman, Bruce, "Change and Continuity in Terrorism," *Studies in Conflict and Terrorism*, Vol. 24, 2001, pp. 417–428.

Jackson, Brian A., "Technology Acquisition by Terrorist Groups: Threat Assessment Informed by Lessons from Private Sector Technology Adoption," *Studies in Conflict and Terrorism*, Vol. 24, 2001, pp. 183–213.

Kitfield, James, "Osama's Learning Curve," *National Journal*, Vol. 33, No. 45, 2001, pp. 3506–3511.

Lutes, Chuck, "Al-Qaida in Action and Learning: A Systems Approach," 2001, available at http://www.au.af.mil/au/awc/awcgate/readings/al_qaida2.htm (last accessed October 21, 2004).

Stern, Jessica, "The Protean Enemy," *Foreign Affairs*, Vol. 82, No. 4, 2003, pp. 27–40.

Thomas, Troy S., and William D. Casebeer, *Violent Systems: Defeating Terrorists, Insurgents, and Other Non-State Adversaries*, Colorado Springs, CO: United States Air Force Academy, United States Air Force Institute for National Security Studies, 2004.

Part I: Case Studies

Prologue

Chapters Two through Six present case studies of organizational learning in five terrorist organizations. The studies draw on information available in the literature and expert interviews to explore the groups' motivations for learning, the areas in which they have chosen to learn, the outcomes of their learning efforts, and—to the extent possible—how they carried out those efforts. In each case study, the author discusses the background of the group, its operations and tactics, its training efforts, its logistics, and its intelligence and operational security practices.

Although the selected terrorist organizations have been studied extensively elsewhere, the information that was available on learning efforts differed among them. Such differences were expected, given the exploratory nature of this study and the fact that organizational learning has not been a primary focus of analytical efforts aimed at these groups. For some, information was available on group motivations and topics of learning but not on the processes through which learning efforts were actually carried out. Available information sources contained almost no insights about some components of group learning—for example, the internal decision-making involved in selecting avenues to pursue—for any of the groups. Particular functions were less relevant to some groups than to others; for example, because of the decentralized nature of the radical environmentalist movement, overarching discussion of logistics practices was not appropriate. These differences and, by extension, their implications for future efforts to better understand terrorist groups' behavior and capabilities are discussed in more detail in Part II of this volume.

CHAPTER TWO

Aum Shinrikyo

John Parachini

Introduction

In 1995, a group known as Aum Shinrikyo used the chemical nerve agent sarin in an attack on the Tokyo subway. The attack marked a fundamental shift in the threat posed by terrorist groups. Prior to this event, terrorists had rarely crossed the threshold of using chemical agents as a weapon to inflict indiscriminate mass casualties. Equally unexpected, the group responsible for the attack was not a recognized terrorist organization, but a religious group that many viewed as a cult. Japanese authorities were surprised by the scale and scope of the group's criminal and terrorist activities. In many ways, these unprecedented activities caught Japanese authorities unaware, as did the September 11, 2001, attacks in the United States.

Shoko Asahara, Aum's self-proclaimed guru, led according to a bizarre philosophy that combined elements of Buddhism, Hinduism, fascination with certain scientific matters, Nostradamus, and millennialism. Over the course of eight years, Aum Shinrikyo evolved from a small organization offering yoga and meditation classes to a multinational entity with hundreds of millions of dollars and programs to develop and procure types of weapons more commonly found in the arsenals of states. In this period, Aum transformed from a mere religious group to a terrorist group determined to fend off Japanese law enforcement authorities by preemptively attacking the subway lines that led to their offices.

Aum's remarkable evolution provides a revealing example of how violent organizations learn. The group's philosophy, organizational structure, finances, recruitment, weapons development and procurement, and the context in which it operated combined to influence its capacity to learn as an organization. Its initial learning patterns were tightly tied to its origins as a small meditation group led by a guru who had considerable persuasive power over its members. Aum's initial learning efforts were tightly tied to the activities of the group, enabling its expansion as a religious organization with a salvation orientation. Its religious endeavors expanded into an apocalyptic mission often associated with the coming millennium. Asahara and his closest associates felt justified in doing anything they believed necessary to achieve this apocalyptic vision—using any means available to achieve the envisioned outcomes. This overall religious motivation accentuated the collective desire of Asahara and his inner circle to use poison to exercise their will over others. Believing that they had divine justification and that death liberated a troubled soul, a key cadre of Aum members embarked upon the task of learning how to make unconventional weapons generally associated with the darkest chapters in the history of state warfare. Thus, a new period of the group's behavior, development, and learning commenced. Members with scientific skills and inclinations were engaged in the study and experimentation that led to the development and deployment of sarin. While this phase of the organization's history involved learning by doing, it also had a significant study component. Aum's organizational learning regarding the functional tasks of developing and testing unconventional weapons provides insights into the way a religiously motivated organization, or any other determined organization with considerable resources, might pursue the violent fulfillment of its vision or prophesies.

Aum proved that a determined group with extensive financial resources, human capital, and a comparatively permissive environment in which to operate can produce weapons and deliver them to vulnerable targets. The outcome of this learning process—a combination of experiences from religious expansion to crude scientific research—was an unprecedented event. Examining Aum's organizational evolution through the lens of the literature on organizational behavior and learning provides new insights into the group's activities. These insights may contribute to the ability of intelligence and law enforcement authorities to assess the relative threat posed by different organizations that engage in violence or that may adopt violent practices.

Background

Aum Shinrikyo began as a 15-person meditation group in 1984 and grew into a movement with almost 50,000 members. Its financial assets amounted to hundreds of millions of dollars, and it had facilities in several different countries, including the United States, Germany, Russia, Taiwan, and Sri Lanka. It also engaged in assassinations, assembled unconventional weapons programs, plotted to overthrow the Japanese government, and contemplated cataclysmic war with the United States. Authorities in Japan, the United States, and Russia did not fully appreciate the scale and scope of the threat the group posed until after the Tokyo subway incident.

While a variety of factors account for this meteoric growth and bizarre evolution, three aspects of the group are particularly significant: First, Aum was the creation of Shoko Asahara, its founder, charismatic leader, and spiritual guru. Second, Aum learned how to raise money, ultimately amassing considerable wealth via donations from followers and its businesses, both legal and illegal. Third, Aum learned to operate in ways that exploited the national and foreign environments in which it functioned. In Japan, Aum appealed to a segment of the young population that craved personal fulfillment, and it exploited Japan's religious tolerance. Abroad, Aum capitalized on Russia's vulnerabilities as a newly created post-communist country and the societal openness of countries such as the United States and Australia.

The evolution of Aum Shinrikyo can be divided into five periods that stretch from its creation to the present day. In the first period, it was an embryonic religious group that attracted Japanese adherents, mostly young people seeking spiritual and personal fulfillment. When asked about the initial appeal of Aum, one follower said that "everyone in Aum was aiming for the same thing—raising their spiritual level—so we had lots in common" (Murakami, 2000, p. 250). Aum members were seeking a more peaceful state of being and freedom from earthly troubles. Members attained a heightened level of spirituality through an ascetic lifestyle and meditation. This formative period lasted until the group's first known killing.

The second period began in fall 1988 and continued until the group's complete failure in the 1990 national election. In October 1988, a young group member died during a harsh initiation ceremony in front of Asahara and several other group members. This death called into question the legitimacy and safety of the organization's practices. Additionally, Aum leaders feared that the death might adversely influence government authorities who were considering an appeal of their decision to delay granting the group certification as a religious organization. The leaders clandestinely disposed of the deceased member's body, which only added to the discomfort of the members who witnessed the death. A few months later, in April 1989, Asahara's most devoted followers killed a group member who had witnessed the earlier fatal incident and wanted to leave the organization. Asahara justified this killing as necessary to allow Aum to flourish and fulfill its mission of salvation. He and his closest followers harbored an intense sense of grandiosity and mission. Asahara's righteousness and the divine destiny he prophesied Aum would reach enabled them to justify violence and paved the way for more murders to follow.

A number of developments following these two deaths served to increase Asahara's feelings of grandiosity and his paranoia about being prevented from achieving Aum's higher ends. The group's membership growth slowed, it faced unfavorable media coverage, and relatives of members organized an Aum Shinrikyo Victims' Society. These developments seemed to confirm a conspiracy against Aum. The Victims' Society retained Tsutsumi Sakamoto, a civil rights attorney who began to investigate a number of Aum activities that he found suspicious. In response, Asahara ordered a small group of his most devoted followers to kill Sakamoto. In the course of the killing, the Aum assassins felt they also had to kill Sakamoto's wife and 14-month-old son.

The third phase followed the group's defeat in the 1990 elections and was marked by an increasing sense of paranoia and the development of an even more delusional worldview. Asahara had believed that the Aum slate of candidates would be elected. When it garnered an embarrassingly small number of votes, he envisioned a variety of conspiracies to explain the devastating defeat. His sense of alienation and rejection increased dramatically following the election. The group's problems were compounded by a decrease in the number of new members and an increase in the number of members who sought to leave. Asahara's rhetoric became increasingly apocalyptic and violent. In many ways, the events of this period established the ideological justification for Aum's increasingly confrontational stance and its robust weapons development and procurement programs. A part of this worldview included justifying killing people in order to "liberate" them and the use of poison as a societal purgative.

In this same period, Asahara repeatedly alleged that the U.S. military was attacking Aum and its facilities with chemical weapons. The organization believed that it needed to acquire sufficient weaponry to battle the forces that jeopardized its divine mission. It was as though Asahara was creating a pretext that justified Aum's own military preparation, particularly its development of chemical weapons. He projected onto a perceived adversary precisely the evil he and his associates were undertaking. In the historical record of terrorist interest in unconventional weapons, there are numerous examples of terrorist groups alleging the use of such weapons by others partly as a justification to pursue them.

The fourth phase began some time after the elections, in 1992–1993, and continued until the 1995 Tokyo subway attack. During this period, the group embarked on an ambitious weapons development and procurement program, using its offices abroad to amass weapons capabilities. Also during this period, Aum's violence extended beyond attacks on its own members and discrete assassinations to include indiscriminate attacks on locales of its opponents. The group progressed from killing members for a higher purpose to assassinations of outside critics and, eventually, to larger and less-focused attacks. In July 1994, Aum members released sarin near a dormitory that housed three judges who were to rule on a land dispute between Aum and local citizens in Matsumoto who sought to prevent the group from entering their community. The attack killed seven people and injured several hundred, including the judges. The case was postponed, giving Aum another example of how it could use violent methods in service of its cause.

The fifth and final phase began with the trials of Aum leaders and key operatives and stretches to the present. Since 1995, the organization has diminished significantly in size and capability. Moreover, it has apologized to the victims of past Aum attacks, changed its name, and broken into at least two factions, one focused on peaceful spiritual activities and the other still devoted to Asahara.

In each phase of its evolution, Aum learned in a variety of ways, expanding and diversifying its capabilities. Some of the changes resulted from the characteristics of the group, and some resulted from pressures or responses of external forces. Most of the following description and analysis concentrates on how Aum acquired capabilities as a violent organization, incorporated them operationally, and wielded them for its purposes.

Competition, Struggle, and Violent Worldview

Aum Shinrikyo was one of many religious movements that emerged in Japan during the 1980s. Some groups grew more rapidly than Aum, while others remained small and obscure. Although Aum's growth as an organization was significant, the group was greatly overshadowed by better-established religious organizations, as well as by other new religious movements. Asahara's deluded view of his divinity and the role of Aum in the cosmos made him very antagonistic toward several other religious organizations he viewed as competitors. Asahara's insecurity about Aum's stature and his competitive sense of survival combined to make him willing to do anything to prevail. As a consequence, he ordered Aum members to attempt assassinations of members of two "rival" religious organizations. These experiences contributed to Aum's organizational learning about struggling with adversaries. Essentially, when the survival of the guru and the organization seemed to be at risk, anything needed to allow Aum to continue its divine mission was considered justifiable. Violent struggle with other religious organizations established a pattern of behavior for how Aum managed relations with all of its adversaries. Defending Aum from critics, which included anyone who could threaten its mission, became, over time, a central objective of the organization's activities.

As the growth of Aum's membership in Japan stalled and was greatly surpassed by that of other religious groups, Asahara and his closest associates struggled with the other new religious groups. In particular, they competed with Kofuku no Kagaku and Soka Gakkai, both of which were much larger organizations. Soka Gakkai had strong links to the Komeito Party, which eventually participated in a coalition of parties that assumed control of the government and continues to the present day. Aum's animosity toward these two organizations became so intense that its members tried to assassinate their leaders (Reader, 2000, p. 184). While other factors eventually influenced Aum's drive to develop and use chemical agents, Aum's early struggles against rival organizations reveal how it managed relations with others whom Asahara and his close associates viewed as obstacles to their divine objectives. Aum's success in perpetrating these attacks and eluding law enforcement authorities reinforced the notion that the organization could commit violence and get away with it.

Aum's struggle with other new religious movements was emblematic of the group's interaction with virtually all organizations that resisted fitting into its worldview. The group struggled with local citizens living near its facilities, local government bodies, the Japanese media, private lawyers representing families seeking to free their relatives from the cult, and foreign hosts who did not readily allow Aum to have its own way. Its grandiose view of its leader and itself as an organization inevitably led to conflict with any individual or organization that disagreed with it.

Aum often prevailed in confrontations with external adversaries, from journalistic critics to governmental regulatory authorities, by aggressively resisting any opposition. Aum's belligerence toward individuals and other organizations probably resulted from a combination of Asahara's personality and the lessons the organization learned in its confrontations. Some scholars note that as a partially blind child, Asahara felt he needed to bully other children to get his way and developed a profound sense of resentment when he failed to be admitted to Tokyo University. Then, as a young man, he developed an antipathy toward government authorities when he was charged with selling fraudulent herb medicines. Surely a variety of other factors and experiences affected his personality development, but these explain in part how he developed a sense of inferiority and victimhood. Aggressive behavior was his way of asserting himself and countering his sense of inferiority. Aum as an organization expressed Asahara's aggressive style for dealing with outside entities. This organizational style was further justified in religious terms that only intensified the righteousness and intensity of the confrontations.

Aum started to come under assault when families united to free their relatives from the organization. Criticism from family groups coincided with Aum's application for designation as a religious organization that would entitle it to tax benefits common to charities. Not only did Aum seek to guard its reputation, it also desperately wanted to obtain these economic advantages. When authorities hesitated to grant it this status, the organization waged an aggressive campaign of protests and accusations. Eventually, authorities gave in to Aum pressure and certified it as a religious organization entitled to the benefits all religious entities enjoy in Japan. The lesson for Asahara and his close associates was that aggressive tactics work and that if Aum was to achieve its vision, it would need to fight for it. This incremental learning experience built upon and reinforced previous experiences in which Aum succeeded by escalating confrontations. Asahara and his close associates were emboldened by each successive confrontation and viewed each incident as affirmation of the divine character of their struggle. Each confrontation was part of a continuous learning process, but when put in the context of Asahara's apocalyptic vision, winning or losing these struggles became transformational experiences for Aum's key leaders. At the tactical level, the group's experiences were incremental, but for a select cadre of the organization, they contributed cumulatively to the desire for dramatic and discontinuous change—the acquisition of weapons capabilities generally associated with states.

Organizational Structure

The organizational structure and leadership style of Aum Shinrikyo profoundly influenced the nature and operations of the group. At the pinnacle of the organization's structure was Shoko Asahara, the group's founder and "ultimate liberated master."[1] Asahara's religious vision and leadership style were critical to the evolution of Aum from a small meditation sect to an organization with 10,000 followers in Japan and more than 30,000 followers in other countries. He was charismatic, had delusions of grandeur, and was paranoid. These personality traits combined to make him a domineering and controlling leader. He was the guru, and group members were devoted to him above all else. As the organization grew in size, a small group of close associates formed around the guru and aided in the management of the group. Asahara, however, reigned supreme in the organization, and all others were his subjects, even those who formed the core of his inner circle.

While this structure was not the product of an organizational learning process, it influenced the character of the organization's ability to learn and adapt. Aum's highly centralized structure and highly disciplined nature allowed it to pursue certain objectives with intense focus. The strength of this focused determination also served to foster an "echo chamber" effect in the organization. No matter how evil and self-destructive Asahara's command or the command of one of his close associates, Aum members obeyed.

The next levels of organizational leadership were also delineated by religious achievement, as defined by Asahara. Members wore different-colored clothes to indicate their levels of religious attainment. Members could rise through the ranks of the organization by paying initiation fees to participate in certain levels of training. To join the broadly defined highest rank, members both paid a fee and had to reject all connections to their previous lives. At this stage, members were frequently urged to give all their assets to Aum.

As the movement grew in size and evolved in character, two classes of members emerged. One class consisted of new recruits drawn to the organization for psychological and religious reasons. The other class developed an affinity for Aum beyond the religious and meditation practices and became totally devoted to Asahara. The guru and their devotion to him became the dominant factor in their participation in the organization. This class of members was called "renunciates" because they renounced their previous life and dedicated themselves to Asahara's service. Of the 10,000 members in Japan, approximately 1,100 were "renunciates." These devoted members could exploit the financial resources, skills, and mere membership of those drawn to the organization on personal spiritual quests. Moreover, their intense devotion to Asahara made them willing to do anything for him, including killing other members and perceived group adversaries.

Within the "renunciates," there was a small circle of long-term followers of Asahara who were key members of the group. In 1994, during the fourth phase of

---

[1] Different sources translate the titles of the various Aum leaders in different ways. This analysis uses the translations provided by Ian Reader (2000).

the group's evolutionary history, Aum established an organizational structure that mirrored the ministry system of the Japanese government.[2] All of Aum's "ministry leaders" were long-time followers who had demonstrated their devotion to Asahara. These leaders and those who worked with them acted as Aum's organizational unit to develop and procure weapons and conduct the group's violent attacks.

This governing structure overlapped with the group's religious hierarchy. As the weapons programs progressed and the leadership of the organization increasingly warred with critics, defectors, the media, and Japanese authorities, Aum's activities were governed by Asahara via these ministries and their leaders.

Operations and Tactics

Even though the Tokyo subway incident and the trials of key Aum personnel revealed a great deal about the organization, many questions remain about its finances and weapons procurement activities. Similarly, many of the details reported in the period immediately following the subway attack have been revised. The fact that many of Aum's bizarre and violent activities were unprecedented contributed to concern about the implications of those activities for how states view the danger of subnational groups and their potential for violence. The novelty of Aum's activities has, in fact, obscured the crudeness and ultimate failure of many of them. There was a considerable gap between what the group envisioned and planned to do and what it was actually capable of doing (Leitenberg, 1999a). Appreciating its learning failures is as important as understanding its learning successes, as insights about the failures may provide information about how future terrorist groups could overcome some of the obstacles that prevented Aum from achieving even greater levels of violence. Additionally, many of Aum's learning failures provided early indications of its illegal and deadly activities. Had Japanese authorities appreciated the implications of some of these mistakes, they might have intervened before the Tokyo subway attack.

Although many Aum members participated in the construction of weapons production facilities at the Kamikuishiki compound, only a few members highly devoted to Asahara were involved in planning, developing, and using the weapons. The key Aum members included the heads of Aum's "ministries" and those involved in the group's "Household Agency" (U.S. Congress, 1996a, p. 57). A U.S. Senate committee report identifies a subset of six "ministry" heads as the key leaders. When Aum announced the ministries, it named twelve ministers, a head of its House Agency, a head of its Secretariat, and Asahara, the founder. The Senate investigators identified 12 people out of a listing of 65 as being "Key Aum Members." In 1990, the group's electoral slate included 25 people, none of whom were group ministers.

---

[2] For a chart depicting the Aum shadow government and the names of the ministers, see Brackett, 1996, p. 104.

Not all of those who were willing to kill on Asahara's orders had skills that were relevant for Aum's unconventional-weapons or foreign-weapons acquisition activities. However, all those involved in these activities seemed to have been willing to kill. While the small size of this group greatly facilitated its operational security, it probably did not make Aum an efficient learning organization. The core group tended to draw upon its own talents instead of seeking outside expertise, which meant in part that a few key people intensively studied a large number of books and manuals on a variety of topics relevant to developing unconventional weapons. The small size of the group probably impeded the development of its capabilities, which may in part explain the crudeness of some of its efforts as well as its failures. A larger group willing to freely exchange ideas might have been able to innovate more effectively.

Biological Weapons Development

Aum's research about and use of biological weapons remain remarkably obscure in official, journalistic, and scholarly accounts, making it difficult to characterize the learning processes that supported those activities. The story of Aum's interest in, experimentation with, and dissemination of biological agents lacks forensic evidence and is largely based on news reports and court testimony. These activities warrant considerably more thorough examination than they have received thus far. There are allegations that Aum sought to cause mass casualties using botulinum toxin in 1990, sought to divert police attention by releasing a biological agent in a train station following the sarin attack on the Tokyo subway, dispersed anthrax from an Aum building in downtown Tokyo, procured Q fever for cultivation, and sought the Ebola virus. Of these events, the only one in which forensic evidence has been openly reported and examined is the 1993 dispersal of a vaccine strain of anthrax and growth medium in the Komeido district.[3] And even this incident presents many puzzling questions about how Aum acquired the critical knowledge and materials needed to carry out what eventually proved to be a harmless action.

Aum's biological program appears to have been small, and the alleged incidents and research and development efforts few. Unless new evidence is brought to light, the scale and scope of Aum's biological weapons program have been overstated.[4] There is no question that Aum's ambitions to develop biological weapons were genuine and potentially dangerous. But the empirical record indicates that the group never produced any biological agents with sufficient toxicity to incapacitate or kill anyone. Even with all of its financial resources, front companies, members with relevant technical expertise, access to foreign scientists and weapons programs, and the

---

[3] The attenuated vaccine strain of anthrax could not produce any harmful effects. As will be discussed further in this chapter, it is unclear why Aum members dispersed this strain.

[4] For a critique of many of the allegations made about Aum's biological weapons program, see Leitenberg, 1999b.

ability to operate in Japan with comparative impunity, Aum could not mount a single deadly attack using a biological agent. This failure highlights Aum's learning weaknesses and the considerable learning required for a subnational organization to be able to develop and successfully deliver biological weapons.

The perpetrator or perpetrators of the October 2001 anthrax attacks in the United States achieved a level of weapons sophistication that far exceeded anything Aum seems to have achieved. Aum lacked some key component and failed to learn it. Significant discontinuous and transformative learning was probably required within the time frame of Aum's existence. Over a longer period of time, or with a more focused and determined effort, Aum might have developed a deadly capability. This insight provides a benchmark for measuring the level of effort a terrorist group must undertake to develop biological weapons and use them in ways that threaten indiscriminate mass casualties.

Two significant sources, one of which cites Japanese National Police Agency (NPA) sources, describe how Aum sought to perpetrate indiscriminate mass casualties in 1990 with botulinum toxin. Three other equally credible sources, including two of the NPA White Papers produced in the two years immediately following the 1995 sarin attack, do not even mention this incident. Allegedly, Aum members drove around Tokyo dispersing botulinum toxin at a time when Asahara was warning of pending apocalyptic events and emphasizing the importance of people joining Aum to survive the coming chaos. Some sources suggest that the botulinum toxin was dispersed at the same time a major Aum retreat was held and was designed to show how Asahara's prophecies were actually occurring. Yet there is no forensic evidence proving that the toxin was disseminated and no pathological evidence indicating that people were sickened or killed by it. Assuming the attacks actually occurred, Aum members most likely mixed up the toxin in a slurry without understanding that it needed to be extracted from the cells. While extracting the deadly agent rather than simply mixing it up in a bowl is a simple operational detail conceptually, it is not so easy to perform operationally. If Aum scientists understood this bench laboratory technique, they were apparently not able to perform it. Alternatively, they may not have realized what they needed to do, which would explain the lack of any reports of people being sickened by the released toxin.

Aum's apparent failure with botulinum toxin may have led the group to seek the starter cultures from university sources that might prove more reliable. Several sources suggest that Aum members obtained the Sterne strain of anthrax (a vaccine strain) from a university. Similarly, some sources allege that it obtained starter cultures of Q fever from a university. And one account suggests that Aum attempted to culture botulinum toxin from a soil sample (Miller, Engelberg, and Broad, 2001, p. 193). Despite reports of several attempts to cause widespread death by dispersing biological agents, none of these alleged attempts resulted in any known casualties (for a chart summarizing Aum's alleged chemical and biological weapons attacks see

Kaplan, 2000, p. 221). The group may have realized that its efforts to culture agents from natural samples would be difficult.

In 1992, a delegation of Aum members traveled to Zaire purportedly on a "good will tour," but later testimony by group members indicated that they sought to obtain a culture of the Ebola virus to use as a biological weapon. Outbreaks of the Ebola virus had occurred in Zaire a few years prior to the Aum delegation's visit and a few years after the visit, but there were none around the time of the visit. Once again, given Aum's capabilities, one would think its delegation would have known that it could not obtain Ebola at that time. It has been suggested that Aum members mistook a Japanese tourist's illness after a trip to Africa for an Ebola infection, when in fact he was suffering from another tropical disease.

Aum's 1993 release of the vaccine strain of anthrax was either a test of dispersal techniques to obtain critical experience for a major attack or a failed attempt from which the group learned the difficulty of perpetrating a major bacterial-agent attack. Detailed examination of this incident reveals the nature of this conundrum. On June 29, 1993, local residents of the Kameido district of Tokyo smelled a pungent odor and notified city authorities at the Department of the Environment that the odor appeared to come from a building housing the Aum headquarters (Takahashi et al., 2004; see also Keim et al., 2001). When environmental authorities attempted to enter the building, Aum members barred them from doing so. The authorities inspected the exterior of the building and took air samples from which they could not detect any "readily apparent risk to human health" (Takahasi et al., 2004, p. 177). Two weeks after the initial reports, city authorities gained access to the building and discovered no laboratory or industrial equipment inside.

While many aspects of this incident remain unclear, later examination of the samples taken by the Department of Health revealed that an attenuated vaccine strain of anthrax and growth medium were dispersed out of the top of the building via a crude pumping system. This is the one case in which Aum used biological material and left forensic evidence to prove it. Evidence of all other biological attacks comes from Aum members' statements after their arrest. While Aum likely sought to perpetrate the attacks claimed by members, it is not clear whether they ever succeeded. Since the attenuated strain of anthrax was harmless, what were the perpetrators of the incident intending to accomplish? It is possible that Aum members did not realize they were working with a harmless strain. The incident occurred during the period when Asahara was predicting Armageddon, leading many to describe it as another attempt to cause mass death to show how the prophesies were coming true. If this was Aum's intent, the attack was a spectacular failure.

There is no indication that the Aum members who participated in this event took measures to protect themselves, such as taking an anthrax vaccine prior to the incident. The comparative ease with which authorities discovered agent material on the side of the building a few weeks after the incident would suggest that Aum members in the building were probably exposed to the results of their effort. If they did not know that the agent they were using was harmless, this lack of awareness provides additional insight into the group's level of expertise.

Another explanation is that they did know they were using a harmless strain and were attempting to perfect their means of dissemination. A sophisticated understanding of the challenge of employing biological weapons effectively would certainly focus on dissemination. Perhaps Aum members were experimenting with dissemination using a harmless strain of anthrax, saving a virulent strain for use in a future attack. But there are no reports that authorities found a virulent strain of anthrax at any of Aum's compounds. Thus, whether Aum was pursuing the use of anthrax in a sophisticated fashion or whether it was fumbling around is an open question. Whatever the stage of development in Aum's efforts with anthrax, this incident is an example of incremental knowledge development. Even if the group was attempting a mass-casualty attack, the results of the experience advanced its understanding in an incremental rather than a transformative fashion. Since this incident was Aum's last significant known effort with biological weapons, it is reasonable to assume that the group understood the difficulty of using them in the way they planned and that other avenues might prove more fruitful for their purposes.

Chemical Weapons Development

In contrast to its troubled efforts to develop biological weapons, the group was, tragically, more successful with chemical agents. Although a great deal more is known about Aum's activities with these agents, many aspects important to understanding how the organization developed the intellectual capacity and assembled the required equipment and material to use them are not well understood.

Some accounts argue that as Asahara's visions became more apocalyptic and Aum's biological program failed to provide the mass-casualty event that would confirm his prophesies, the group decided to try another type of unconventional weaponry (Kaplan and Marshall, 1996). Some accounts also indicate that Asahara had grown dissatisfied with Seichi Endo, who headed the biological program, because he failed to meet the guru's expectations. While Asahara may indeed have become disenchanted with Endo, there is no evidence to indicate that the group switched to chemical weapons after having failed to meet its objectives with biological weapons. Rather, it seems likely that Aum embarked on a full set of weapons programs at roughly the same time and that different programs advanced as opportunities arose. Even if there were setbacks in one weapons category and advances in another, the group seemed to keep all of them alive at different paces of development. When Japanese authorities raided Aum facilities at the Kamikuishiki compound, they discovered construction materials and laboratory equipment believed suitable for assembling a "clean room" for work with biological material. This evidence suggests that Aum may have continued its biological program even after several apparent failures.

Its pursuit of nuclear weapons was much less intense than either its biological or chemical weapons efforts. The group simply explored opportunities as they arose without ever ruling anything out. Producing chemical weapons proved much easier than producing either biological or nuclear weapons because the required skills were easier to master and dual-use chemicals that could be fashioned into weapons were easy to obtain.

Several accounts indicate that in the spring of 1993, Asahara ordered Endo and Masami Tsuchiya, the group's chief chemist, to work with Hideo Murai to develop a plant that could produce sizable quantities of chemical agents. As Murai, who later was designated Aum's minister of science and technology, began the construction of a facility large enough to produce these quantities, Endo and Tsuchiya launched a research and testing program that took the group to a remote sheep ranch in the Australian outback.

Aum's activities in Australia are another example of its attempts to develop knowledge even though the funds it used for those attempts could have been used to more efficiently to acquire the knowledge from external sources. In May 1993, Aum established two Australian companies. Their operations included the purchase of a 500,000-acre ranch in the outback, almost 400 miles north of Perth. While this property may have contained some uranium, which interested Aum, it was ultimately used for testing chemical agents on sheep (U.S. Congress, 1996b). Aum inquired about the price for a nuclear weapon from Russia, but the group spent considerable sums searching for the radioactive ore on its own. When uranium proved too hard to develop, the group turned to using the vast ranch for other deadly purposes. Aum was flexible as a learning organization to the extent that when it encountered obstacles, it focused on easier options that it could manage.

In September 1993, Asahara and 25 of his followers traveled to the ranch. The entourage paid a huge sum for excess baggage, and in addition, Australian authorities fined two of the members for clandestinely attempting to ship toxic chemicals in containers marked "hand soap." With Asahara dressed in brightly colored robes, traveling with five women under the age of 15 and carrying excess baggage, some of which contained highly toxic chemicals, the group drew the attention of Australian authorities. Despite its nefarious activities, Aum did not seem to adopt even modest operational security procedures during this trip. Either its members believed that the rightness of their mission would safeguard them from the authorities or they were incredibly naïve. Both explanations may account for the way they operated. They drew so much attention that the next time Aum members sought to travel to Australia, they were denied visas. A few eventually did succeed in obtaining visas, however, and went to the ranch to conduct a series of tests of toxic agents on sheep.

Australian authorities who conducted a forensic investigation of the ranch after the 1995 Tokyo subway incident discovered that sarin was the agent used to kill the sheep. The investigation revealed that Aum was able to test its chemical agents on a large scale (U.S. Congress, 1996b, pp. 610–657). The ability to conduct these tests in such a remote location likely enabled Aum members to learn things that would have been difficult to obtain from mere bench tests. Aum sought to produce chemical weapons in a quantity that would result in mass death. Batch processing entails scaling of chemical engineering processes and poses different challenges than bench-level production experiments do. By analogy, cooking a recipe for two people is a different challenge from that of cooking the same recipe for a group of 50 people. Thus, while Aum may not have obtained the nuclear material it sought, it advanced its chemical weapons program by conducting large-scale open tests of chemical agents against sheep. Its activities in Australia are yet another example of the group's willingness to simultaneously pursue more than one area of interest. In this case, it was able to make more progress with chemical agents than with other means of destruction.

Aum's most significant learning occurred when it obtained the Russian formula for synthesizing sarin. No physical copy of a Russian blueprint for sarin has ever been publicly acknowledged, however, and it has been suggested that a Russian expert may have visited Aum's sarin production facility. Both are possible and they may have occurred at different stages of Aums efforts. Like some of the other details of Aum's sarin program, it is not clear when Aum obtained the information, but a number of different sources suggest that the knowledge transfer occurred. Given Aum's large membership and its access to Russian officials, the idea that this knowledge came from Russia seems credible. The most telling evidence is that the samples of sarin examined by Japanese Defense Agency (JDA) chemical weapons experts revealed that it was synthesized in a fashion that is unique to the Soviet arsenal of chemical agents.[5] Getting the blueprint or formula from an external source may explain why Aum was able to produce sarin in such large quantities, why it was the agent they used with the greatest deadly success, and why Asahara refers to it in so many of his writings. His fascination with sarin may have resulted as much from the group's possession of critical knowledge about how to produce it as from any historical or idiosyncratic interest.

Aum also used the chemical agent VX in assassinations in Japan. Presumably, group members made the agent themselves, but not in large quantities. The quantity of VX they produced is not known, but the production process is much more difficult than that of sarin, and bench-scale quantities seem to have been the extent of the effort. NPA experts believe that Tsuchiya began researching how to make VX in January or February 1994.[6] Tsuchiya used foreign books to guide his research, but his initial attempts were not successful. NPA experts reported that he was able to de-

---

[5] Personal interview with a senior JDA official, Tokyo, January 2004.

[6] Personal interview with a senior NPA official, Tokyo, November 2003.

velop his own synthesis pathway, one that was different from the technique described in the foreign texts, when he discovered the formula for a VX precursor in a chemistry magazine. Some time prior to July 1994, he informed Asahara that he could produce the agent but that it would require a different facility from the one in which sarin was produced. In late July, Tsuchiya produced one gram of VX and Asahara named the agent "Jintsuriki," meaning divine power. By early September, Tsuchiya managed to produce 20 grams. The purity of the agent was still not very high, which accounts for the group's failed assassination attempt using VX in November 1994. A month later, Aum used VX to kill one of its members, who was believed to be a spy (Reader, 2000, p. 206).

Other Weapons Programs

While Aum emphasized unconventional weapons in its growing military program, it also sought to develop ordinary military capabilities such as the use of small arms and explosives. Aum's training with Russian Spetznaz forces and its purchase of blueprints for the production of AK-74 rifles suggest that Aum planned to assemble a military to parallel the organizational structure of the Japanese government. In addition to the training and plans to produce rifles, many chemicals were found at the Satian-7 facilities that could have been used for explosives (Tu, 1999, p. 66). With enough time and freedom from pressures from Japanese authorities, Aum might have attempted to assemble a classic insurgent force inside the country.

Training

Aum pursued two types of training for its violent purposes, one formal and generally sought from foreign entities offering training services commercially and another informal in the form of repeated experimentation. The few instances of formal training focused on specialized expertise in how to operate things. The informal training focused on activities Aum generally wanted to keep secret, such as how to make weapons, including chemical agents. Fortunately, most of Aum's training was performed in-house. The time it had to invest in weapons development and its failure rate from such trial-and-error learning retarded its weapons development programs. Moreover, the informal learning was generally incremental. Nevertheless, the group was able to maintain a high degree of operational security by keeping only a small group of people involved in weapons development.

Aum usually trained members unfamiliar with tasks relevant to its weapons program by having them serve as assistants first—a form of apprenticeship. For example, Aum closed its animation division and moved those people into the science division, which eventually became its ministry of science and industry. Members who once worked on book publishing and illustrating were now assigned to assist with metal construction. These individuals did not know how to weld metal for assembling large metal tanks, so they were initially assigned to assist those who did. Many of these assistants injured themselves while working because of their inexperience with welding (Murakami, 2000, pp. 325–326).

The training Aum sought illustrates how the organization exploited aspects of the environment unique to the countries providing the training. In post-Soviet Russia, where a Cold War–sized military was struggling for resources and meaning, offering training courses to whomever might pay was understandable. Some Aum members received training from Russian Spetznaz forces, but it is not known what they learned, and the impact of the training on Aum operations is unclear. By the time the training took place, Aum had already engaged in several attempted assassinations, including one successful one.

Aum members were getting pilot training in Florida at about the same time, as part of the effort to attain the capabilities the group was attempting to assemble. Aum purchased a civilian version of a military helicopter in Russia and had it disassembled and shipped to Japan. One source speculated that Aum planned to use the helicopter to disseminate chemical or biological weapons. While Aum members may have thought about this, the actual use of a helicopter for this purpose is difficult to imagine. Like the September 11 hijackers who investigated the possibility of purchasing a crop-duster aircraft, Aum members may have had a vision of nefarious uses, but the practical implementation of that vision remained incomplete.

Tragically, the Aum precedent of using the Florida flight training schools did not attract the attention of American law enforcement authorities. Perhaps this is because it is not clear that the Aum pilots ever had a chance to apply their skills. They do not seem to have ever used the helicopter they purchased in Russia. In contrast, flight training was at the core of the September 11 hijackers' attack mission. They sought the training and methodically employed it for their deadly purposes.

While it is not clear whether Aum's formal training was ever put to use, its informal training was central to the attack that eventually brought the group international attention.

An interesting aspect of Aum's training is the options it did not exercise. Given its resources and contacts in Russia, it is surprising that Aum was unable to lure a former Soviet scientist to work in its program or train some of its personnel. In the early 1990s, there was tremendous international fear that former Soviet scientists who were facing dire economic conditions would sell their expertise. The available evidence suggests that Aum was willing to buy such potentially transformational knowledge—and presumably did buy the Russian formula for sarin—but either it did not need to involve Russian expertise further or it believed that the potential benefit was not worth the security risk. The members at the center of Aum's military programs showed enormous hubris by believing they could develop what Asahara requested. In the end, it appears that they did not know the extent of their own knowledge. Moreover, former Soviet weapons scientists may not have been as willing to sell their expertise to the highest bidder as many feared, and additional restraints may have kept them from connecting with Aum in the ways many feared. Additionally, Aum was basically uncomfortable with people outside the organization.

Perhaps Aum would have shifted from trial-and-error research to more formal training in the development of specialized weapons if it thought it could have done so without revealing the nature of its activities. And the realization that it could benefit from particular experts or specialized training might have come later.

Logistics

Aum's logistical capabilities as a terrorist organization were enhanced by its legitimate business activities, the protections it received as a religious organization, and its tremendous wealth. These three factors contributed to all phases of its logistics operations, from procurement of materials for its businesses and weapons development to the actual execution of its attacks.

Aum leveraged the institutional learning it undoubtedly acquired in its legitimate business activities and applied that learning to its nefarious activities. As the group's business activities and overseas religious programs expanded, Aum members learned how to operate in the international trading environment. Similarly, legitimate business activities and religious activities provided the group with contacts that it eventually exploited to procure weapons capabilities. For example, Aum had two companies that purchased chemicals for its chemical weapons programs without attracting unwanted attention. It also ran several hospitals and clinics that could be used by scientists to obtain pathogen cultures for seemingly legitimate purposes.

Aum's status as a religious organization shielded it from scrutiny in Japan and other countries. Because of Japan's history of tremendous tolerance for religious organizations after World War II, Japanese law enforcement authorities sought very high standards of evidence before undertaking investigation of some of Aum's activities. Aum's status as a religious organization also helped it avoid taxes on some of its businesses and thereby accumulate considerable wealth. Additionally, its involvement in charitable medical services was perfectly consistent with the activities of religious organizations. The thought that a group would exploit its medical clinics to develop biological weapons was beyond the imagination of most people. Religious organizations generally are not perceived as dangerous organizations. In testimony before the U.S. Congress, American intelligence personnel indicated that they did not follow Aum because they did not perceive a religious organization in an allied nation to be a likely threat. Thus, Aum operated in Japan and abroad under a veil of presumed innocence. Its American branch contacted several producers of sensitive dual-use equipment and sought to make purchases. Producers did not hesitate because of suspicions about a Japanese religious organization attempting to make the purchase.

Aum's financial resources enabled it to buy capabilities and move them around with comparative ease. The group's entry into Russia and its success in gaining access to political leaders and military equipment there would not have been possible without large sums of money. Without its wealth, it is unlikely that Aum would have been able to set up a laboratory in the Australian outback and conduct extensive tests of chemical weapons. Similarly, Aum's wealth enabled it to assemble the industrial capability to produce enough toxic chemicals to conduct indiscriminate mass attacks in Matsumoto and Tokyo. While the tragic results of these two attacks were relatively modest in comparison with other recent catastrophic terrorist attacks, Aum intended to cause many more casualties.

Fundraising

Aum had several different means of generating revenue. Its meditation classes, books, and other publications were the initial sources of revenue. As the organization grew, it diversified into a number of businesses that proved quite lucrative, including copy shops, noodle shops, computer assembly and sales, and real estate. Several of these businesses were natural developments of its growth as a religious organization. The incremental learning experiences in businesses such as publishing and medical care contributed to the group leaders' grandiose vision about their destiny. Several of the key leaders had left technical, commercial, and legal careers, which they naturally applied in furtherance of Asahara's vision. Fulfillment of his vision required money, and they had skills to establish businesses. Aum's entry into the computer business just as the sector was expanding proved enormously profitable. Its entry into this sector was natural, given the many people with technical backgrounds who joined Aum, but it was also serendipitous. Eventually, however, Aum's business activities evolved in ways that served Asahara's delusional and apocalyptic visions. The later businesses were launched not to make money for the organization, but rather to procure materials for weapons development.

Before Aum's business activities became robust, it relied on contributions or "initiation fees" from its members. Achievement of higher levels of spiritual attainment was integrally linked to fees members paid to the organization. Fees for different religious items, rituals, and training courses provided a stream of revenue.[7] Eventually, people totally devoted to Asahara and the organization handed over all their worldly possessions and financial assets. Such "renunciation" was the greatest act of devotion. Member contributions continued throughout the life of the organization, even when its formal business activities were booming.

---

[7] For a list of Aum products and initiations, see Brackett, 1996, p. 73.

In its business activities and transactions, Aum wished to avoid association with its religious nature or to hide it entirely; thus it conducted business through separately incorporated companies or in the names of individual group members. Hasegawa Chemical and Tokyo and Beck, Inc., were established in Yamanashi Prefecture to purchase the chemicals the group used in its weapons program (Brackett, 1996, p. 90). These companies eventually purchased the precursor chemicals used in the sarin attacks.

Most of the international procurement for Aum's computer business and its nefarious military activities was conducted via a company named Mahaposya.[8] The group also used businesses established in foreign countries to facilitate local buying, generally countries where it was easy to establish such businesses—i.e., Australia, Taiwan, and the United States. In the United States, the organization first established a nonprofit entity, then established several for-profit entities at the same location and engaged a purchasing agent to facilitate procurement of items such as gas masks.

International Activities

Aum's involvement in Russia was one of the most spectacular aspects of the group's evolution. Aum's most successful recruitment of members occurred in Russia. In 1992, Asahara and an entourage of several hundred Japanese members made a "Salvation Tour," which sparked a tremendous wave of interest in Aum. In the 18 months following Asahara's tour, the group's Russian membership surged. Over the course of a three-year period, the group attracted between 30,000 and 40,000 Russian followers, including several hundred who renounced their previous lives and devoted themselves to Aum. In the immediate post-Soviet period, 70 years of religious suppression gave way to a plethora of new religious movements. The allure of Asian religion and Aum's considerable wealth and willingness to spend it on buying access, organizing spectacular events, and purchasing considerable radio and television time all combined to swell the organization's Russian ranks.

Aum used its tremendous wealth to gain access to high officials, including the Russian Vice President, the head of the Russian Parliament, and the Secretary of the Security Council, and to buy weaponry, weapons production plans, and military training. It was estimated that Aum paid "$12 million in payoffs to well-placed officials" (Olson, 1999, p. 515). Russian press reports claimed that Aum's overall investment in Russia "amounted to some $50 million" (Kaplan and Marshall, 1996, p. 106). Oleg Lobov, the Secretary of Security Council and a close associate of Boris Yeltsin, significantly facilitated Aum's entry into Russia. Lobov promoted Russian-Japanese business contacts via a leadership role he had at the Russia-Japan University,

---

[8] For a list of Aum companies and facilities, see U.S. Congress, 1996a, pp. 86–87.

one of several quasi-educational institutions that built upon the Soviet practice of using such institutions to interface with foreign organizations. But in the dawn of the new Russia, every contact with a foreign organization with money was a business opportunity. Lobov encountered Aum leaders in Japan and seized upon their eagerness to use their money to build alliances in Russia. While Lobov met with many organizations in Japan, few were as ready and willing as Aum to put cash into a relationship.

Aum's activities in Russia declined as swiftly as they rose. In August 1994, the Russian government revoked the group's status as a religious organization. A few days prior to the sarin attack on the Tokyo subway, Russian authorities raided Aum's Moscow offices, confiscating much of the group's property as reimbursement for damages determined during the course of several legal cases (Reader, 2000, pp. 176–177). A small cadre of devoted followers continued the organization, but in a greatly diminished fashion. The influence of Aum's investments in the early 1990s could start the organization in Russia but could not sustain it. Moreover, the Tokyo sarin attack stained the group's reputation so badly that the small number of people who sought to continue the organization essentially went underground.

Aum sought to establish itself in Sri Lanka in much the same way as it did in Russia, but the experience proved to be very different. Asahara wanted a base of operations in South Asia because of the Buddhist roots in the region, but the group found it too difficult to arrange the type of situation it desired in India. What it sought was the situation it encountered in Russia, where its money and Asian origins appealed to important people and prospective recruits. In India, Aum's Hindu roots were viewed with derision, and its Asian origins did not hold the same appeal as they did in Russia. Aum's leaders wanted a less-structured society amenable to giving it what it wanted for the right price. Foremost among Aum's delusional desires was to be viewed as a great world-saving religion. This was, of course, accompanied by a desire to make money to further the group. Later, the group wanted to procure materials for its defense and to bring about Asahara's vision of a violent apocalypse.

Aum purchased a tea plantation in Sri Lanka with the intention of setting up a lotus village similar to its compound at the base of Mt. Fuji. The leaders sought meetings with government officials and offered to make substantial investments in the country as part of the lotus village project. Sri Lankan officials did not prove as accommodating as their Russian counterparts. Political, economic, and cultural conditions were sufficiently different that Aum's efforts in Sri Lanka largely failed. The tea plantation was retained as an investment, but it was never developed into the planned lotus village.

Aum's operations in the United States were launched in October 1987, comparatively early in the group's evolution. As noted above, it initially established a nonprofit corporation in New York and eventually established several commercial enterprises that operated from the same location. Aum seemed like just another of the many Eastern religions New Yorkers can take part in, however, and it never attracted many followers. The group's presence in the United States ultimately proved more valuable for purchasing equipment and obtaining training. A few members attended helicopter flight school, but whether they became proficient pilots is not known. In 1993 and 1994, Aum's New York office purchased gas masks via a purchasing agent in California, arranged to test chemical-potency-enhancing software from a San Diego company, and sought special lasers from a company in Connecticut.

Intelligence and Operational Security

The presence of Aum members working in a number of important Japanese and Russian government, scientific research, and commercial entities is frequently cited as an example of how the organization had unique insights into the activities of law enforcement authorities and access to sensitive military capabilities. However, evidence that these workers gained unique insights or access is scant. A number of Japanese media sources and some book-length accounts allege that Aum acquired classified information from the JDA, obtained a list of addresses of all the police stations in Japan, and discovered that the NPA had been taking environmental samples from around the Satian-7 sarin production facility (Kaplan and Marshall, 1996, pp. 188–189). These reports do not provide named sources for these allegations. In an interview, senior NPA officials indicated that reports of Aum infiltration of official bodies were not accurate.[9] Aum's intelligence operations in Japan are difficult to assess. The group's bold use of its wealth and the nature of Japanese and Russian society were probably more decisive for Aum's operations and their weapons procurement activities than was advance notice of the plans of law enforcement authorities.

Aum's intelligence operation involved attentive monitoring of the open press. Information on the pending raid on Aum facilities may have come from stories in the news media rather than from infiltration of the JDA and the NPA. Law enforcement authorities periodically leak information indicating their pending activities so that the media will cover them extensively. In March 1995, press accounts revealed that Japanese authorities planned to raid Aum facilities in two days. Those two days gave Aum enough warning to conduct an attack on subway lines running toward the NPA building in order to forestall the NPA raid by striking first (Reader, 2000, p. 214).

Starting in 1993, Aum faced difficulties recruiting new members, and an increasing number of current members, including some who had risen high in the religious structure, began to leave or at least attempted to leave. Asahara became very

---

[9] Personal interview with a senior NPA official, Tokyo, January 2004.

paranoid about spies within the organization. At least one individual may have been killed because of Aum's perhaps mistaken belief that he intended to defect. Aum leaders feared that his defection might create new problems if he talked to law enforcement authorities. The killing sent a strong signal to other members that the organization was willing to maintain a high state of operation security and no longer tolerated defections, particularly defections that could compromise some of the group's nefarious activities.

Conclusions

The rise of Aum Shinrikyo from a small religious group to a terrorist organization conducting mass-casualty attacks in an unprecedented fashion offers a number of important lessons for efforts to combat terrorism. Several of these lessons emerge as a result of assessing the group's learning activities. An equally valuable finding from this case is that Aum's failures reveal a great deal about what the group did not learn and what learning opportunities it overlooked. Understanding the successes, failures, and missed opportunities could provide a map of moves terrorist groups might make in the future.

In-house production of weaponry by terrorist groups, as opposed to procuring it off the shelf, may provide warning indicators. Production accidents, failed tests, and failed attempts at delivering unconventional weapons were all indicators of Aum's pernicious activities. Many of the accidents and failed efforts went undetected by authorities, but a series of failed experiments contributed to law enforcement authorities' focus on Aum after the release of sarin in Matsumoto. After local citizens near the Satian-7 facility complained about a foul odor coming from the group's compound, soil samples taken by authorities from near the facility contained chemical residues that were similar to those found in Matsumoto following the July 1994 incident. When terrorists are trying to master the production of a sophisticated weapon, there is a great chance that an event will occur that provides warning about their activities. Law enforcement and intelligence authorities need to make sure they have the technical capabilities and investigative orientation to capitalize on such indicators. Japanese authorities lacked some technical capabilities that might have enabled them to be more confident at an earlier date in their suspicions about Aum's activities.

Even though Aum found the production and dissemination of biological agents too difficult to perform successfully, they were able to produce and disseminate significant quantities of deadly chemicals, including conducting two deadly indiscriminate mass attacks with sarin. The failed attacks or tests, whichever they were, were indicators of pernicious activities. Failures should not be discounted—even flawed efforts can prove deadly. Aum's method of releasing sarin on the Tokyo subway was far less sophisticated than its mode of dissemination in the Matsumoto attack, where they dispersed the aerosolized agent from a converted refrigerator truck. Had they been able to employ this dissemination technique on the Tokyo subway, the number of fatalities and injuries might have been much higher.

The nature of the organization's leadership—both Shoko Asahara and the small circle of devoted followers who planned the group's nefarious activities—provided an unusually high degree of operational security that proved important to Aum's weapons procurement and testing activities but probably impeded its ability to capitalize on unintentional knowledge. Asahara's complete control over his key followers and associates enabled him to command them to engage in violence they might not have undertaken otherwise. Several group members who demonstrated extreme devotion to Asahara admitted after they were arrested that they were personally troubled by his orders to kill, but they explained their obedience in two ways. First, they believed in Asahara's vision and believed that by killing, they were furthering a higher divine purpose. Whether the purpose was to free the victim from a corrupt earthly life or to block the actions of judicial or law enforcement authorities who sought to impede Aum's activities, the mission justified the action. Second, they feared being punished, perhaps physically, if they disobeyed.

As an organization, Aum engaged in a tremendous amount of incremental learning, many aspects of which remain poorly understood. Much of its chemical and biological weapons development involved extensive testing. The records Aum must have kept on these efforts should be examined from the perspective of how it learned as an organization. Similarly, the group's books and manuals on exotic weapons and warfare, which seem to have been important to its operations, should be evaluated from the same perspective. What can we infer from notes they may have made in the margins of these books? What were the limitations of their book knowledge, and how did they overcome those limitations?

Aum's most significant discontinuous learning probably accounts for its most deadly mass-casualty attack, although the importance of the Soviet formula to Aum's chemical weapons program is still not well known. Was the group unable to manufacture sarin at all prior to obtaining this formula, or did the formula help it achieve larger-scale production? Did the formula only confirm what the group already knew? Answers to these questions may provide valuable insights into the danger of specific-knowledge proliferation. What is clear, based on the available public record, is that Aum's sarin attacks occurred after it conducted incidents involving biological agents that did not cause any casualties. Additionally, Aum's sarin attacks occurred after the group had grown substantially in Russia and had synthesized sarin via a process that was unique to the Soviet arsenal of chemical agents.

While Aum's tremendous wealth enabled it to procure weaponry commonly associated with the militaries of states, the organization did not use its wealth to recruit foreign scientists to work in the weapons development programs or to obtain training for some of its own scientists in foreign weapons labs. The reasons for this are not clear. The group may have felt that it did not need this type of assistance—it had its own scientific capabilities and, theoretically, the money to purchase whatever material or equipment it needed. Additionally, the leaders did not want to risk revealing their evil activities. Aum may also have tried to get outside support but found that foreign scientists and institutions were not willing to accommodate the request. It is possible that someone with the Soviet formula for making sarin was willing to sell the instructions, which would probably have been less risky than actually providing the training. This transformational piece of knowledge may have been just enough for Aum to reach beyond its limitations as an incremental learning organization. The group's inflated self-perception, paranoia, and conscious operational security limited its inclination to learn from outsiders on key topics critical to its weapons development programs.

References

Brackett, D. W., *Holy Terror: Armageddon in Tokyo*, New York: Weatherhill, 1996.

Chevrier, Marie Isabelle, "Preventing Biological Proliferation: Strengthening the Biological Weapons Convention," available at http://library.fes.de/fulltext/id/00714009.htm (last accessed December 22, 2004).

Kaplan, David E., "Aum Shinrikyo (1995)," in Jonathan B. Tucker (ed.), *Toxic Terror: Assessing Terrorist Use of Chemical and Biological Weapons*, Cambridge, MA: MIT Press, 2000, pp. 207–226.

___, and Andrew Marshall, *The Cult at the End of the World: The Terrifying Story of the Aum Doomsday Cult, from the Subways of Tokyo to the Nuclear Arsenals of Russia*, New York: Crown Publishers, 1996.

Keim, Paul, Kimothy L. Smith, Christine Keys, Hiroshi Takahashi, Takeshi Kurata, and Arnold Kaufmann, "Molecular Investigation of the Aum Shinrikyo Anthrax Release in Kameido, Japan," *Journal of Clinical Molecular Biology*, Vol. 39, 2001, pp. 4566–4567.

Leitenberg, Milton, "Aum Shinrikyo's Efforts to Produce Biological Weapons: A Case Study in the Serial Propagation of Misinformation," *Terrorism and Political Violence*, Vol. 11, No. 4, 1999a, pp. 149–158.

___, "The Widespread Distortion of Information on the Efforts to Produce Biological Warfare Agents by the Japanese Aum Shinrikyo Group: A Case Study in the Serial Propagation of Misinformation," College Park, MD: Center for International Security Studies, University of Maryland, unpublished, 1999b.

Miller, Judith, Stephen Engelberg, and William Broad, *Germs: Biological Weapons and America's Secret War*, New York: Simon & Shuster, 2001.

Murakami, Haruki, *Underground: The Tokyo Gas Attack and the Japanese Psyche*, New York: Vintage Books, 2000.

Olson, Kyle B., "Aum Shinrikyo: Once and Future Threat?" *Emerging Infectious Diseases*, Vol. 5, No. 4, July–August 1999, pp. 513–516.

Reader, Ian, *Religious Violence in Contemporary Japan: The Case of Aum Shinrikyo*, Honolulu, HI: University of Hawai'i Press, 2000.

Takahashi, Hiroshi, Paul Keim, Arnold F. Kaufmann, Christine Keys, Kimothy L. Smith, Kiyosu Taniguchi, Sakae Inouye, and Takeshi Kurata, "Bacillus Anthracis Incident, Kameido, Tokyo, 1993," *Emerging Infectious Diseases*, Vol. 10, No. 1, January 2004, available at www.cdc.gov/eid.

Tu, Anthony T., "Anatomy of Aum Shinrikyo's Organization and Terrorist Attacks with Chemical and Biological Weapons," *Archives of Toxicology, Kinetics and Xenobiotic Metabolism*, Vol. 7, No. 3, Autumn 1999.

U.S. Congress, Senate, Committee on Governmental Affairs, Permanent Subcommittee on Investigations, *Global Proliferation of Weapons of Mass Destruction*, Part I, Washington, DC: U.S. Government Printing Office, 1996a.

___, "The Australian Investigation of the Aum Shinrikyo Sect," Exhibit 14.b, *Global Proliferation of Weapons of Mass Destruction*, redacted copy, Washington, DC: U.S. Government Printing Office, 1996b, pp. 610–657.

CHAPTER THREE

Hizballah, the Party of God

Kim Cragin

Introduction

This chapter examines Hizballah's organizational learning from the group's inception in 1982 until the Israeli withdrawal from southern Lebanon in May 2000. Hizballah's learning can be divided into three distinct phases. In the first phase, from 1983 to 1988, there was relatively limited incremental learning, most of which can be attributed to training from external actors or was unique to a few isolated militias. The second phase, from 1989 to 1995, was a time of substantial incremental *and* discontinuous or transformational learning. During this phase, Hizballah's leadership re-organized its structure in response to Israeli counterterrorism successes, and it also established a command and control mechanism that could transfer the "learning by doing" that occurs in the field to multiple units. Finally, from 1996 to 1999, Hizballah returned to a period of learning focused on continuous improvement of its current activities, especially with regard to the adaptation of weapons systems. This chapter analyzes these events as a means of contributing to our understanding of how terrorist groups learn, the conditions that give rise to certain forms of learning, and the effects of different patterns of learning in terrorist organizations.

Background

Hizballah is a militant organization based in southern Lebanon that has conducted terrorist attacks and guerrilla operations against Western and Israeli targets since 1982. Until recently, Hizballah's stated goal was the withdrawal of the Israeli military from southern Lebanon. Unlike many militant organizations, Hizballah has achieved its primary objective: The Israeli military unilaterally withdrew from southern Lebanon in May 2000. Since then, Hizballah has concentrated on turning itself into a political organization. Hizballah members first ran for parliament in 1992, winning eight seats in the election. The group expanded its political base after the 2000 victory, especially in the Christian-dominated areas of Lebanon, and it now holds nine affiliated and three nonaffiliated seats in parliament.

Hizballah is governed by a 17-member Supreme *Shura* Council. It has both a political wing, overseen by a 15-member Politburo, and a military wing, referred to as Islamic Resistance, controlled by regional commanders (Hajjar, 2002). Although Hizballah reportedly has between 20,000 and 25,000 supporters, its core fighting force has ranged from approximately 500 to 4,000 members throughout its existence.

Hizballah's structure has changed over the years. It currently organizes its 50-man units according to geography and task.[1] For example, members drawn from villages in southern Lebanon might be involved in intelligence-gathering along the border, while those in the Lebanese diaspora might be responsible for fundraising and/or black-market purchases. In addition, Hizballah has only had two major leaders during its 20 years of operation. Israeli security forces assassinated the first leader, Abbas al-Musawi, in February 1992, after which Hassan Nasrallah, Hizballah's current leader, took over the leadership.[2]

In the 1970s and early 1980s, Palestinian guerrillas used southern Lebanon as a base of operations for attacks against Israel. During this time, Palestinian militants established camps in the area to help train their own fighters as well as militias drawn from the local Lebanese Muslim (Shi'ite) population. The Israeli military, in turn, provided military aid to the Southern Lebanese Army (SLA), which consisted primarily of Maronite Christians. In 1982, the Israeli military invaded and occupied southern Lebanon in an effort to eliminate incursions by Palestinian guerrillas into Israel.[3] The local militias clearly faced a much greater military challenge with the Israeli occupation To counter this challenge, some of Iran's Revolutionary Guards began to train and organize the militias, one of which became known as "Hizb' Allah," or "Party of God." Although Hizballah began to operate as a guerrilla organization in 1982, the group as it is known today did not take shape until fall 1988. At that time, a conference of Hizballah officials was held in Tehran, resulting in the development of a central command for the various militia groups associated with Hizballah ("Focus on Hizballah," 1993, p. 6).

Ideologically, Hizballah is an Islamic, Shi'ite organization. It articulates a universalistic view of the *ummah*[4] that incorporates Arab and non-Arab Muslims, but it

---

[1] Personal interview with a journalist in Tel Aviv, April 2004.

[2] For background information on Hizballah, see Saad-Ghorayeb, 2002, and Jaber, 1997.

[3] For more information on Israeli counterterrorism activities during this time, particularly in southern Lebanon, see Black and Morris, 1991.

[4] The term *ummah* (or *umma*) usually refers to the "community of believers," or the Muslim community. In many cases, it is used to refer only to the Arab world, especially in the lexicon of pan-Arabism in the mid-twentieth century. For more information, see Sivan, 1985, or Kurzman, 1998.

also maintains that Ayatollah Khumayni[5] was the divinely inspired ruler of the *ummah* and Ali Khamini'i[6] is the true "Legal Guardian of the Muslims" today (Saad-Ghorayeb, 2002, pp. 64–87). This concept—referred to as *Wilayat al-Faqih*—places Iran at the center of Hizballah's religious and pan-Islamic worldview, a position that Sunni Muslims oppose. Hizballah combines this Islamic outlook with strong nationalistic rhetoric vis-à-vis Lebanon. In this sense, Hizballah is not purely pan-Islamic. Similarly, Hizballah may publicly sympathize with Islamic revolutions in, for example, Algeria, but it has not adopted these movements into its lexicon of "our *ummah*." According to Hizballah, the only movement that requires a pan-Islamic jihad is the Palestinian resistance movement (Saad-Ghorayeb, 2002).

In 1982, Hizballah conducted its first terrorist attack, bombing the Israeli military headquarters in Tyre and killing 141 people. Significantly, other militant groups also operated in Lebanon at this time. Hizballah's biggest competitor was a group called Amal. In fact, in many ways, Hizballah was a splinter of the original Amal group. Hizballah's first leader, Musawi, once belonged to Amal, but he rejected its willingness to negotiate and/or compromise with Israel. Fierce fighting often broke out between the groups until 1988. At that point, Syria stepped in and forced a truce between the different Lebanese factions. Yet even with Syria's intervention, Hizballah was able to negotiate a concession to this truce: It could continue its militant activities against Israel in southern Lebanon until the Israeli military withdrew ("Syrian Troops Enforce South Beirut Truce," 1988).

In this context, the situation in southern Lebanon was different from that of any of the other terrorist groups examined in this study. By occupying southern Lebanon, the Israeli military attempted to create a buffer zone between terrorist groups and the Israeli civilian population. Ironically, the buffer zone became the greatest source of tension between Lebanese militias and the Israel Defense Forces (IDF) and forced the Israelis into a defensive position. Because the rest of Lebanon was under the protection of Syria, any offensive action by Israel beyond its occupation zone would risk a major confrontation with Syria. This defensive line, therefore, limited the IDF's range and forced it to rely increasingly on technological advances to maintain its defensive posture. Thus, the defensive line also allowed Hizballah to seize and retain the initiative during much of the hostilities.[7] This initiative is seen most clearly in Hizballah's psychological warfare: The group was able to establish a

---

[5] Ayatollah Khumayni, also spelled Khomeini, was the leader of the 1979 Iranian Revolution.

[6] Khamini succeeded Khumayni as the Supreme Leader of the Islamic Republic of Iran in 1990.

[7] It could be argued that Hizballah was able to seize the initiative because it received money and weapons from state sponsors, such as Syria and Iran, and that this is the key difference between it and other terrorist organizations in this study. While Hizballah did benefit greatly from its relationship with Syria and Iran—and these benefits are discussed in greater detail throughout this chapter—the main observation at this point is that Syria's protective umbrella allowed Hizballah to innovate.

tit-for-tat retaliation strategy that acted as a deterrent against tougher Israeli measures. For example, the leader of Hizballah made a statement in 1996 promising that "any new aggression against Lebanon will drag the occupying Israeli army back into mud and into a quagmire where bombs are not made of iron but of human bodies" (quoted in Ranstorp, 1998, p. 103).

In fact, Hizballah, Syria, and Iran were similarly constrained by regional dynamics. Hizballah could not conduct major attacks in Israel without risking retribution against its sponsor states. Syria could not let Hizballah get too powerful for fear of creating chaos inside its Lebanese neighbor. And Iran could not take too active a role with Hizballah without disrupting its own relationship with Syria.

From an analytical viewpoint, these constraints are important for a number of reasons. First, they explain some discrepancies in Hizballah's behavior. For example, Hizballah's inconsistent use of a particular tactic did not necessarily mean that the group could not perform it effectively. Rather, Syria and Iran might have asked Hizballah to not provoke Israel in that way. Second, the relationship between Hizballah and its sponsor states provided the opportunity for the organization to make comparative leaps in its learning process, relative to other militant groups that lacked state sponsors. However, it is still possible to place identifiable boundaries around shifts in Hizballah's behavior and thus make it possible to understand both the incremental and transformational learning processes that occurred in particular phases of Hizballah's history.

Operations and Tactics

From its inception, Hizballah's operations demonstrated a high degree of commitment, ingenuity, and skill. But this does not mean that the group has remained unchanged since that time. During its first operational learning phase (1983 through 1988) Hizballah conducted kidnappings and suicide bombings against U.S., French, and Israeli targets in Beirut and southern Lebanon. Its degree of skill was quite high for a new organization, but that level apparently remained static during this period. Notably, from 1985 to 1989, Hizballah was embroiled in a power struggle with Amal and other local militias which occupied most of its resources and energy at the time. Thus, we do not discuss these three years in detail below.

The second learning phase (1989 through 1995) was a time of upheaval and significant, discontinuous learning for Hizballah. This period was marked by intensive counterterrorism activities by the Israeli military. While some analysts view Hizballah's actions during this period as primarily responsive, clear patterns exist in how and why Hizballah accelerated or reduced its violence (Ranstorp, 1998, p. 107). In the escalation and counterescalation, Hizballah not only adopted new weapons and developed a sophisticated psychological warfare campaign, it also restructured itself in order to deal with increased Israeli pressure. Indeed, this effort to survive appeared to create almost a "survival of the fittest" scenario for Hizballah's top leaders: The Israeli military weeded out the weaker ones, and only the most capable survived.[8] Finally, Hizballah engaged in a substantial incremental learning phase from 1996 to 1999 that ultimately ended with the Israeli military withdrawal.

Phase I: Suicide Bombings, Kidnapping, and Other Hostage-Taking Tactics (1983–1988)

Suicide bombings have been a hallmark of Hizballah's operational success. For example, in March 1983, Hizballah members drove a truck filled with approximately 1,000 pounds of explosives next to an Israeli military convoy and detonated it, killing or injuring all 120 members of the convoy as well as the terrorists themselves. Similarly, in October 1983, Hizballah conducted another suicide vehicle bombing against U.S. Marines and French troops in Beirut, crashing a car packed with approximately 1,000 pounds of explosives into the peacekeepers' barracks. At the time, Hizballah's leader, Musawi, did not claim responsibility for either attack, but he indicated his support for the action by declaring, "The French and Americans came to Beirut to help the Phalangists and Israelis—our enemies—against the Muslims. They evacuated the Palestinians to enable the Israelis to enter Beirut" (quoted in Kramer, 1990). Despite Musawi's denial, most analysts agree that Hizballah was the first terrorist organization to successfully integrate and employ suicide bombings into its wider guerrilla campaign.[9]

According to the RAND Terrorism Chronology, Hizballah engaged in 19 (of its total of approximately 30) suicide attacks between 1983 and 1988. Most of these 19 attacks were conducted against Israeli, French, and U.S. targets between spring 1983 and summer 1985 (Kramer, 1990). Hizballah appears to have then begun a move toward more guerrilla-like warfare against Israeli troops in southern Lebanon. This shift is interesting from the viewpoint of organizational learning. If the suicide-bombing tactic was successful, why did Hizballah stop using it? And, perhaps more important, once Hizballah stopped using this tactic, did its capabilities deteriorate? If not, how was it able to retain this knowledge? These questions are explored further below.

In addition to suicide bombings, Hizballah also engaged in a number of kidnappings during this phase. Its targets included western journalists, embassy officials, and professors at the American University in Beirut, whom the kidnappers often ac-

---

[8] The irony of this situation was mentioned by a number of Israeli scholars (personal interviews in Israel, April 2004).

[9] Why and how Hizballah was able to integrate this tactic are discussed further below.

cused of being spies or foreign agents. A number of these kidnappings are listed below:[10]

- March 7, 1984. Jeremy Levin, the CNN Beirut bureau chief, was abducted by Hizballah. He eventually escaped.
- March 16, 1984. William Buckley, a political officer at the U.S. embassy in Beirut, was kidnapped by Hizballah members. His body was never recovered.
- March 16, 1985. Terry Anderson, the chief Middle East correspondent for the Associated Press, was abducted. Islamic Jihad (Hizballah) claimed responsibility. Anderson was released in early December 1991.
- March 22, 1985. Marcel Fontaine, vice consul of the French mission, was abducted by three men while walking to his office in West Beirut. He was driven away in a car similar to one used in three other kidnappings during the same period. Later on that day, an embassy spokesman said that another French diplomat, Marcel Carton, and an embassy employee, Danielle Perez, had failed to report to work and were reported kidnapped. Islamic Jihad (Hizballah) claimed responsibility. Danielle Perez was released on March 31.
- May 27, 1985. British professor Dennis Hill was abducted from the American University by armed militants. He apparently tried to escape, and his body was later found with four bullet holes in the back of the neck.
- May 28, 1985. Hizballah claimed responsibility for kidnapping David Jacobsen, the American director of the American University medical center. Six gunmen are believed to have been responsible. After 17 months in captivity, Jacobsen was released on November 2, 1986.
- September 26, 1985. Two British women, Amanda McGraw, a teacher at the American University of Beirut, and Hazel Moss, a former manager of a Beirut restaurant, were kidnapped. They were released 13 days later.
- September 12, 1986. Joseph J. Cicippio, an American banker working for the American University of Beirut, was kidnapped from the university's guarded campus in West Beirut. He was released in December 1991. The Revolutionary Justice Organization, a group believed to be linked to Hizballah, claimed responsibility.

Notably, these kidnappings did not necessarily require significant skill or learning.[11] In most cases, the victims were not well protected and were kidnapped during

---

[10] For information on specific terrorist attacks, see the RAND Terrorism Chronology.

[11] In 2003, RAND published a report that outlined types of attacks that could be used to categorize terrorist groups' sophistication. In order, from lowest to highest capability rankings, these are: kill or injure 50 or more people in a single attack, intentionally target unguarded foreign nationals, kill or injure 150 or more people in a

a normal, predictable work routine. Moreover, militias during this period were already conducting kidnappings to obtain revenue, hiding the victims in areas of Lebanon outside Beirut controlled by the various militant groups. Thus, Hizballah's members needed only to acquire a certain amount of training in reconnaissance and the use of weapons to conduct their attacks successfully.

Some of Hizballah's hostage-taking incidents were more sophisticated. One of the most sophisticated was the hijacking of an American commercial airplane: In June 1985, three Hizballah members hijacked a TWA flight on its way from Athens to Rome with more than 100 American passengers aboard.[12] The hijackers demanded the release of 766 Shi'ite militia members being held by the Israeli security forces and eventually released all but 41 of the hostages.

In addition to its campaign of suicide bombings and hostage-taking within Lebanon, Hizballah also engaged in attacks overseas. For example, in April 1984, Hizballah detonated a bomb in a restaurant frequented by members of the U.S. armed services based in Torrejon, Spain. They also placed a remote-detonated car bomb at the Kuwait International Airport in 1983, attacked an El Al office in Turkey in 1985, and hijacked an Iraqi airliner en route from Baghdad to Saudi Arabia in December 1986. This second hijacking was conducted by four individuals, two of whom died when the plane crashed after a grenade exploded in the cockpit. These international attacks, along with the suicide bombings and hostage-taking, illustrate Hizballah's impressive capability in its early years.

A closer look at the kidnapping and hostage-taking events reveals that the group was segmented according to skill. This segmentation was likely the result of Hizballah's structure at the time, i.e., a loose network of militias. Most analysts agree that one subset of the group was responsible for the "special operations" attacks, but these individuals were all drawn from the same militia, making it more like a fraternity than segmentation according to skill. Segmentation would become institutionalized in later years. Notably, relatively low-skill-level kidnappings were not unique to Hizballah. Prior to 1982, Palestinian terrorists often kidnapped officials for the release of prisoners or for money, so it is likely that any member of Hizballah could have conducted the attacks in Beirut without additional training or knowledge acquisition. The 1985 hostage event, however, did demonstrate a high degree of planning and skill. According to Israeli experts, members of Musawi's inner circle perpetrated this attack. Thus, even at a fairly early phase in Hizballah's development, its members had a diversity of skills that they were able to employ appropriately.

Hizballah's early years are interesting in terms of terrorists' organizational learning because the group began its activities with relatively difficult operations.

---

single attack, strike at guarded targets, successfully coordinate multiple attacks. For more information, see Cragin and Daly, 2003.

[12] For more information on specific terrorist attacks, see the RAND Terrorism Chronology.

Most analysts attribute this to training provided by the Iranian Revolutionary Guards (Jaber, 1997). Indeed, Musawi's own writings speak about the Guards' camps and the indoctrination that took place,[13] and Israeli experts have observed that the military kept finding individuals who had trained in Palestinian camps during the early 1980s. It appears that in this first phase of learning, most of the key operatives were drawn from Musawi's own militia, which fought during the period prior to the 1982 invasion. These individuals were also sent to Iran for further training. The small, clique-like nature of Hizballah's core of skilled operatives is also the likely explanation for the highly effective command and control the group evidenced even in the early 1980s. These characteristics would continue throughout Hizballah's existence, but they appear to have become institutionalized only after 1988.

Phase II: Guerrilla Warfare (1989–1995)

In May 1988, Syria stepped in and forced a truce between Amal and Hizballah. This intervention would eventually lead to the dissolution of Amal and the ultimate supremacy of Hizballah among the local militias. It also apparently allowed Hizballah to concentrate resources on increasing its own capabilities, not only in traditional guerrilla warfare, but also in deception and psychological operations. For example, during this time, Hizballah began to systematically infiltrate the SLA and to expand its support networks in southern Lebanon. Between 1988 and 1991, Hizballah repaired more than 1,000 homes damaged by Israeli military incursions in the area (Ranstorp, 1998, p. 106). This repair would become a standard activity after subsequent IDF operations, including Operation Accountability in 1993 and Grapes of Wrath in 1996 ("Massive Israeli Assault Ravages South Again," 1993, p. 2). Syria also attempted to negotiate the release of Western hostages during this truce, with some success. Operationally, this is the point at which Hizballah began to shift its attention away from international targets in Beirut and to increasingly focus on Israeli targets in the south.

By the early 1990s, Hizballah had begun to successfully attack and engage with Israeli military outposts in southern Lebanon.[14] It also appears to have begun to institutionalize its learning, probably due in part to a shift in the group's operating environment and the expansion of its membership. Hizballah began to draw more members from the south, rather than from its traditional strongholds in the Bekka Valley.[15] Because southern Lebanon was less tribally oriented, Hizballah's leadership could reorganize the group on the basis of operational needs, rather than interper-

---

[13] Ibid.

[14] Personal interviews with an Israeli academic, Tel Aviv, April 2004. See also the RAND Terrorism Chronology.

[15] Personal interviews with a Hizballah expert, Tel Aviv, April 2004.

sonal relationships.[16] To engage military outposts, Hizballah had to operate in areas with less popular support; thus, the group had to be concerned with operational security and the safety of its members.

Hizballah's leaders divided the membership into small units of approximately 50 members each, on the basis of skills and tasks. They also began to incorporate specialized units drawn from residents of the southern villages. The fact that Hizballah ran summer camps and soccer leagues in the area helped its leaders to identify the most athletic and intelligent recruits. Figure 3.1, adapted from an article on Hizballah's structure published in *The Lebanon Report* ("Focus on Hizballah," 1993, p. 7), shows how the military units were divided into regional commands and indicates the variety of nonmilitary activities that strengthened Hizballah's presence and recruitment activities in southern Lebanon.

Hizballah's process of learning by doing began to be institutionalized as more-mature members passed on lessons learned to talented new recruits.[17] The group's use of rockets demonstrates this learning. Although most analysts agree that the Ketusha rocket unit consisted of members with the lowest skill set, it was still able to

Figure 3.1
Organizational Structure of Hizballah

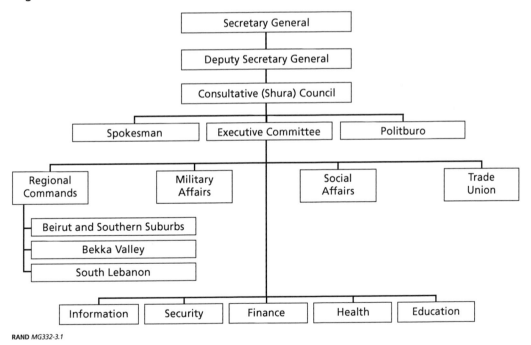

RAND *MG332-3.1*

---

[16] Ibid.

[17] Personal interviews with a Hizballah expert, Tel Aviv, April 2004.

improve the accuracy and range of its rockets, as indicated by the range of its attacks: Rocket attacks initially hit targets only in southern Lebanon, but by 1996 Hizballah was accurately targeting sites in northern Israel and the Galilee, and experts believe that by the time of Israeli withdrawal, the group could have successfully hit Haifa.[18]

At this time, Hizballah was also under pressure from Israeli counterterrorism operations, which included attacks against villages that supported Hizballah as well as direct attacks against Hizballah itself. In February 1992, Israeli security forces killed Musawi (Hirshberg, 1992). His death resulted in a struggle for control of Hizballah, which Nasrallah, the current leader, eventually won. From an institutional learning perspective, Musawi's death did not appear to have resulted in much "lost" knowledge. Indeed, a newspaper report at the time observed that while the number of Hizballah attacks did not increase during the year immediately following the death of Musawi, the number of deaths it achieved per attack and the sophistication of the attacks continued their upward progression (Hirshberg, 1992). It is arguable that Musawi, although a key leader, did not contribute to the continuity of knowledge within the organization, and some have even suggested that his assassination increased the group's learning by allowing the younger, more adaptable cadre to assume control.

In retaliation for the Musawi assassination, one month later, Hizballah bombed the Israeli embassy in Buenos Aires. Two years later, Hizballah conducted another suicide attack in Argentina against a Jewish cultural center ("Buenos Aires: A Prime Target," 1994). These suicide attacks are interesting for a number of reasons. First, they illustrate that Hizballah had the capability to reach Israeli and/or Jewish targets outside its immediate area of influence in southern Lebanon and northern Israel. To many experts in Israel, the attacks represented an effort on the part of Hizballah to deter any future assassination attempts against its leadership. This argument is not unreasonable. Indeed, in August 1993, IDF Chief of Staff Ehud Barak announced that an agreement had been reached between Hizballah and Israel: Hizballah would stop its rocket attacks against northern Israel and the Galilee, and the IDF would stop its bombing campaign against Hizballah villages in southern Lebanon ("What Security for the South?" 1993).

Other experts have noted that the attacks occurred during a period in which Hizballah was literally besieged by the Israeli military.[19] From February 1992 to July 1993, the IDF launched a campaign to target and remove Hizballah leaders, forcing the organization's leadership to isolate the military wing from the political wing to improve its operational security. Unable to mount a significant guerrilla response, Hizballah resorted to terrorism against soft targets outside the region. Of course,

---

[18] Personal interviews with an Israeli academic, Tel Aviv, April 2004.

[19] Personal interviews with counterterrorism experts, Haifa and Herzilya, April 2004.

either or both of these explanations for the group's expansion of its area of operations could be correct. The relevance for this study is that Hizballah was able to retain its ability to conduct fairly sophisticated terrorist attacks even during a period in which it was concentrating on developing its guerrilla-warfare tactics.

Phase III: Ketusha Rockets, Kidnapping Israeli Soldiers, and Ultimate Victory (1996–1999)

By 1996, Hizballah had convinced the Israeli public that it was winning skirmishes with the Israeli military every day.[20] Of course, this perception was not necessarily accurate. It is difficult to determine which side is winning in a low-intensity conflict, but Hizballah was able to project the image primarily through kidnappings and the remotely detonated roadside bombs it used to pick off Israeli soldiers one by one. If Israel retaliated with air strikes against Hizballah bases and injured civilians (and civilians almost always were injured), Hizballah would respond with Ketusha rocket attacks against Israeli neighborhoods in the north.[21] These operations did not necessarily require any new guerrilla-warfare techniques or skills. Hizballah needed only to sustain its capabilities for this war of attrition to succeed. Moreover, the group demonstrated that it was capable of conducting terrorist attacks against soft Israeli targets overseas, which also served as a deterrent. The organization did, however, improve its intelligence-gathering and communication structure. This incremental learning is discussed further below.

Training

Training has been an important factor in Hizballah's ability to learn and to retain its members' skills. Training provided by external players is evident at various stages of Hizballah's development. As mentioned above, most analysts attribute Hizballah's early operational successes to the training provided by Iran's Revolutionary Guards. For example, newspapers observed in 1999 that the group had begun to use a new weapon, the BGM-71 TOW (tube-launched, optically tracked, wire-guided) missile. Commentators noted that the weapons had probably come from Iran via Damascus, along with some initial training (Susser, 2000).

When the Revolutionary Guards provided training, Hizballah members did not need to develop their own learning process; lessons were simply handed to them. Later, however, Hizballah demonstrated that it was able to take a new weapon, gather information in the field on its most practical uses, and employ these lessons throughout multiple units. (For more information on how these improvements were

---

[20] Personal interview with an Israeli journalist, Tel Aviv, April 2004.

[21] See the RAND Terrorism Chronology.

transmitted across multiple units, see the section on intelligence and operational security below.)

For example, Hizballah incorporated a learning-by-doing regimen with the TOW. News articles note that after several weeks, Hizballah members moved from shooting the TOW in open spaces to firing from inside villages, where the guerrillas were under cover and therefore able to guide the missiles accurately (Susser, 2000).

Hizballah apparently had a two-track training program: It trained everyday fighters in its own camps and incorporated lessons learned from its skirmishes with Israel, but it also sent elite troops to Iran for specialized training.[22]

During the late 1970s, many—if not most—of Hizballah's core fighters also trained in Palestinian camps, a number of which still exist, especially those tied to Palestinian refugee camps. Hizballah quickly established its own bases as well and has since provided training to various Palestinian groups, including Islamic Jihad and the Popular Front for the Liberation of Palestine-General Council (PFLP-GC) (see, for example, Matar, 2000b). A number of examples exist to demonstrate how Hizballah's training has clearly benefited Palestinian terrorists. Experts note that in the recent al-Aqsa Intifada, Palestinian groups used a homemade claymore device based on Hizballah's innovations (from approximately 1995).[23] In March 2004, Hamas smuggled two suicide bombers in shipping containers out of Gaza and into the Israeli port of Ashdod, where they attempted to detonate near a series of fuel storage tanks in the area. The attack failed, but evidence indicates that it was instigated, perhaps even planned, by Hizballah (for more information, see Schiff, 2004). These two examples indicate not only that Hizballah's training has benefited its own group and operations, but also that Hizballah had the ability to transmit the lessons to other groups operating in different environments.

Logistics

Hizballah has demonstrated three different patterns of logistics operations. First, Syria and Iran provided money and weapons to Hizballah to support its guerrilla campaign against Israel. Second, Hizballah has an international infrastructure that includes weapons trafficking and money laundering, as well as some involvement in the drug trade. Finally, Hizballah provides monetary support for a variety of different charities in Lebanon that provide the group with new recruits as well as political support in elections.

---

[22] Personal interview with an Israeli counterterrorism expert, Tel Aviv, April 2004.

[23] Ibid.

Support from Syria and Iran

As with training, Hizballah's logistical network receives outside support from Syria and Iran. The benefit of these state sponsors is not only the new weapons these state sponsors provide, but also the availability of a secure supply line that includes money, weapons, and ammunition. Hizballah has had the freedom to innovate because it has not needed to focus as much of its resources on weapons as other terrorists have. For example, Hizballah was able to obtain the TOW missile from Iran and then dedicate time and resources to improving its use.

Similarly, during the second phase of its learning, Hizballah took advantage of an established logistical network to compete with Israel in the escalation-counterescalation that took place between 1989 and 1995. For example, in the early 1990s (approximately 1993), IDF forces noticed that Hizballah had begun to introduce remote-detonated bombs into its arsenal. Guerrillas would plant these bombs along the roads in southern Lebanon and detonate them as IDF patrols drove by ("Hizballah and Israelis Wage Electronic War in South Lebanon," 1995). Although the source of the weapons is unknown, it was likely Iran by way of Damascus. In response, the IDF began to detonate the bombs early, using the same radio frequency as Hizballah. Rather than give up the weapon and/or tactic, Hizballah went back to its logistics network to obtain a weapons upgrade. The result was a remote-detonated bomb with scrambling devices, as well as a bomb detonated by a computer that provided multiple-frequency transmissions.[24] This example illustrates a different type of organizational learning than simply learning to use certain types of weapons. It exemplifies how Hizballah learned to interpret difficulties with a particular weapon and resolve those difficulties in order to continue its guerrilla campaign against Israel.

In addition to utilizing new types of remote-detonated devices, Hizballah also introduced an innovative tactic. After detonating a small bomb along the roadside, causing IDF troops to leave their vehicles to take cover in surrounding terrain, Hizballah would detonate a homemade claymore filled with nails and other small metal scraps.[25] Newspaper reports during this period frequently indicate frustration on the part of IDF officers at Hizballah's ability to identify weaknesses in IDF standard operating procedures (in this case, the soldiers' deployment after the first roadside bomb) and use those weaknesses to its own advantage. Thus, Hizballah demonstrated that it was able to invent its own devices as well as take full advantage of the supply network established by Iran and Syria.

---

[24] For more information, see "Hizballah and Israelis Wage Electronic War in South Lebanon," 1995.

[25] "Hizballah and Israelis Wage Electronic War in South Lebanon," 1995; personal interview with an Israeli counterterrorism expert, Herzilya, April 2004.

International Black-Market Infrastructure

To supplement the support that it has received from Iran and Syria over the years, Hizballah established its own black-market network. Most of its activities, which range from involvement in the drug trade to weapons trafficking to smuggling contraband products, focus on generating funds for the organization. Hizballah's global activities demonstrate how easy it would be for other terrorists to tap into its knowledge even outside Lebanon. Hizballah has slowly begun to draw more and more on its international black-market infrastructure, not necessarily to replace aid from Iran, but perhaps to reduce its reliance on external sources.

Hizballah's international infrastructure also includes contraband smuggling cells in the United States. In July 2000, North Carolina authorities discovered a Hizballah cigarette-smuggling ring in Charlotte (Emerson, 2003). This group was traced to similar cells in Detroit, Michigan, and three individuals were eventually indicted. Authorities contend that these individuals were engaged primarily in money laundering, as well as providing false documents, communications gear, explosives, and other equipment to Hizballah.[26] Hizballah also is well known for its money laundering and weapons trafficking in the tri-borders area between Paraguay, Argentina, and Brazil. The tourist area near Iguazu Falls is one of the central black markets in Latin America. Terrorist organizations frequently use the tri-borders area to smuggle weapons and drugs in and out of the region. Hizballah has representatives there, and also in Panama City.[27]

The interesting question is, Why would Hizballah, with the support it receives from Syria and Iran, risk establishing an international logistics network? Hizballah is substantially different from other large terrorist groups, such as PIRA, on this issue. Yet it follows the logistical patterns of similarly sized groups. As mentioned previously, part of the explanation might be its desire to retain some independence from its state sponsors. This independence might become more important as Hizballah integrates into Lebanon's political system. It is also possible that Hizballah has learned to supplement external support with its own weapons and money supply. Either way, it is an interesting paradox that should be studied further.

Local Charities

Finally, Hizballah's logistical infrastructure also includes the distribution of funds to the poorer areas of Beirut and southern Lebanon. In the early 1990s, Israel began a concerted campaign against Lebanese villages in the occupied zone. The purpose of this campaign was to induce resentment and anger against Hizballah in an effort to cut local support. Indeed, this campaign appeared to work in the beginning, then in

---

[26] For more information, see Burger and Shannon, 2003.

[27] For more information on these black markets in Latin America, see Cragin and Hoffman, 2003.

response, Hizballah devoted substantial resources to shoring up its local support (Jaber, 1997). If the IDF bombed local villages, Hizballah would repair the damaged homes.[28] In fact, the organization has a unit called the Campaign for Reconstruction Institution just for repairing homes. Hizballah also has a Martyrs' Foundation for the widows and children of martyrs and a Resupply Committee involved in relief to the poor ("Focus on Hizballah," 1993, p. 7). Hizballah's charitable activities include medical care, schools, and general food aid.

As with the remote-detonated bombs, this example illustrates how Hizballah was able to identify the source of a potential problem and counter it. Hizballah threatened Israeli towns in the Galilee in response to IDF attacks against Lebanese villages—a significant deterrent, which contributed to Hizballah's eventual success in southern Lebanon. In addition, its charitable activities have contributed to growing support, even among Lebanese Christians, and have allowed it to begin the transformation to a political organization.

Intelligence and Operational Security

The final category of learning discussed here is that of intelligence, counterintelligence, and operational security. As with the other categories of learning, Hizballah's use of intelligence has evolved over the past 20 years. Moreover, it has been an important factor in Hizballah's success against Israel.

The early Iranian Revolutionary Guards training included basic operational security practices. For example, Hizballah members were taught to disguise the fact that they were Shi'ites by shaving their beards and dressing in Western clothing (Jaber, 1997). Hizballah did not begin to expand its intelligence network, however, until the early 1990s. At that time, people were recruited from villages near and within the occupied zones to warn Hizballah members of upcoming IDF attacks. This informal intelligence-gathering network expanded in parallel with Hizballah's popular support in the south.

Earlier in this chapter, we discussed Israel's occupation of southern Lebanon and how the circumstances with Syria and Iran forced it into a defensive position. The IDF's military standard operating procedures actually worked against it in the early to mid-1990s. Villagers familiar with the geography and terrain apparently began to observe and understand the IDF's routines and reported them to Hizballah. More important, this intelligence network provided the basis for most of the innovations discussed above. For example, the integration of small remotely detonated devices with claymores was successful because Hizballah knew that once a small bomb detonated, the IDF soldiers would leave their vehicles to take cover.

---

[28] For more information, see Cragin and Daly, 2004.

Hizballah also used its intelligence network to infiltrate its operatives into the SLA during the mid- to late 1990s. This infiltration was evidenced by the fact that Hizballah distributed lists of SLA officers throughout southern Lebanon. The purpose of this activity was to demoralize the SLA, and indeed, a separate information unit was established to publicize the desertion of SLA soldiers (Ranstorp, 1998, p. 111).

By the third phase of Hizballah's development, its intelligence network had become institutionalized; that is, specific individuals in the Hizballah organization were assigned to intelligence collection. Hizballah still recruited the individuals from local villages and areas that they would eventually be responsible for watching, but the recruits were paid a salary and were integrated into the formal Hizballah structure. This appears to have allowed Hizballah to rapidly increase its intelligence-collection capabilities, causing concern on the part of the Israeli security apparatus. For example, in 1998 Israeli intelligence officials commented on Hizballah's superior intelligence-gathering skills when testifying before a Knesset subcommittee: "The bottom line is who gets to the point of ambush first. . . . If we do, then we hit the Hizballah group carrying the bomb. If they do, they place the bomb. It's often a question of who had better intelligence" ("IDF Plans to Beef Up Lebanon Intelligence," 1998). Hizballah capitalized on both the IDF's defensive position and its own growing local support to better integrate intelligence collection into its guerrilla campaign.

The establishment of an intelligence-gathering core also appeared to allow the group to adopt and use new technologies better. For example, interviewees observed that at about this time Hizballah obtained night-vision goggles from either Syria or Iran.[29] Although these new technologies did not represent a transformation of Hizballah's intelligence, they did allow the group to improve its capabilities on a step-by-step basis. The combination of a restructured intelligence core and these new technologies provided a foundation for Hizballah's transformational learning in the mid-1990s and its successful escalation-counterescalation in the late 1990s. Indeed, IDF Major General Gabi Ashkenazi expressed a similar concern stating, "We must avoid routine like the plague . . . We have to change our modus operandi all the time" ("IDF Plans to Beef Up Lebanon Intelligence," 1998).

Hizballah also appears to have used its television and media network to conduct disinformation campaigns against the Israeli government. Some commentators observed that during the 2002 negotiations between Hizballah and Israel over a prisoner swap and the release of IDF prisoners' bodies, Hizballah leaked the possibility that some of the IDF prisoners might actually be alive. This leak put tremendous pressure on the Israeli government and strengthened Hizballah's position in the negotiations. Notably, this disinformation campaign was not necessarily a new element

---

[29] Personal interview with a Hizballah expert, Tel Aviv, April 2004.

in Hizballah's campaign—it had earlier used its ability to hit soft Jewish targets on a global scale to deter Israeli assassination attempts against its leaders. The group, therefore, learned early on to manipulate or pressure the Israeli government. The use of disinformation illustrates how Hizballah's leaders learned to integrate intelligence and the information it gathered throughout its organization—from a high, strategic level to the tactical needs of local militants.

Finally, most experts agree that Hizballah's success in taking advantage of its intelligence network was due to the nature of its command-and-control structure. In addition to its *Shura* Council and regional commanders, "fighting clerics" were another important factor in the strict control that Hizballah leaders maintained over their fighting force.[30] Each unit within Hizballah's regional command apparently has its own cleric, who derives his authority from the *Shura* Council and, to a certain degree, Iran. These clerics do not hold a political position inside Hizballah. They are not part of the *Shura* Council or the Politburo, but they are trained in guerrilla-warfare tactics and communicate with each other across units and up the hierarchical chain. Thus, the parallel (but separate) religious, political, and military structures in Hizballah—from the very top to the very bottom of the organization—have made it easier for the group to translate strategic decisions into tactical practice.

Conclusions

In sum, Hizballah faced a capable opponent in the Israeli military. The IDF pressured Hizballah in a variety of ways, ranging from threats against its leadership to technological measures designed to disrupt its ability to conduct successful attacks. It is therefore arguable that Hizballah's success was due, in great measure, to its ability to learn and integrate new knowledge into its daily practices on multiple levels. The examples discussed above demonstrate that Hizballah was able to take training provided by a state sponsor and adapt it to specific circumstances on the ground. It also showed its ability to observe weaknesses in its own tactics—or challenges mounted by the IDF—and make the necessary changes to survive, whether those changes were transformational or incremental. Finally, the suicide bombings reveal Hizballah's ability to store knowledge, for years if necessary, and reapply it when the situation demands.

What factors contributed to Hizballah's ability to learn and apply knowledge at such a high level? Clearly, its relationship with Syria and Iran was a key factor in its learning, though not so much the actual lessons provided by these state sponsors as the confidence they built. Having reliable outside support, Hizballah could focus more of its resources on innovating, rather than simply maintaining a certain level of

---

[30] Personal interview with a Hizballah expert, Tel Aviv, April 2004.

activities. The second factor appears to have been its ability to operate freely in southern Lebanon and the support of local villages. Hizballah's emergence in Lebanon during a time of upheaval allowed it to establish training camps, which it could then use to emphasize and institutionalize new lessons learned. The popular support also gave Hizballah an intelligence edge, allowing it the opportunity to study, understand, and even anticipate its adversary. Finally, Hizballah's hierarchical structure—and the religious nature of that hierarchy—provided its leaders with a high degree of control. Thus, strategic decisions for change made at the top translated easily throughout the organization.

References

Black, Ian, and Benny Morris, *Israel's Secret Wars: A History of Israel's Intelligence Services*, New York: Grove Weidenfeld, 1991.

"Buenos Aires: A Prime Target for Pro-Iranian Terror," *Jerusalem Report*, August 11, 1994, p. 6.

Burger, Timothy, and Elaine Shannon, "Hizballah Is Moving Up the Threat Chart," *Time*, February 25, 2003.

Cragin, Kim, and Sara Daly, *The Dynamic Terrorist Threat: Assessing Group Motivations and Capabilities in a Changing World*, Santa Monica, CA: RAND Corporation, 2004.

Cragin, Kim, and Bruce Hoffman, *Arms Trafficking and Colombia*, Santa Monica, CA: RAND Corporation, 2003.

Emerson, Steven, *American Jihad: The Terrorists Living Among Us*, New York: Free Press, 2003.

"Focus on Hizballah," *The Lebanon Report*, Vol. 4, No. 3, March 1993, pp. 6–7.

Hajjar, Sami, *Hizballah: Terrorism, National Liberation, or Menace?* Carlisle Barracks, PA: U.S. Army War College, Strategic Studies Institute, thesis, August 2002.

Hirshberg, Peter, "Getting Smart," *Jerusalem Post*, December 17, 1992.

"Hizballah and Israelis Wage Electronic War in South Lebanon," *Jane's Intelligence Review*, February 1, 1995.

"IDF Plans to Beef Up Lebanon Intelligence," *The Jerusalem Report*, September 14, 1998, available at LexisNexis.

Jaber, Hala, *Hizballah: Born with a Vengeance*, New York: Columbia University Press, 1997.

Kramer, Martin, "The Moral Logic of Hizballah," in Walter Reich (ed.), *Origins of Terrorism: Psychologies, Ideologies, Theologies, States of Mind*, Washington, DC: Woodrow Wilson Center Press, 1990, 1998.

Kurzman, Charles, *Liberal Islam: A Source Book*, London: Oxford University Press, 1998.

"Massive Israeli Assault Ravages South Again," *The Lebanon Report*, Vol. 4, No. 8, July 1993, pp. 2–4.

Matar, Joseph, "Paying for the Cause," *The Jerusalem Report*, April 24, 2000a.

___, "The Hizballah Model," *The Jerusalem Report,* November 20, 2000b.

Ranstorp, Magnus, "The Strategy and Tactics of Hizballah's Current 'Lebanonization Process,'" *Mediterranean Politics*, Vol. 3, No. 1, Summer 1998, pp. 103–134.

Saad-Ghorayeb, Amal, *Hizbu'llah: Politics and Religion*, London: Pluto Press, 2002.

Schiff, Ze'ev, "Hizballah Had a Role in Ashdod Bombing," *Ha'aretz*, March 28, 2004.

Sivan, Emmanual, *Radical Islam: Medieval Theology and Modern Politics,* New Haven, CT: Yale University Press, 1985.

Susser, Leslie, "Hizballah Masters the TOW," *The Jerusalem Report*, March 13, 2000, p. 18.

"Syrian Troops Enforce South Beirut Truce; Inter-Shiite Fighting Ends," *World News Digest*, June 3, 1988, available at LexisNexis.

"What Security for the South? Syrian Displeasure Limits Army's Deployment," *The Lebanon Report*, Vol. 4, No. 9, September 1993, p. 5.

CHAPTER FOUR

Jemaah Islamiyah

John C. Baker

Introduction

Jemaah Islamiyah (JI) is a militant Islamist group operating in Southeast Asia that uses terrorism to pursue its goal of creating a pan-Asian Islamic state centered in Indonesia. JI has been closely linked with al Qaeda, both before and since the 9/11 attacks. In recent years, JI operatives are suspected of having undertaken major bombing operations in Indonesia, the Philippines, and Singapore. Since 2001, many JI leaders and members have been arrested, convicted, and imprisoned, including the group's spiritual leader, Abu Bakar Ba'asyir. Others have been killed resisting arrest. The remaining JI members have demonstrated a continuing ability to execute major terrorist attacks. Assessing the relatively short but violent history of JI raises several questions concerning its capacity for organizational learning:

- What are the sources of operational and tactical learning related to JI's bombing attack operations?
- How has the JI leveraged the organizational knowledge and skills of other terrorist groups, such as al Qaeda and militant groups in Southeast Asia?
- Is the JI's operational and tactical learning experience best described as a form of continuous improvement or has the group also exhibited forms of discontinuous change?

This case study focuses on JI's operational and tactical learning, with particular attention to its bombing attack operations and the operational practices most relevant to such attacks.

Why Focus on JI?

JI offers a good case for examining tactical and operational learning by terrorist organizations for several reasons. First, it is one of the many extremist groups in Southeast Asia that employ violent means to advance their aims. However, JI's regional scope of operations, broader political goals, and close working relationship with al Qaeda make it distinctive among the groups in the region that have engaged in acts of terrorism.

Second, JI conducted a sustained bombing campaign between mid-2000 and mid-2004. Although JI members have undertaken other types of violence, such as participating in the sectarian fighting that sporadically flares up in different parts of Indonesia, the bombing attacks, both those accomplished and those foiled, offer particularly useful insights on learning in this terrorist organization. This time frame is notable because of the major changes that occurred in the security environment facing JI following the 9/11 attacks and the October 2002 Bali nightclub bombings.

Third, assessing the close ties between al Qaeda and JI presents an opportunity to better understand how learning occurs among terrorist organizations that have significant interactions with each other. It is useful to examine how JI's access to the knowledge and resources of al Qaeda has affected its development as a terrorist group, an aspect that JI might share with other groups associated closely with al Qaeda.

Finally, a growing amount of information is available on JI from both official and nongovernmental sources. Supplemented with interviews of experts in the region, such information is key to understanding JI's terrorist activities.

Organization of This Chapter

The remainder of this chapter is organized as follows. First, background information is presented on JI's goals and organization (e.g., structure, leadership personnel), as well as some context on the domestic conflicts that have attracted JI involvement. JI's connection to other terrorist groups, both al Qaeda and regional Islamic separatist groups that have provided organizational learning opportunities, is also assessed.

Next, the organizational learning implications of how JI attack operations have evolved from the late 1990s through 2004 are analyzed. In particular, we examine JI bombing operations and how they evolved into more sophisticated—but not necessarily more successful—attacks over time. Subsequently, JI operational decision-making is discussed, and several other functional areas in which JI has operational and tactical learning experience, including training, logistics, and intelligence and operational security, are examined.

The chapter concludes with observations on patterns of organizational learning identified for the JI and their implications for the choices the group could make to deal with the challenge of having to operate in a new, more robust counterterrorism environment.

Background

This section describes the goals, key leadership, and structure of JI. It highlights organizational developments that have shaped JI as a terrorist organization and reviews JI's connections with other regional militant Islamic groups and with al Qaeda.

JI's Goals

JI's ultimate goal is to establish an Islamic state, or regional caliphate, within Southeast Asia that would be centered in Indonesia, with its Muslim majority, but could also encompass Islamic communities in Malaysia, Singapore, the southern Philippines, Brunei, and southern Thailand. Establishing an Islamic community or "Jemaah Islamiyah" is a major step toward this long-term goal (*Report of the Inquiry into the Australian Intelligence Agencies*, 2004, p. 36), and undertaking jihad is viewed as an essential part of the process for realizing the JI vision of a pan-Asian state based on Islamic law (Abuza, 2003b; International Crisis Group, 2002a).

The use of violence by militant Muslims seeking an independent Islamic state has a long history in certain Southeast Asian countries, such as Indonesia and the Philippines, that have deep-seated religious and ethnic conflicts (Jones, Smith, and Weeding, 2003). Following World War II, the Darul Islam movement attempted unsuccessfully to create a separate Islamic state in the West Java region of what became Indonesia (Abuza, 2003b). Antigovernment activities associated with this movement continued through the early 1960s.[1] Bolstered by the Islamic resurgence over the past several decades, some radical Islamic separatist groups emerged by the late 1980s that were more willing to engage in terrorism, including the Moro Islamic Liberation Front (MILF) and the Abu Sayyaf Group (ASG) in the southern Philippines. By the mid-1990s, JI had coalesced as an increasingly organized network of individuals operating outside the law who were willing to undertake terrorist attacks and other forms of violence to achieve their goals (International Crisis Group, 2002b). JI's rapid development as a terrorist group was facilitated by its ties with other Islamist separatist groups operating in Southeast Asia, as well as by its direct connections to al Qaeda.

JI's Leadership and Organization

JI grew out of the efforts of two radical Muslim clerics, Abdullah Sungkar and Abu Bakar Ba'asyir, who saw themselves as the descendants of earlier Muslim separatist movements, such as Darul Islam, and spent decades working to promote Islamic fundamentalism in Southeast Asia (Abuza, 2003b, p. 126). These Indonesian clerics

---

[1] Muslim separatist movements in the Philippines have been active for centuries, fueled by resistance, initially to the Spanish colonial authorities and subsequently to the Americans. The Philippine Muslims in the southern regions of Mindanao and the Sulu archipelago, known as the Moros, have a very long tradition of fighting for autonomy (Tan, 2003).

provided the intellectual leadership and organizational skill for the fundamentalist Islamic movement that spawned JI.[2] They viewed JI as one of many means for achieving an Islamic state that could bring together Islamic true believers residing in different Southeast Asian countries. JI has also been shaped by individuals who gained practical jihad experience in Afghanistan and fostered close ties with al Qaeda.

Starting in the early 1970s, Sungkar and Ba'asyir laid the groundwork for a militant Islamic movement; their work resulted, eventually, in the establishment of JI cells in several countries and the development of a dedicated, well-trained following. Their task was complicated by the fact that many Indonesians have traditionally adhered to a relatively moderate form of Islam (Rabasa, 2004, pp. 369–370). However, more-radical Islamic movements were galvanized by the suppression of Islam as a political force during the Suharto regime. At the same time, international developments were encouraging Muslims to view jihad as the only real solution to the problems in their societies. These developments included the 1979 Iranian revolution and the *mujahidin* resistance against the Soviets in Afghanistan, which is estimated to have involved up to a thousand Muslims from Southeast Asia. This growing militancy was also fostered by the global spread of some fundamentalist Islamic schools (*madrasas*) and boarding schools (*pesentrens*), as well as by the spread of radical mosques (Abuza, 2003b).[3]

In the years prior to the JI bombing attacks that began in mid-2000, the group's key organizational priorities were

- Recruiting and indoctrinating JI members
- Creating an organizational structure
- Establishing ties with other terrorist and militant Muslim groups, including al Qaeda

Recruitment and Indoctrination. Many individuals who later emerged as JI terrorists began their association through religious training provided by Sungkar and Ba'asyir in Indonesia or Malaysia. In the 1970s, the clerics established a religious boarding school near Solo, Central Java, known as Pondok Ngruki (ICG, 2002a; Abuza, 2003b). The school was devoted to teaching *Salafism* and a very conservative interpretation of Islamic principles. Time and again, key JI operatives apprehended by authorities following terrorist attacks turned out to be part of the "Ngruki network." These individuals had been students, disciples, and assistants of Sungkar and Ba'asyir. The clerics could exploit the strong personal loyalty that typically develops

---

[2] One source marks the JI's founding officially on January 1, 1993, when the more-militant JI members separated from the long-standing Darul Islam movement (International Crisis Group, 2004b).

[3] On the galvanizing effect of the Islamic victory over Soviet troops in Afghanistan and the deeper historical roots of the radical Islamic movement, see Benjamin and Simon, 2003, pp. 102–105.

between teachers and students in Southeast Asia (Abuza, 2003b; Sageman, 2004), and in addition, ties among key JI members were often reinforced through relationships based on kinship and marriage.

In 1985, Sungkar and Ba'asyir fled to Malaysia to avoid being sent to prison by the Suharto regime.[4] They found Malaysia to be tolerant of their preaching of violent jihad as the best path for achieving an Islamic state (Abuza, 2003b, p. 126). They also were in a good location to facilitate the travels of Indonesians and Malaysians to Pakistan and Afghanistan. Many devout Muslims not only were interested in advancing their knowledge of Islam at one of the *madrasas* in Pakistan but also engaged in training and even fighting alongside the Afghan and foreign *mujahidin* against the occupying Soviets troops.[5] The lengthy religious training offered by Sungkar and Ba'asyir provided opportunities to recruit and indoctrinate individuals for militant Islamic activities, including becoming members of JI (Ramakrishna, 2004). During its early years, JI was selective in its recruiting and patiently dedicated to building up its organizational base (Abuza, 2003b, p. 129).

After the Suharto regime ended in mid-1998, the two radical clerics returned to Indonesia. Sungkar died of natural causes the following year, and Ba'asyir assumed leadership of JI, which was soon to undertake its first known terrorist attacks.[6] Assisting Ba'asyir in these organization-building tasks were the radical clerics known as Hambali and Abu Jibril.[7] Both engaged in recruiting, preaching, and building up the network of militant cells in various countries. Each had spent time in Afghanistan. Equally important, both men served as key connections between the fledgling JI group and the well-established al Qaeda. Until his arrest in 2003, Hambali was viewed as having important leadership roles in both JI and al Qaeda and was responsible for JI operations for some time. His unique role as the link between JI and al

---

[4] The two radical clerics had been arrested by the Suharto regime earlier, in 1978. They were sentenced to nine years in prison but were released in 1982 on the basis of a second court ruling. In 1985, however, the Indonesian Supreme Court ruled against them and reimposed the original nine-year sentence, prompting them to flee to Malaysia (Abuza, 2003b, p. 126).

[5] One expert notes that all JI members came through the religious schools and that many JI operatives were also graduates of secular education programs, including Indonesian and Malaysian technical universities (Abuza, 2003b, p. 14).

[6] Ba'asyir was arrested by Indonesian authorities following the Bali attacks in October 2002 and has been held in custody since then on various charges in the expectation of being brought to trial for involvement in JI terrorist acts ("Indonesian Cleric to Be Charged," 2004).

[7] Hambali (also known as Nurjaman Riduan Isamuddin) is an Indonesian cleric best known for his management skills. He became a senior JI leader while serving Sungkar and Ba'asyir in Indonesia and Malaysia. Similarly, Abu Jibril (also known as Mohammed Iqbal Abdul Rahman) is a JI senior operative with Afghanistan war experience. He has been described as a "fiery orator" and a preacher for the JI cause; he was a leading recruiter and took a leadership role in JI's jihad activities in Indonesian sectarian conflicts. Abu Jibril was instrumental in recruiting JI members and managing their progression through the training and indoctrination process (Ressa, 2003, pp. 75–76, 94–96, 150–151, 181–184; and Abuza, 2003b, pp. 128–129). Both Hambali and Abu Jibril have been arrested.

Qaeda is highlighted in the 9/11 Commission report (National Commission, 2004, pp. 150–152). Abu Jibril was considered JI's top recruiter and the second in command, with responsibility for managing the group's operations (U.S. Department of State, 2003a; Abuza, 2003b, pp. 127–130).

Creating an Organizational Structure. The JI organizational structure that took shape in the mid-1990s reflected the group's regional aspirations. This structure, as it was revealed following the arrests of JI members starting in late 2001,[8] embodies both functional components and geographically based units. How much this structure has changed under the pressure of increased counterterrorism operations in recent years is uncertain.

JI's top leadership consists of the Amir, or supreme leader, and the Regional *Syura*, a consultative council of senior JI members. Abu Bakar Ba'asyir served as the JI's Amir at least until he was arrested and taken into custody by Indonesian authorities in October 2002.[9] Some accounts view him as the group's spiritual leader rather than its top decisionmaker. Ba'asyir's own public statements suggest that he plays an inspirational role in educating and exhorting the radical Muslims who resort to violence.[10] He has said, "I make many knives and I sell many knives, but I'm not responsible for what happens to them" (Ressa, 2004). However, recent investigations of bombing incidents suggest that Ba'asyir was deeply involved in JI attacks, because operatives sought his approval, or at least his acquiescence, to legitimize their attack plans (Rabasa, 2004, p. 399).

The Regional *Syura* involves the JI's senior personnel and serves as a top policymaking group. In some respects, this group parallels the *Shura Majlis*, or consultative council, that al Qaeda has used for its top deliberations. It is supported by a series of functional components (i.e., operations, security, recruitment work, economy wing, and communications) that report to it (Gunaratna, 2002, pp. 27, 57; Ressa, 2003, pp. 75–76). The operations and security units are critical to JI's ability to undertake terrorist operations. Recruitment and indoctrination of JI members is the responsibility of a particular work unit. The economy wing or unit generates the

---

[8] The arrests in late 2001 and mid-2002 of JI members involved in various foiled bombing plots against targets in Singapore resulted in the public release of specific details on JI's organizational structure (White Paper, 2003).

[9] Following Ba'asyir's arrest, Abu Rusdan was believed to have served as the caretaker leader of the JI, but he was arrested by Indonesian authorities in April 2003 and charged with complicity in the Bali bombings ("Indonesia Sentences JI Leader," 2004; Ressa, 2003).

[10] Along with his clandestine role as Amir of JI, Ba'asyir has assumed a public role as head of the Mujahidin Council of Indonesia (MMI), an umbrella organization that seeks to coordinate numerous militant and hard-line Islamic organizations that support the idea of establishing an Islamic state by implementing the *sharia* into Indonesia's national laws. Some analysts view the MMI as essentially a front organization for JI that can assist with its recruitment and financing needs (Abuza, 2003b, pp. 141–144).

funds needed to finance the group's activities, managing front businesses and procuring arms and materials.[11]

Consistent with its regional focus, JI also established a series of territorial groups (or districts) known as *mantiqis*, with responsibilities for JI operations throughout Southeast Asia. They include

- *Mantiqi 1.* This group, which is centered in Malaysia with a branch in Singapore, has been central to JI's development. It has worked closely with the Malaysian militant group known as the Kumpulan Majahidin Malaysia (KMM). *Mantiqi 1* performs a primary role in recruiting and indoctrination of JI members, particularly through the Islamic boarding school operated in Johor, Malaysia.
- *Mantiqi 2.* Although this group covers most of Indonesia, relatively little is known about it. However, it is probably the source of many JI operatives, and it undoubtedly played an important role in supporting JI activities in Indonesia's sectarian conflicts through Islamic paramilitary groups (Abuza, 2003b, p. 140).
- *Mantiqi 3.* This group has been important for training JI personnel and supporting its logistical network, including the use of MILF training facilities in Mindanao (Abuza, 2003b, pp. 136–138, 149).
- *Mantiqi 4.* This territorial group in Australia focuses primarily on recruiting and fundraising in the large Indonesian diaspora community.[12]

These territorial groups consist of several branches known as *wakalahs*, which comprise operations cells, or *fiah*, that usually consist of four or five JI members (White Paper, 2003, p. 10; International Crisis Group, 2002b, p. 1). Reliance on individual cells makes JI less vulnerable to arrests and penetration by counterterrorist operatives. Although JI's organizational structure suggests a hierarchical organization, there is evidence that strong differences of perspective have existed within the organization, as will be discussed later.

JI's organizational structure, with different groups responsible for large areas of Southeast Asia, reflects both its vision for creating a regional Islamic state and its plans for a long-term regional struggle. The geographical scope of the JI organization creates a need to convey expertise and organizational knowledge among many components while guarding against security breaches in particular locations.

---

[11] JI is known to make use of a diverse range of funding sources, including cash deliveries from al Qaeda, funds from Islamic charities, front companies, *hawala* shops, petty crime, and donations (Abuza, 2003a, p. 171).

[12] One indication of the JI leadership's interest in developing a presence in Australia is that Sungkar and Ba'asyir reportedly made 11 visits to Australia during the 1990s (Abuza, 2003a, pp. 136, 177–178). Although none of the JI plots for violent actions in Australia progressed very far, several JI members have been arrested and charged with running makeshift training camps there (Tarabay, 2004; Abuza, 2003b, p. 177).

JI Ties with Regional Militant Islamic Groups. On its own, JI would have faced major obstacles in pursuing its long-term goals. However, its regional aspirations provided it with incentives and opportunities to leverage other militant Islamic groups operating in Southeast Asia to enhance its own knowledge and capabilities for undertaking violent acts. Several regional militant Islamic groups (e.g., MILF and KMM) have been willing to share training facilities and provide JI with other forms of support (Rabasa, 2003, pp. 25–62; Abuza, 2003b, pp. 89–101, 124–125, 140–147, 171–177). An indication that JI aspires to become something more than another Muslim separatist group is the important role its leaders have played in forming a regional alliance of jihadist groups known as the Mujahidin Coalition (*Rabitatul Majahidin*).[13] JI also has close connections with jihadist groups that are actively involved in Indonesia's ongoing sectarian conflicts.[14] These regional relationships have provided JI with access to secure training facilities, increased logistical support, and opportunities to undertake joint operations, thereby expanding the resources available to it for acquiring the knowledge and materials required to shift to armed conflict.

JI Connections to al Qaeda. In addition to its ties with regional militant Islamic groups, JI has had a strong connection with al Qaeda dating back to the early 1990s. Al Qaeda took advantage of a relatively benign security environment in Southeast Asia to support its own operations, including the 9/11 attacks, as well as to collaborate with local Islamist militant groups. Within this context, al Qaeda and JI forged a close connection that was instrumental in shaping JI as a terrorist group and that expanded its opportunities for organizational learning.

JI's connections to al Qaeda began when Abdullah Sungkar traveled to Afghanistan and met with Osama bin Laden some time in 1993–1994 (Gunaratna, 2002, pp. 174, 194). Over the next few years, the two organizations engaged in a number of activities that benefited both of them (see Table 4.1). The key benefits for JI were access to al Qaeda's training facilities, financial support, and the ability to plan and carry out joint operations, which increased its operational knowledge. JI also sought approval for its plans from al Qaeda leaders, an action that yielded both technical advice and a sense of legitimacy for JI undertakings.

Some analysts believe that the organizational learning and more-tangible benefits that JI gained from these dealings came at the price of being gradually co-opted

---

[13] One analyst contends that despite its very informal and loose nature, the Mujahidin Coalition serves as a "potentially force-multiplying extension of the JI" and that its effect has been seen in collaborative terrorist attacks (Ramakrishna, 2003, p. 312).

[14] These include jihadist groups directly supported by JI, such as *Laskar Mujahideen* and *Laskar Jundullah*. Other jihadist groups, such as *Laskher Jihad*, have played prominent roles in these conflicts (Rabasa, 2003, pp. 28–31). A competing jihadist group known as *Mujahidin KOMPAK* operated in the Poso area of Indonesia's Central Sulawesi province and made use of some disenchanted JI members.

by al Qaeda into supporting its global jihadist agenda in ways that are similar to al Qaeda's relationship with several other local terrorist groups prior to 9/11 (Gunaratna, 2002, pp. 186, 194). At a minimum, JI became an affiliate of al Qaeda through joint activities that benefited both organizations. These close ties were fostered by a strong doctrinal compatibility between the two groups.

Any al Qaeda effort to co-opt JI in the years before the 9/11 attacks would have benefited from having individuals such as Hambali and Abu Jibril, who had gained experience in Afghanistan, within JI's top leadership. These leaders shared with al Qaeda the idea of undertaking jihad against Western interests, particularly the United States, sooner rather than later.

Al Qaeda also gained from this relationship by being able to take advantage of JI's covert infrastructure to support terrorist attacks on targets in the region and elsewhere. JI members, including Hambali, hosted the infamous meeting in Kuala Lumpur in January 2000 that involved several high-level al Qaeda operatives, including two 9/11 hijackers and others who were involved in planning the attack on the USS *Cole* in October 2000 (Abuza, 2003b, p. 123; Gunaratna, 2002, pp. 195–196). Similarly, al Qaeda's plans for undertaking bomb attacks on U.S. and western interests in Singapore in late 2001, which were eventually foiled, depended heavily on JI's clandestine infrastructure and local knowledge for surveillance of the targets and for building the truck bombs.

Table 4.1
Key Interactions Between JI and al Qaeda

Date	Key Interaction
1993–1994	JI is formed by Abdullah Sungkar after a meeting with Osama bin Laden in Afghanistan.
1999–2000	Singapore Fiah Ayub cell leader goes to Afghanistan for training in mid-1999 and later briefs the al Qaeda leadership on JI preparations for a bombing attack on a rail station in Singapore that is routinely used by U.S. military personnel.
January 2000	Hambali, serving both JI and al Qaeda, helps arrange a meeting in Kuala Lumpur that involves some top al Qaeda operatives involved in the 9/11 plot as hijackers and the USS *Cole* attack.
2000–2002	Omar al-Faruq, al Qaeda's senior representative in Southeast Asia, works with the JI to undertake surveillance of the U.S. embassies in Jakarta and Kuala Lumpur in preparation for a car bomb attack.
2001	JI member Yazid Sufaat spends several months trying to cultivate anthrax as part of the al Qaeda biological weapons program at a laboratory in Afghanistan.
September 2001–October 2001	JI's Fiah Musa cell in Singapore is approached by JI leaders and al Qaeda operatives to assist in a plan to bomb specific targets in Singapore (e.g., embassies, U.S. business offices); the plan calls for JI personnel to undertake surveillance and bomb preparations and support activities for al Qaeda suicide truck bombers.

SOURCES: Gunaratna, 2002, pp. 186–199; White Paper, 2003, pp. 4–5, 9–12; National Commission, 2004, pp. 149–152; Ratnsar, 2002.

In the aftermath of the 9/11 attacks, the relationship between al Qaeda and its associated groups changed considerably. Al Qaeda no longer enjoys the use of a safe haven in Afghanistan, and it has suffered substantial attrition through combat fatalities and the capture of operatives in many countries. As a result, it is more isolated from other organizations, and the center of gravity for terrorist activities has shifted to a looser patchwork of jihadist groups, including the degraded but still dangerous JI (Gunaratna, 2004, pp. 119–123; International Crisis Group, 2003, pp. 29–31; Black, 2004). Some regional groups are attempting to sustain the terrorist campaign against the United States and its allies. However, this is complicated by the fact that groups such as JI have suffered significant leadership losses since 9/11 and must adapt to operating in a more hostile counterterrorist environment.[15]

Although JI was not a creation of al Qaeda, its leadership looked to al Qaeda for inspiration, training, and financial assistance during JI's formative years. At least one faction within JI, headed by Hambali, had exceptionally close connections with al Qaeda, although other JI factions do not seem to have shared al Qaeda's global jihadist priorities. Whether al Qaeda and JI, or at least an aggressive faction within JI, still maintain ties with significant implications for operational and tactical learning is uncertain. Nevertheless, the connections that JI forged with al Qaeda and key regional groups such as MILF during its first decade of development have been important sources of operational and tactical learning.

Operations and Tactics

Starting in mid-2000, JI planned a series of bombing attacks—some of which were successful and some of which were not—that defined it as a terrorist group and signaled its willingness to use violent methods for advancing its aims. These JI bombing attacks, as well as the evolving communication practices that have supported the group's bombing operations and other organizational activities, are examined below. Particular attention is given to operational decisionmaking. The examination is then extended to other important functional areas, including training, logistics, and operational security practices. It is important to note that while the bombing attacks have attracted substantial attention, they were only one aspect of the many activities JI has undertaken as a militant Islamic organization. The group has also been heavily engaged in building up its base of recruits and supporters through "missionary work,"

---

[15] Since 2002, JI has suffered from a steady loss of senior leadership. Its leader Ba'asyir and several mid-level leaders, including Hambali, Abu Jibril, Abu Rusdan, and the leaders of the Bali bombing operations, Imam Samudra and Mukhlas, have been arrested. In addition, a senior JI operative and bomb-making expert, Fathur Roman al-Ghozi, was arrested and later killed while attempting to avoid capture after escaping from prison.

as well as other jihad activities, such as sending JI members to participate in the sectarian conflicts in eastern Indonesia.

JI Bombing Attacks

One of the defining features of JI as a terrorist group has been its willingness and ability to undertake major bombing operations. Since 2000, JI bombing operations of varying sophistication have been conducted against a broad range of target types in Indonesia, the Philippines, and Singapore.

Table 4.2 lists the most significant bombing attacks known to have been undertaken by JI to date, from the first known JI attack in mid-2000 in Jakarta to the bombing of the Australian embassy in Jakarta in September 2004. It also includes the foiled plot to bomb locations in Singapore, including the U.S. and Israeli embassies, because this was a fairly well-developed effort by the time it was interrupted by arrests made by Singapore authorities. Although JI is suspected of having been involved in a few other bombings throughout Southeast Asia in recent years, there is no definitive confirmation and little available information on the details of the attacks.[16]

Table 4.2
JI Bombing Attacks, 2000–2004

Date	Target and Location	Type of Attack and Results
August 1, 2000	Residence of the Philippine ambassador to Indonesia (Jakarta)	Single car bomb: 3 killed, 17 wounded
December 24, 2000	Churches and priests in Indonesia (11 cities across Java and Sumatra)	Christmas Eve bombings—38 bombs (20 detonated): 15 killed, 94 wounded
December 30, 2000	Metro Manila, including the light rail train	Five near-simultaneous bombings; 14 killed, 70 wounded
Late 2001	Foreign embassies (U.S., Israel, UK, Australia), U.S. naval ships, and other Western interests in Singapore	Six large truck bombs: foiled by Singapore police arrests in December 2001
October 12, 2002	2 Bali nightclubs (Kuta, Bali) and the U.S. consulate (Sanur, Bali)	One large car bomb and two smaller bombs: 202 killed, over 500 wounded
August 5, 2003	J.W. Marriott Hotel (Jakarta)	Single car bomb: 12 killed, numerous wounded
September 9, 2004	Australian embassy (Jakarta)	Single truck van bomb: 9 killed, nearly 100 wounded

SOURCES: *Report of the Inquiry into the Australian Intelligence Agencies*, 2004, p. 41; White Paper, 2003; various *TEMPO Magazine* articles.

---

[16] Determining which bombing attacks were undertaken by JI is complicated by the fact that JI does not take public responsibility for its attacks, and numerous bombings in Southeast Asia could be attributed to any of a large number of groups that also do not typically claim responsibility for their violent actions. The bombing operations attributed to JI are based on what can be confirmed with confidence, using open sources. Additional bombing incidents may have been undertaken or supported by JI in the areas of sectarian conflict. For example, there are reports that JI members were involved in an effort to bomb churches in Medan, Indonesia, in May 2000; JI, with MILF assistance, may also have been largely responsible for the two Davao City bombings in the Philippines in March and April 2003 that killed more than 40 people (International Crisis Group, 2004b, pp. 18, 23–24, 28).

To provide a better sense of JI's evolving approach to bombing operations, the major JI operations are described below.[17]

Philippine Ambassador's Residence in Jakarta. On August 1, 2000, JI operatives exploded a car bomb outside the Jakarta residence of the Philippine ambassador to Indonesia. A car laden with explosives was parked at an entrance to the residence and remotely detonated as the ambassador's car drove by it.[18] The operation was managed by Fathur Roman al-Ghozi, one of JI's leading bomb experts at the time (Ressa, 2003, p. 102; McBeth, 2001, p. 28).[19] Three people were killed and 17, including the Philippine ambassador, were wounded in the attack. This early JI bombing operation was somewhat atypical, because it involved discriminate targeting that was apparently intended to assassinate one individual.[20] Some analysts believe that JI carried out this attack as a favor to MILF, which had recently suffered reverses when the Philippine army attacked its training camps in Mindanao. Thus, the attack is consistent with JI's priority at the time of promoting regional collaboration among the newly created Mujahidin Coalition of militant Islamic groups, which JI was instrumental in forming.

Christmas Eve Bombings in Indonesia. JI undertook a very ambitious operation on December 24, 2000, that involved more than three dozen bombs at religious targets in 11 Indonesian cities. The bombs were delivered as parcels and bags to churches and the homes of priests, and most of them exploded at around 9 p.m. on Christmas Eve (ICG, 2002b, pp. 5–6, 15–18, 27–29; Ressa, 2003, pp. 102–103).[21] The bombers used timers or relied on remote detonation using cell-phone devices. The bombings killed 15 people and wounded more than 90. The casualties would have been higher, but only 20 of the 38 bombs exploded. Although JI did not publicly take responsibility for these attacks at the time, information obtained during later arrests of JI operatives provided details on the group's involvement in the operation, which provided several JI leaders and operatives, many of whom were involved in subsequent attack operations, including the Bali bombings, with an important

---

[17] In addition, there have been public reports of failed JI plots, including plans to attack the U.S. and Australian embassies in Bangkok and popular Thai beach resorts, and surveillance of the site of the APEC meeting of world leaders in Bangkok in October 2003. However, these plots are not analyzed in this chapter because arrests by Thai authorities stopped them from progressing very far, and few details are publicly available on the preparations that might have been undertaken (Ressa, 2003, p. 217; "Hambali 'Eyed Bangkok Embassies,'" 2003.)

[18] Personal interview with an academic expert, Jakarta, May 2004.

[19] Al-Ghozi was one of Ba'asyir's students and who went on to receive training in Afghanistan and Pakistan to become an explosives expert. Al-Ghozi had close relations with MILF. He procured needed explosives for terrorist operations and managed some of the initial JI bombing attacks (Ressa, 2003, pp. 135–136).

[20] This early bombing involved a tactical operational security blunder by JI operatives, who failed to erase the registration number on a vehicle slated to be used to deliver the attack. Indonesian authorities subsequently used this information to link the vehicle to a JI operative who was later involved in the Bali bombings (BBC Monitoring Asia Pacific, 2003).

[21] Personal interview with a counterterrorism official, Singapore, June 2004.

learning experience. Hambali was reportedly responsible for overall management of this wide-ranging operation.

This early incident highlighted the fact that JI had much to learn about staging effective bombing operations, as one operative was killed by a premature detonation and another was killed while transporting the bombs.[22] These mixed results reportedly prompted Hambali to undertake an after-action review session to improve JI skills (Ressa, 2003, p. 103).[23]

Metro Manila Bombings. A series of bombs were detonated around the metropolitan Manila area on December 30, 2000, the nation's Rizal Day holiday. Five bombs detonated at nearly the same time, killing 14 people on a light railway train and wounding some 70 others (White Paper, 2003, p. 7; International Crisis Group, 2004b, pp. 18–19; Ressa, 2003, pp. 102–103). This operation was reportedly managed by Fathur Roman al-Ghozi (International Crisis Group, 2004b, pp. 18–19; White Paper, 2003, p. 7). One bomb was exploded at the plaza in front of the U.S. embassy, probably for symbolic reasons (Turnbull, 2003).

Foiled Singapore Bombings. In late 2001, the JI cells in Singapore engaged in a joint operation with al Qaeda to attack multiple targets, using truck bombs. The key targets of interest to al Qaeda were the U.S. embassy, the Israeli embassy, and naval facilities in Singapore being used by U.S. naval forces. The JI operatives suggested additional possible targets, including the Australian and British High Commissions, as well as American companies with offices in commercial buildings in Singapore (White Paper, 2003, pp. 12–13; Ressa, 2003, pp. 158–160).[24]

As part of the joint plan, the JI's local cells began conducting reconnaissance with an al Qaeda representative, Mohammed Mansour Jabarah, on selected targets; the reconnaissance included making video recordings. JI was tasked with handling the major logistical requirements of the operation, including procurement of 17 tons of ammonium nitrate to make explosives that would be used in up to six truck bombs (White Paper, 2003, pp. 13, 27).[25] Al Qaeda was providing planning and financing for the operation and was planning to provide suicide bombers to deliver the truck bombs to their targets. While the JI operatives were mainly serving in a support role, one of the Singapore cells (Fiah Musa) indicated that it was ready to participate in the attacks. The plot was derailed when Singapore's Internal Security Department arrested several JI members in December 2001 (White Paper, 2003).

---

[22] One senior JI member, known as Jabir, was killed when the bomb he was carrying detonated prematurely. He apparently failed to change the card inside his own cell phone, which was being used in a bomb. Several other JI members were also killed while working on or transporting bombs (International Crisis Group, 2002b, p. 17; Turnbull, 2003).

[23] Personal interview with a counterterrorism official, Jakarta, May 2004.

[24] Personal interview with a counterterrorism official, Singapore, May 2004.

[25] Personal interview with a counterterrorism official, Singapore, June 2004.

The 2001 arrests were followed by the arrests of more JI members and other terrorist suspects in August 2002; this was a major setback for JI in Singapore. In addition to the joint attack with al Qaeda, JI's operations chief Hambali had been pressing for attacks on Singapore's infrastructure installations, including water pipelines and the national airport, hoping to somehow implicate Malaysia and provoke a war between Singapore and Malaysia. JI members also conducted reconnaissance and videotaped some of these potential targets (White Paper, 2003, pp. 28, 30–31; Ressa, 2003, pp. 156–157).

Bali Bombings. The JI's most destructive bombing attack to date took place on the Indonesian island of Bali on October 12, 2002. As detailed in Table 4.3, multiple bombs were used to produce mass casualties at two nightclubs in the Kuta section of Bali at around 11 p.m. (local time). At the same time, another bomb was detonated near the U.S. consulate in Sanur, Bali. The JI attack team placed a small bomb in Paddy's Bar and a much larger bomb (50 to 150 kilograms) in a van parked on the street outside the Sari Club. The near-simultaneous detonations on a crowded evening killed 202 people and wounded more than 500 (Australian Federal Police, "Operation Alliance," n.d.). To ensure that the large bomb would work, the JI team outfitted it with four separate detonation mechanisms (Ressa, 2003, p. 186). The third bomb was exploded at a street curb near the U.S. consulate but caused no casualties. There is evidence that the JI team that planned the Bali attacks used suicide bombers. If this is correct, the Bali attacks signaled a discontinuous change in JI's operational bombing approach. It was JI's first known use of suicide bombers.

The team that managed the Bali bombings was coordinated by an experienced JI field commander, Imam Samudra, who had been involved in the Christmas Eve bombing along with others in this group (Ressa, 2003, pp. 183–185). The leader of the entire operation was Mukhlas (Ali Gufron), a senior JI member with Afghanistan

Table 4.3
Operational Details on the Bali Bombings (October 12, 2002)

	First Bombing	Second Bombing	Third Bombing
Target	Paddy's Bar	Sari Club	U.S. consulate
Time	~11:05 p.m.	~11:05 p.m.	~11:06 p.m.
Location	Kuta, Bali (inside bar)	Kuta, Bali (outside bar on street)	Sanur, Bali (on street curb near consulate)
Bomb type	500 g–1 kg TNT	50–150 kg TNT	500 g–1 kg TNT
Delivery means	Bomb delivered inside bar	L300 Mitsubishi van with added explosives driven by a suicide bomber	Bomb left on curb and remotely detonated using a cell phone
Casualties	Total for both clubs: 202 killed, 500 wounded		No casualties

SOURCES: Australian Federal Police, "Operation Alliance," n.d.

experience, who was capable of handling the financial and logistical needs of the operation.[26] Some JI members claimed that their motive was to attack the United States and other Western adversaries by striking a location where "white" Westerners were known to congregate. The bomb outside the U.S. consulate was intended to signal that the Bali bombings were linked to the United States (Australian Federal Police, "Bali Bombing Trials," n.d.).

Through a combination of good police work and the use of surveillance technologies, Indonesian authorities found and arrested the leaders of the Bali bombing operations and most of their team members in the weeks and months following the bombing. The Indonesian authorities and their police forces received vital assistance from foreign investigators and particularly benefited from technical services provided by Australia.

J.W. Marriott Hotel Bombing. Despite the arrests of its Indonesian operatives following the Bali bombings, JI demonstrated theability to still conduct major bombing attacks, even under greater scrutiny by government counterterrorist assets. On August 5, 2003, JI operatives detonated a large car bomb in front of the J.W. Marriott Hotel in downtown Jakarta (McBeth et al., 2003, pp. 12–16). The bombing resulted in 12 killed and many wounded and might have produced much higher casualties among the lunchtime crowd in the hotel, which had a large glass facade, but the driver of the bomb-laden truck encountered difficulties in approaching the building and the bomb was exploded a short distance from it. The attack was reportedly managed by Dr. Azahari Husin, with assistance from Noordin Mohamed Top (Wiljayanta, 2003, pp. 16–19; Ressa, 2003, pp. 214–215), both Malaysians with bomb-making experience. The JI member driving the truck is believed to have been a suicide bomber. Azahari remotely detonated the bomb from a distance and then made his escape on the back of a motorcycle.

Australian Embassy Bombing. On September 9, 2004, JI undertook another car bombing, this one at the Australian embassy. At a minimum, this attack demonstrated JI's continuing capabilities for executing major bombing attacks. However, if the operational and political intent of the attack was to inflict substantial casualties on Australian embassy personnel, particularly foreigners, it fell quite short of the desired result. In the attack, which occurred during a mid-morning business day, a minivan estimated to be carrying about 200 kilograms of explosives was detonated approaching the embassy front gates on an adjacent side street. The explosion resulted in substantial casualties (seven killed and nearly 100 seriously wounded), including embassy security personnel, Indonesian police guarding the embassy perimeter, passersby, and numerous individuals in surrounding buildings who were hurt by

---

[26] The Bali bombing operation also highlighted the willingness of JI operatives to rely on a tightly knit group of comrades, including family members. Mukhlas' two younger brothers, Amrozi and Ali Imron, were deeply involved in the logistics and bomb-making aspects of the operation (Ressa, 2003, pp. 183–184; Turnbull, 2003).

shattered window glass. Most of those wounded and all of those killed were Indonesians. While the explosion ravaged the embassy's facade, no Australian personnel were killed.[27]

Indonesian police officials believe that the bombing was again the work of JI operatives Azahari and Top, who had gained experience in the earlier Bali and J.W. Marriott Hotel bombing attacks. The two operatives had narrowly avoided being arrested by the police on various occasions while operating in Indonesia's Central Java region in the months prior to the embassy attack (McBeth, 2004; Davis, 2004). As in the Bali and Marriott Hotel attacks, there are indications that a suicide bomber delivered the bomb to the target location. There are also reports that JI has a cell of newly recruited suicide bombers available (McBeth, 2004).

In summary, most of the JI bombing attacks since 2004 have involved multiple or large bombs aimed at indiscriminately producing substantial numbers of casualties. Although the delivery mechanisms vary somewhat, car and truck bombs have been prominently used, particularly to deliver larger amounts of explosives to target sites. In most cases, the JI bombers left the attack scene before or after the explosion occurred, but in at least three instances (the Bali, J.W. Marriott Hotel, and Australian embassy bombings), there is evidence that suicide bombers were used. Finally, in the case of the foiled plot to bomb Western interests in Singapore, the JI personnel were performing a support role as part of a joint operation with al Qaeda.

Operational Decisionmaking

The formal organizational structure of JI suggests a top-down decisionmaking process for making choices about where, when, and whether to undertake bombing attacks, yet available sources suggest a more complex form of operational decisionmaking.

Although all of the JI bombing attacks since 2000 have been consistent with the group's militant separatist agenda, a disagreement over priorities seems to have emerged among its members in recent years. Some analysts believe that a split occurred within JI when one faction embraced the idea of making a quick transition to undertaking terrorist attacks as part of the global jihad strategy favored by al Qaeda and another faction favored the long-term strategy of building up the organization through recruitment and indoctrination and the participation of JI members in local sectarian conflicts in Indonesia (International Crisis Group, 2004a, pp. 1–3; Jones, 2004).

In this context, the operational decisionmaking of the JI leadership concerning bombing attacks is the result of competing influences. Al Qaeda has been able to gal-

---

[27] It is possible that the attackers were more intent on demonstrating JI's continuing presence than on inflicting maximum casualties among the foreign embassy personnel, who were relatively protected within the embassy grounds.

vanize certain JI factions into terrorist attacks by providing needed financial resources and technical expertise. Some top JI leaders, including Hambali, were known to have pressed for moving more rapidly toward achieving an operational capability for terrorist attacks, particularly against targets consistent with the global jihadist strategy promoted by al Qaeda. Others within JI seemed to favor a "go-slow" approach that is more consistent with the long-term plan reportedly contained in the JI's basic guidelines document.[28] Thus, external encouragement and pressure from al Qaeda appears to have influenced the timing of JI terrorist attacks and their targets.

In this internal debate, JI's Amir, Abu Bakar Ba'asyir, appears to have favored the go-slow approach. However, he was apparently unable or unwilling to prevent JI leaders (e.g., Hambali and Mukhlas) from proceeding with large bombing attacks. Not surprisingly, the JI operatives who undertook the Bali bombing were closely associated with Hambali and had worked with him previously, in the Christmas Eve bombing (Ressa, 2003, pp. 183–184). But despite the group's internal disagreements, it is likely that Ba'asyir, as its spiritual leader, had some knowledge of and influence over major attack plans.

Another operational decisionmaking issue confronting the JI's top leaders has been whether to attack high-value protected targets, such as U.S. embassies and naval targets in Southeast Asian countries. Since the 9/11 attacks, JI has explored opportunities for attacking U.S. embassies, including those in Manila and Jakarta. Prior to the Australian embassy bombing in mid-2004, JI apparently concluded that attacking well-protected targets was beyond its capabilities and instead opted for attacks on relatively unprotected soft targets.[29] Without the distinctive advantages enjoyed by al Qaeda, such as a safe haven for developing a well-funded and highly professional terrorist organization, the JI leadership apparently lacked the confidence or capabilities required to emulate al Qaeda's attacks, despite a desire to do so. To some degree, JI's inability to attack highly protected targets reflects a lack of necessary operational and tactical knowledge and skills and an inability to acquire them from al Qaeda or develop them on their own. The failure of the attack on the Australian embassy to inflict devastating damage while expending JI's finite resources may suggest a lack of organizational learning.

Information on how specific JI teams are used for bombing operations is somewhat limited. However, the organization appears to rely on the basic approach favored by al Qaeda, separating the final attack team members from the teams engaged

---

[28] This document, *General Guidelines for the Jemaah Islamiyah Struggle* (known as the PUPJI), appears to have been written by JI founder Sungkar and other Afghan veterans. It lays out the JI organizational structure and basic guidelines for recruiting new members and other activities (International Crisis Group, 2002b, pp. 11–12).

[29] The only time the JI came close to bombing a protected target was in late 2001, when its local cells were assigned to support their al Qaeda counterparts in undertaking strikes on the U.S. embassy and other facilities in Singapore. This plan, which was foiled by a series of arrests made by Singapore's internal security police in late 2001, relegated the JI operatives to a supporting role to al Qaeda (White Paper, 2003, pp. 27–28).

in target surveillance and supporting logistics. This approach was apparent in both the Bali bombings and the foiled Singapore attack, where al Qaeda was to provide the suicide bombers to deliver the truck bombs and the Singapore cell of JI was responsible for target surveillance and logistical support. There are some indications that JI has formed a unit known as *Laskar Khos* (special force), which appears to have been involved in the J.W. Marriott Hotel bombing. This unit is believed to be headed by Zulkarnaen, JI's current military operations chief, who is still at large (Davis, 2004). *Laskar Khos* seems to have the authority to draw together JI members from any part of the organization to undertake its missions (International Crisis Group, 2002b, pp. 11–12).[30]

Bomb-Making Practices

JI seems to have settled for making incremental improvements to its basic bomb design and approach rather than striving for more innovative designs and techniques. Even though there has been a steady improvement in its design and delivery techniques, JI's bombing capability in its 2003–2004 attacks is not fundamentally different from that in the attacks of 2000. Its basic bomb design and vehicle delivery system probably are based on knowledge received at al Qaeda training camps in Afghanistan or later at MILF training camps in the southern Philippines. As noted earlier, many of the bombs used in the Christmas Eve bombings either failed to detonate or exploded prematurely, killing several JI operatives.

The later JI bombings (e.g., the Bali, J.W. Marriott Hotel, and Australian embassy attacks) show some notable improvements. The destructive effects of the large bomb used in the Bali attack were enhanced by packing the delivery vehicle (a Mitsubishi L300 van) with a dozen plastic filing cabinets filled with a mix of explosive materials. In addition, JI bomb-makers rigged the bomb with four separate detonation mechanisms to ensure that it would detonate as planned.[31] Similarly, the bomb used in the attack on the J.W. Marriott Hotel the following year was packed with a combination of explosives and additional materials to enhance its lethal effects (Manggut, 2003, p. 20; Wijayanta, 2003, pp. 17–20).[32]

JI appears to rely heavily on the experience of one of its top bomb-makers, Dr. Azahari Husin, a former university lecturer and British-trained engineer who was involved in the Christmas Eve, Bali, and J.W. Marriott Hotel bombings (and probably the Australian embassy bombing). He reportedly attended an advanced bomb-

---

[30] Personal interview with an academic expert, Jakarta, May 2004.

[31] The mehanisms included a mobile phone rigged for detonation, a direct trigger switch to be pulled by the suicide bomber, a timer system, and a trigger in one of the filing cabinet drawers set to go off if the drawer was opened (Ressa, 2003, pp. 186–187).

[32] One analyst has suggested that the large bombs used by JI were intended to eliminate all material evidence that could be important to forensic investigations after the explosions (Yusuf, 2003, p. 16).

making course in Kandahar, Afghanistan, during 2000 ("Azahari's Tracks," 2003, p. 15) and seems to have developed a method to take advantage of household materials, such as soap bars, and a compact design to significantly boost the destructive effects of composite bombs (Wijayanta, 2003, pp. 17–20).

Some Western experts, along with the police who assessed the Bali bombings, have contended that the JI bombs are not sufficiently well designed to make full use of their potential explosive power.[33] However, it is possible that JI operatives consider these bombs "good enough" for their purpose of undertaking terrorist attacks on soft targets and supporting jihadist operations.

Two other factors could also be shaping JI's approach to bomb making. The first is JI's tendency to look to al Qaeda for support and guidance, having received its basic bomb-making training from al Qaeda instructors in Afghanistan. Given this continuing relationship, JI might not have had a strong incentive for improving its bomb designs and delivery systems until relatively recently, when its connection to al Qaeda likely has been disrupted. Second, JI has not enjoyed a safe haven where it could develop and test improved bombs and weapon delivery systems without compromising its security. Whatever the reason, from 2000 to 2004, JI focused on the use of bombs whose destructiveness and reliability were continuously (but modestly) improved over time.

Communications

Reliable communications are the lifeblood of any organization, and terrorist groups have a special need for secure communications to build up their infrastructure and to undertake major attack operations. Like most terrorist organizations, JI has relied on a combination of traditional and modern communication techniques to link diverse organizational components. As noted in the discussion of bombing attacks, however, JI has had significant problems in achieving secure communications.

By relying on a cell structure to enhance its operational security, JI creates a special need for communications that are both reliable and secure. It has reportedly made use of the following types of communications:

- **Face-to-face communications.** The JI's cell structure has enabled it to use direct communications to disseminate messages and orders. In addition, like al Qaeda, JI has relied on couriers to deliver communications (Gunaratna, 2002, p. 76).
- **Internet communications.** Some JI operatives have taken advantage of the Internet, including talk channels, to communicate with other operatives and even to appeal to fellow Muslims to engage in jihadist activities in the Ambon and Poso conflicts (Ressa, 2003, p. 184).

---

[33] According to Australian Federal Police officials, only about a third of the material in the main Bali bomb exploded; the rest of it simply burned ("Bali Bomb 'Failed to Fully Explode,'" 2003).

- **Cell phones and text messaging.** One of the more modern communication technologies available to JI has been cell phones. Although operatives use the verbal communications features, they have found the text messaging function particularly useful for contacting other JI colleagues.
- **Codewords.** JI operatives reportedly rely on codewords to protect their messages from outsiders who might be listening in on their communications.[34,35]

The communication practices of the JI "field commander" for the Bali bombing operations, Imam Samudra, offer some insights into how modern communication technologies can be used to support terrorist attacks. One account notes that

> Samudra not only used the Internet to coordinate his operatives; he also added an Asian twist, text messaging on cellular phones. According to law enforcement officials in the region, this is one of the hardest forms of communication to trace (Ressa, 2003, p. 185).

However, following the Bali bombings, the Indonesian police investigators, with technical surveillance assistance from the Australian Federal Police, were able to take advantage of the JI members' use of cell phones to identify the suspected bombers, track them down, and arrest them. JI apparently adapted to this new counterterrorism capability by gradually changing its communication practices to reduce the risks that attackers would be identified and apprehended by the Indonesian police.

Thus, JI's communications have evolved over time as the group learned through painful experience that counterterrorism forces could effectively exploit its earlier shortcomings in maintaining secure communications. In addition to secure communications, however, JI's attack capabilities depend upon other functional areas, including training, logistics, and operational security, that must be mastered to support repeated and effective terrorist operations. These functional areas are examined next.

Training

Training serves multiple purposes for JI. Religious study is an integral element of its recruitment and indoctrination process,[36] and JI also wants some of its members to

---

[34] Personal interview with a counterterrorism official, Singapore, June 2004.

[35] For example, the suspected suicide bomber in the attack on the J.W. Marriott Hotel in 2003, a JI operative known as Asmal, reportedly sent a coded e-mail message expressing an intention to "marry as soon as possible," which Indonesian police interpreted to mean he was ready to launch a suicide attack ("Police Identify Driver of Van Used in Jakarta Bombing," 2004).

[36] One report notes that the JI recruits were expected to undergo two stages of religious training: religious classes for the general audience, and a more targeted recruitment process for identifying potential recruits for the

have the knowledge and skills required to participate in terrorist attacks and other types of armed warfare, such as fighting local sectarian conflicts.[37]

JI members who attend training camps receive physical conditioning and are trained in the use of the following types of weapons and tactics (International Crisis Group, 2004b, p. 16; Ressa, 2003, pp. 102–103):

- Basic firearms (pistols, automatic rifles, mortars, etc.)
- Military tactics
- Explosives, including the safe handling of explosive materials and the use of improvised explosive devices
- Assassination techniques

In addition, JI members are likely to have received training in surveillance of targets and operational security to protect them from having their activities observed or penetrated by security forces.

Over the past decade, JI has relied on a combination of venues to address its training needs. This has created opportunities for organizational learning, as JI members have worked and trained with experts from other Islamic militant organizations. The most important training venues available to the JI have been

- Al Qaeda training camps in Afghanistan
- MILF camps in the southern Philippines
- Jihadist camps in Indonesia and Malaysia

Al Qaeda Camps in Afghanistan

During its initial years, JI sent promising members to Afghanistan to advance their knowledge of and commitment to jihad. These individuals could receive general training or they could be given training tailored for terrorist operations based on the al Qaeda manual, *Declaration of Jihad Against the Country's Tyrants (Military Series)*, which covers weapons, espionage, and operational security (Gunaratna, 2002, pp. 71–72). At that time, JI was able to take advantage of the extensive training camps al Qaeda had developed as part of the safe haven it enjoyed under the protection of the Taliban regime. The training senior JI operatives received at camps in Afghanistan contributed to their organizational effectiveness and group cohesion.

---

exclusive unit committed to jihad. The recruitment process could take up to 18 months (White Paper, 2003, p. 15).

[37] JI's insistence on extensive religious training prompted some jihadists anxious to participate in the sectarian conflict in Poso, in Indonesia's Central Sulawesi province, to join with *Mujahidin KOMPAK*, a competing jihadist group that provided a quick military training course and relied more on learning by doing (International Crisis Group, 2004a, pp. 8–9).

However, sending JI members to Afghanistan for training was expensive and required providing false documentation to facilitate their travel. It also became increasingly risky over time. After the U.S. embassy bombings in 1998, arrests of individuals transiting through Pakistan for training purposes increased (Gunaratna, 2004, p. 119), and al Qaeda began looking for more-secure regional training facilities. As a result, militant Islamic groups were encouraged to establish training camps that also would be available for training al Qaeda operatives.

MILF Training Camps in the Philippines

During the mid- to late 1990s, JI benefited from sending its members to MILF's Camp Abu Bakar, in Mindanao in the southern Philippines. This camp was made available for training of foreign jihadists, including JI and al Qaeda personnel.[38] Within the camp, JI was allowed to establish a separate training facility known as Camp Hodeibia (or Camp Hudaibiyah), where its members had access to a full range of courses, including training in handling firearms and explosives (White Paper, 2003, p. 8; Ressa, 2003, pp. 7–9, 134–137). Other foreign jihadists received training in different parts of the Camp Abu Bakar complex.

The working relationship of JI and MILF was strengthened by the involvement of Fathur Rohman al-Ghozi. Until his death in 2002, he was an important liaison between JI and MILF. By 1998, MILF and JI essentially created an Islamic military training academy within the larger Camp Abu Bakar infrastructure. At this facility, Indonesians and Filipinos served as both trainers and students for an 18-month course in weapons training, explosives handling, tactics, and religious studies. The students also received "jihad exposure" by briefly serving on the front line between MILF and the government forces (International Crisis Group, 2004b, pp. 15–17). This collaborative training arrangement lasted at least through mid-2000, when the camp was overrun by the Philippine army. Some observers have suggested that JI continues to train its operatives in Mindanao, despite this setback.[39]

Other Training Camps

Along with training at these formal camps, JI has provided basic training for its members in other venues in Malaysia and Indonesia. JI recruits received rudimentary training in a "jungle training" camp in the Negri Sembilan region of Malaysia, where they had the opportunity to engage in physical training and to learn basic military

---

[38] One analyst notes that the "importance of the training in the MILF camps to the development of Jemaah Islamiyah cannot be overstated," because of the large numbers of JI personnel who gained relevant terrorist skills, including bomb making, weapons training, surveillance, sabotage, communications, and cell formation at these camps (Abuza, 2003b, p. 138).

[39] Personal interviews with a counterterrorism official, Singapore, June 2004, and an academic expert, Jakarta, May 2004.

skills. However, at this camp, JI avoided the use of firearms, which could attract undue attention to its activities and could prompt Malaysian authorities to take action. Similarly, JI reportedly has been able to take advantage of the ongoing sectarian conflicts in Indonesia to use the military training camp run by its associated paramilitary arm, the Laskar Jundullah. Al Qaeda operatives also reportedly have been associated with such local training camps as well (Gunarata, 2004, pp. 119, 127).

These training activities have been integral to developing JI's organizational learning capacity. Along with acquiring the necessary skills and knowledge for undertaking terrorist operations, training provides opportunities for reinforcing indoctrination and exposing members to jihadist situations (Ramakrishna, 2004, p. 42). Training also enables JI members to interact with external groups that possess needed knowledge and skills. The sharing of training camps and expert instructors creates opportunities for collaboration with other regional militant groups and has also provided JI with access to al Qaeda's substantial expertise.

Logistics

Logistics, broadly defined, is another functional area in which terrorist groups need to acquire knowledge and experience. Key logistical tasks include the acquisition of arms and materials for creating weapons, such as bombs, and meeting the general material needs of operations. These tasks have been more challenging for JI than for some other groups because, despite its successes in bombing attacks, JI has lacked a robust and reliable structure for providing logistical support and financing its bombing operations.

In most of JI's bombing operations, an individual or an individual cell was assigned the lead responsibility for managing the logistical needs of the attack team. These needs include supplying the explosive materials to the bomb-making team, acquiring and delivering the vehicle to be used (if the bomb is to be delivered by car or truck), and making arrangements for secure accommodations for the operatives on the attack team (Australian Federal Police, 2003).

The shortage of funds has hampered efforts to provide adequate and timely logistical support for JI's larger bombing attacks. Earlier operations, including the foiled attempt to attack western targets in Singapore in late 2001, benefited from injections of al Qaeda funding, either directly or through an Islamic charity. However, by the time of the Bali bombings a year later, JI had to rely on criminal activities, including the robbery of a jewelry store, to generate the cash it needed (Australian Federal Police, 2003). Even when external financing was available, the amounts received were not always sufficient, and critical bomb-making materials had to be purchased in a piecemeal fashion (White Paper, 2003, pp. 27–28).

The logistical arrangements for supporting JI bombing operations have also been somewhat haphazard. For example, the plans for accumulating explosive materials for the joint al Qaeda and JI attack on targets in Singapore involved scheduling travel through four neighboring countries.[40] To some degree, the southern Philippines has been the logistical hub for JI because weapons (e.g., automatic rifles), explosive materials (e.g., TNT), and bomb components (e.g., blasting caps, timers) were readily accessible there, and JI safe houses for arms caches could be established without arousing as much suspicion as in neighboring countries.[41] In addition, the relative ease of travel among the littoral countries of Southeast Asia has facilitated the transnational trade in weapons-related contraband.

Intelligence and Operational Security

Intelligence Gathering to Support Attack Operations

The success or failure of a major terrorist operation can depend on whether sufficient knowledge concerning the target is available to the attackers. A distinguishing characteristic of the JI bombing operations to date has been an emphasis on extensive target identification and surveillance. JI's proficiency in this functional area results from several sources of learning, including the al Qaeda training of senior JI operatives, the study of al Qaeda training manuals, and learning by doing over the course of several different bombing operations.

Insights into JI's target identification and surveillance practices come primarily from JI operatives who have been arrested and sent to trial. The limited information available suggests that even though JI realizes the importance of undertaking target surveillance, its practices can vary by local circumstances. For example, prior to their arrests in late 2001 and early 2002, the JI operatives in Singapore accumulated years of experience in casing potential targets, both Western targets, such as the U.S. embassy and naval facilities, and a wide range of Singapore government facilities and critical infrastructure.

As a White Paper prepared by the Singapore Ministry of Home Affairs notes, the JI operatives engaged in a variety of target identification and surveillance activities, including making photographs and sketches of potential targets. They also used modern information technologies to create an electronic record:

---

[40] The Singapore bombing plan involved acquiring TNT from a supplier in the Philippines, which then had to be smuggled through Indonesia and Malaysia before arriving clandestinely in Singapore. This time-consuming process constrained JI's ability to support the al Qaeda plan (White Paper, 2003, pp. 27–28).

[41] One arms cache seized in the General Santos City region in January 2002 yielded "more than a ton of explosives, detonating cords, blasting caps, and seventeen M-16 rifles packed in grease to prevent corrosion from seawater" (International Crisis Group, 2004b, p. 23).

The JI "casing" (reconnaissance) methodology included a reliance on video recordings of the targeted sites as preparation. Such video reconnaissance and recordings were conducted over many times and final composite video would then be produced for use to finalise the operation.[42]

The video recordings provided actual images and the opportunity for JI operatives to edit the tapes and provide voice-over commentary. This was particularly useful to the attack personnel who could not be involved in target surveillance activities for operational security reasons. The videotapes also added to JI's institutional memory by providing a permanent record that retained valuable information.

Maintaining an electronic record of target surveillance activities can be risky from an operational security perspective. For example, the JI videotape recording of target reconnaissance in the vicinity of Singapore's Yishun mass transit station (routinely used by U.S. military personnel and their families) was discovered in the rubble of the home of Mohammed Atef (also known as Abu Hafs) in Afghanistan during Operation Enduring Freedom. This recording helped provide solid evidence of a connection between JI and al Qaeda that was useful in galvanizing stronger counterterrorism activities by Southeast Asian countries, particularly Singapore (White Paper, 2003, pp. 28–29; Ressa, 2003, pp. 155–156).

Other incidents of known JI target identification and surveillance activities reflect a determined but somewhat different approach from that taken in the Singapore case. In casing the Bali bombing targets, the JI operatives appear to have made more expedient choices of specific soft targets (particularly nightclubs) based on a series of drive-by tours of the tourist areas of Kuta weeks before the bombings, followed by a close-up visit just two days before the attack (Ressa, 2003, p. 185; Turnbull, 2003). The apparent absence of photography or a video-recording device in this case might indicate a difference among JI's territorial groups and branches in learning the benefits of this technique. Alternatively, it could indicate a greater concern for operational security on the part of the JI bombing teams in the post-9/11 period.

With a few notable exceptions, the JI bombing attacks conducted since 2000 have been well focused on their intended targets. Perhaps the most questionable case of JI target selection was that of the bombing of the Australian embassy in Jakarta, given that this major attack produced relatively limited casualties among embassy personnel. This poses the question of whether the embassy was the original target or the attack was poorly conceived and executed. The casualties were limited for several reasons, including the building's setback distance and orientation from the street, the protected perimeter of walls and a guarded entrance gate, the time of day when the attack occurred, and blast-resistant windows (McBeth, 2004; Manggut and

---

[42] White Paper, 2003, p. 28fn. For an excerpt of the detailed JI commentaries that accompanied a video recording, see Gunaratna, 2002, pp. 188–189.

Gunawan, 2003). In addition, there does not appear to have been an effective effort to breach the embassy gates beyond possibly crashing the explosives-laden vehicle near the gate. These factors suggest the possibility that the attack was poorly executed. Another possibility is that the JI planners changed their target selection at the last minute because of an increased security alert in Jakarta.[43]

Unless the JI attack on the Australian embassy was largely intended to demonstrate JI's continued presence, it appears to have fallen quite short of achieving its intended result. It is difficult to see the bombing as a major success for the JI. By creating numerous Indonesian casualties, it provoked Indonesian public anger and denouncement by political parties, including the Muslim political parties (Jones, 2004), in a way that reportedly had not occurred with earlier JI attacks. These mixed results suggest the possibility that JI has a constrained learning capability in terms of developing the skills needed to conduct effective bombing attacks against well-protected targets.

Operational Security Practices

Since the early 1990s, the JI leadership has faced the challenge of sustaining the organization within an increasingly hostile security environment. Following the 9/11 attacks, the Southeast Asian countries where JI traditionally operates came to recognize that JI presents a serious terrorist threat and started taking more-effective counterterrorism measures, including arrests and trials of JI members. In terms of security practices, JI appears to have a mixed record of initial operational success followed by a series of tactical shortfalls that have diminished its ranks.

Success at the Operational Level. The JI successfully operated "under the radar" of the authorities in Indonesia, Malaysia, the Philippines, Singapore, and Australia, where its presence grew over several years. As Gunaratna observed:

> By maintaining a low numerical strength, operating in the religious milieu, refraining from acquiring weapons until immediately before targeting, and strictly conforming to operational security, JI terrorist cells operated below the intelligence radar screen of Southeast Asian governments and public for nearly a decade until their detection in Singapore in December 2001 (Gunaratna, 2004, p. 126).

Before the Singapore government arrested JI cell members operating in Singapore in December 2001, there was little international recognition that JI existed as a group

---

[43] JI may have intended to attack a less-protected target, such as a hotel, but was thwarted when security measures were increased following a U.S. embassy warning the week before that "identifiably Western hotels" were at increased risk of terrorist attack (McBeth, 2004). Another possibility is that JI had been weakened by arrests over the previous two years and had fragmented into several subgroups capable of only low-tech (but high-impact) bombing attacks (Jones, 2004).

that perpetrated violent acts, including terrorist attacks. Part of the problem was the difficulty of distinguishing the nascent JI organization from the multitude of better-known outlawed militant or legal groups such as the Mujahidin Council of Indonesia (MMI), an umbrella organization that Ba'asyir established in 2000 to coordinate militant and hardline Islamic groups in Indonesia after the fall of the Suharto government (Abuza, 2003b, pp. 141–142).[44]

Although the proselytizing activities of Ba'asyir and his JI followers for a radical Islamic vision were widely known in Malaysia and elsewhere, JI's clandestine growth into a terrorist organization went largely unrecognized. It apparently was not clearly identified as an emerging threat by either Southeast Asian or foreign governments, including those of the United States and Australia, despite being responsible for a series of bombing attacks in Indonesia and the Philippines during 2000.[45] Only after the 9/11 attacks did Singapore and the Philippines recognize JI as a terrorist group and begin taking effective counterterrorism actions. Even then, neighboring Indonesia was slow to accept the idea of a significant terrorist threat arising from a local militant Islamic group; it did not launch a vigorous counterterrorism effort against JI until after the Bali bombings.[46]

While JI's learning sources are uncertain, it is likely that Sungkar and Ba'asyir were strongly influenced by the postwar experience of the Darul Islam separatist movement in Indonesia, from which they learned to maintain a low profile to avoid provoking government action. Similarly, JI might well have learned from al Qaeda ways of maintaining an ambiguous identity while building up its capabilities. One technique the JI leadership seems to have consciously adopted was that of avoiding undertaking any overt JI military or terrorist training in countries such as Malaysia, where it needed a safe haven for its organizational building activities.[47]

Shortfalls at the Tactical Level. JI has suffered some major setbacks because of shortfalls in its security practices at the tactical level. For example, Indonesian authorities, drawing on technical assistance from foreign countries such as Australia, were able to identify the JI operatives through their cell-phone communications in

---

[44] A good indication is that JI is not identified in public sources, including terrorist databases and press reports, before the 9/11 attacks, which drew greater international attention. For a related observation, see *Report of the Inquiry into the Australian Intelligence Agencies*, 2004, p. 36.

[45] As noted by the Australian government, "Little was known of the JI, under that name, before a major security operation undertaken by Singapore security authorities in December 2001 resulted in the arrest of 13 individuals suspected of planning large-scale terrorist strikes against US and other Western interests in Singapore and of being members of an organisation called Jemaah Islamiyah" (*Report of the Inquiry into the Australian Intelligence Agencies*, 2004, pp. 36–42).

[46] For a country-by-country assessment of the increasingly vigorous counterterrorism efforts of various Southeast Asian countries, see Rabasa, 2004, pp. 395–405.

[47] The JI leadership's desire to avoid drawing host government attention to its activities helps to explain the fact that there were no overt forms of military training or the use of firearms at the JI camp at Negri Sembilan in Malaysia (personal interview with a counterterrorism official, Singapore, June 2004; Gunaratna, 2002, p. 186).

the aftermath of the Bali bombings (McBeth, 2003). The Bali bombers also underestimated the government's ability to track them down using the vehicle registration number found in the truck debris scattered at the scene of the explosions. The government's ability to reconstruct the vehicle registration number, despite the efforts of the JI operatives to erase it prior to the bomb detonation, was a major break in the investigation. This important forensic evidence helped identify the JI members involved in the bombings and led directly to their arrests (McBeth et al., 2003).[48]

In addition to these shortfalls in operational security, JI has endured significant leadership attrition, as many of its top leaders have been captured or killed in counterterrorism operations since the 9/11 attacks.[49] However, it is unclear whether the ability of government authorities to find and arrest these leaders and other top operatives indicates a systemic shortfall in JI operational security practices or is simply the result of hard work and good luck on the part of the domestic intelligence agencies.

The JI learning experience in operational security against domestic and international counterterrorism efforts demonstrates both operational success and tactical shortfalls. The group took effective steps aimed at reducing the risk that government authorities would discover its steps in building a terrorist organization and undertaking its early bombing operations. It was able to go unnoticed, not only by the intelligence and police services of the countries where it was operating, but also by foreign intelligence services. However, JI appears to have not achieved similar success in its organizational learning of the tactical uses of operational security, since it was unable to protect a significant portion of its top leadership from being identified and captured.

Conclusions

Whatever course JI pursues in the future, its organizational effectiveness and survival will be strongly influenced by its operational and tactical learning capabilities, since it will be operating in a much more challenging counterterrorism environment than that which existed in the group's formative years.

---

[48] Initial reports from the forensic investigation of the Australian embassy bombing suggest that the police were able to recover the chassis number of the van used to deliver that bomb as well (Aglionby, 2004).

[49] These losses have included operations chief Hambali (arrested in Thailand, August 2003); Fathur Roman al-Ghozi (arrested in Manila in January 2002, later killed in a shootout after escaping from prison); and Abu Jibril, the JI's leading recruiter (arrested in January 2002 in Malaysia) (Ressa, 2003, pp. 162–163, 215–216).

Sources of Operational and Tactical Learning

JI's learning behavior as a terrorist organization has been shaped by a combination of internal processes and external influences. The most important drivers underlying its operational and tactical learning have been the following:

- **Learning by doing.** Over the course of its numerous bombing operations, the JI has continuously improved its capabilities for delivering deadly force, even though it has failed to achieve maximum possible casualties. This steady improvement reflects growing expertise gained through learning by doing. Likewise, JI has learned from its failures in key areas, including operational security. A good example is that the JI ceased communication practices that had enabled Indonesian authorities to identify and arrest key JI members involved in the Bali bombings.
- **Jihadist experience.** JI members have acquired knowledge and skills through their involvement in jihadist activities. The earlier generation of JI members gained this jihadist experience in Afghanistan. More recently, members have participated in internal Indonesian conflicts with the paramilitary organizations that JI has supported by providing fighters and trainers.
- **External influences.** One of the most important sources of operational and tactical learning for the JI has been its close connection with external groups. More than any other group in Southeast Asia, JI has been shaped by its close ties with al Qaeda, which was instrumental in its origins and development as a terrorist organization. The JI leadership has looked to al Qaeda as a model for terrorist operations and organization and has sought its blessings and support for operations. JI members have also benefited from training with al Qaeda operatives and closely worked with al Qaeda in the foiled 2001 plot to attack Western targets in Singapore. They also enjoyed a close working relationship with MILF, which permitted JI to conduct terrorist training at its camps in the southern Philippines.

While the diversity of JI's learning sources has enhanced the organization's overall operational and tactical learning, it appears to have come at the price of fostering distinct factions with different operational priorities. As noted earlier, one faction, which includes Hambali and others with experience at the al Qaeda training camps in Afghanistan, seems more favorably inclined toward the global jihadist strategy espoused by al Qaeda than do the JI members who received their training in the MILF camps or by participating in jihadist activities in Indonesia's sectarian conflicts. JI most likely acquired important knowledge and training in military tactics and skills by working with MILF.

Limits on Learning from Other Groups

However, there are limits to the process of learning from outside sources. JI's connections with al Qaeda and more-experienced regional militant groups help to explain how it was able to develop rapidly and become capable of undertaking relatively ambitious and deadly bombing attacks in multiple countries as early as 2000. Through collaboration, training, and mimicry, JI adopted some of al Qaeda's defining organizational and operational characteristics, including its basic organizational structure and approach to terrorist operations (e.g., mass-casualty attacks focused on Western targets).

Yet, despite these similarities, JI has fallen quite short of replicating al Qaeda's attack potential because it lacks the experience, financial resources, and operational flexibility that al Qaeda had uniquely acquired prior to 9/11. This difference is particularly evident in a comparison of their achievements. Although JI conducted numerous bombing attacks between 2000 and 2004, it concentrated on relatively soft targets, such as hotels, nightclubs, churches, and passenger trains. In comparison, al Qaeda demonstrated its capability to attack protected, hard targets (e.g., the U.S. embassies in East Africa) and to carry out very demanding operations, including the 9/11 attacks and the attack against the USS *Cole*. Whereas al Qaeda has demonstrated a unique flexibility to select targets on a global basis, as well as the ability to undertake effective attacks in different geographical locations, JI has operated within a particular regional context that constrains its potential selection of targets. Similarly, JI has not demonstrated the operations-driven learning that would enable it to attack protected targets effectively. Despite apparent interest in high-value Western targets in Southeast Asia, such as embassies and military assets, JI has been unable to achieve much success to date. The attack on the Australian embassy in Jakarta suggests an inability to mount effective attacks against protected or hard targets.[50]

JI's Forms of Organizational Learning

JI has exhibited both continuous improvement and discontinuous change in its operational and tactical learning, although for the most part, its attack operations are characterized primarily by continuous improvement, rather than by the fundamental transformations associated with discontinous change. Since JI began conducting bombing attacks in 2000, it does not appear to have made any notable efforts to develop or acquire new types of weapons for use in its attacks. Instead, its operations have been largely characterized by incremental improvements:

---

[50] The closest the JI came to attacking a protected target prior to the attack on the Australian embassy was when its local cells agreed to support al Qaeda in preparing for bomb attacks on Western embassies in Singapore in late 2001, which were never carried out.

- **Target surveillance.** JI has developed solid target surveillance practices, including "eyes-on" surveillance, over a period of years. The group has been innovative in its use of recording cameras and electronic media (e.g., DVDs) to record and edit images of potential targets for identification and attack planning purposes.
- **Weapon systems.** JI has used bombs almost exclusively as its weapon system. The improvement process it undertook between 2000 and 2004 did not fundamentally change the composition or efficiency of its bombs, but JI did improve on its bomb delivery system to increase its reliability and to reduce the safety hazard posed to its operatives by premature detonations. The bombing threat posed by JI has not changed substantially over time, even though the bombs have grown in size and their design has incrementally improved to ensure higher reliability.
- **Operational security.** The set of basic operational security practices that served JI well when it was still operating largely under the radar of the security services in various Southeast Asian countries (e.g., operating in cells, using codewords) did not prevent the arrests of a significant number of JI members, including some top leaders, following the 9/11 attacks and the Bali bombings, when counterterrorism efforts were substantially increased. JI appears to have taken steps to learn from its mistakes in operational security practices, e.g., it has shifted to face-to-face communications rather than relying on cell phones.

Although JI has exhibited determined efforts to improve its attack operations and address shortfalls, it has not been particularly innovative in adopting new weapon systems or strategies for its terrorist attacks. Hence, JI's most recent bombing attacks during 2002 to mid-2004 (i.e., the Bali attacks and the bombings of J.W. Marriott Hotel and Australian embassy in Jakarta) are not fundamentally different from its initial attacks undertaken in 2000 (i.e., the Philippine ambassador's residence and Christmas Eve bombings).

Not all of JI's terrorist actions can be accurately characterized as only incremental improvements over previous operations. Indeed, JI has demonstrated some advances in its learning behavior that are suggestive of discontinuous change. One is its transition from a radical Islamic group participating in local sectarian conflicts by supporting volunteer fighters to a terrorist group undertaking major attacks. The Christmas Eve bombings (i.e., 38 bombs delivered to targets in 11 cities across Indonesia), for example, represented discontinuous change in that they demonstrated JI's organizational capability to execute a relatively sophisticated attack plan involving a large number of widely dispersed and nearly simultaneous bombings. The group's desire and ability to undertake such an ambitious attack probably reflects its close association with al Qaeda at the time. Similarly, JI appears to have been one of the first Islamic militant groups operating in Southeast Asia to use suicide bombers.

Adoption of this tried-and-true tactic used by Hizballah and al Qaeda indicated a major change in JI's operational pattern. Although some uncertainty exists, the evidence suggests that JI used suicide bombers in the attacks on the J.W. Marriott Hotel and the Australian embassy, and probably in the Bali bombings.

Nonetheless, JI's propensity for continuous improvement does not preclude the possibility of discontinuous change occurring in the future.[51] It is possible that JI will abandon its bombing operations in favor of lying low and building a foundation for a regional militant Muslim movement. This would be consistent with reports that some JI factions favor a go-slow approach. Another possibility is that JI will engage in discontinuous change by adopting different terrorist tactics, such as political assassinations and hostage-taking of Westerners. Such tactics could draw on the expertise of other terrorist groups or could simply involve copycat actions based on public knowledge.[52] Finally, another possibility that should not be discounted is that JI will turn to unconventional weapons, such as chemical, biological, and radiological weapons or to large-scale use of poisons. Although JI is known to have produced a manual on chemical and biological weapons, there has been no firm indication to date of JI attempts to acquire and use such weapons.[53,54] Nonetheless, its doctrinal compatibility and established working relationships with al Qaeda make JI a good partner for receiving unconventional weapons provided by al Qaeda sources or for assisting al Qaeda operatives in employing such weapons against regional targets.[55] Any of these alternative courses of action would represent discontinuous change for JI as a terrorist organization.

Operational and tactical learning could figure prominently in whatever path JI chooses to take. Its past patterns of organizational learning will shape the feasible choices facing the its leadership in adapting to operating under unprecedented coun-

---

[51] Of course, JI could also continue its current approach. However, undertaking major bombing operations has become more challenging, given the vigorous counterterrorism activities occurring among Southeast Asian countries, the problem of securing the necessary resources now that al Qaeda support is less reliable, and the loss of several high-ranking JI operatives who were probably critical in encouraging bombing attacks.

[52] Some news reports suggest that JI is preparing to turn away from large-scale car bombs and toward simpler tactics, such as assassinations of public figures, diplomats, and business people, particularly Westerners (Greenlees and McBeth, 2004, pp. 16–19). In addition, JI members collectively possess the necessary training gained in al Qaeda or MILF camps, and experience gained in jihadist activities in Ambon and Poso, for undertaking these types of violent actions.

[53] Personal interviews with a counterterrorism official, Singapore, June 2004, and an academic expert, Jakarta, May 2004.

[54] According to some reports, JI might have been indirectly connected to the arrest of a Thai man in Bangkok in 2003 who was trying to sell cesium-137, a substance that could be used to make a radiological dispersal device, or "dirty bomb." Following this arrest, Thai authorities arrested three men with alleged JI ties (Andreoni, 2003).

[55] As noted in Table 4.1, Yazid Sufaat, a U.S.-trained biochemist and JI member who was captured in December 2001 returning to Malaysia from Afghanistan, is believed to have worked on the al Qaeda program in Kandahar that was seeking to develop biological and chemical weapons ("Al-Qaeda Program to Make WMD Halted by Afghan War," 2004).

terterrorist efforts for the foreseeable future, as domestic security agencies work much more closely with foreign intelligence agencies to disrupt, track down, and capture JI leaders and members. Better understanding of the tactical and operational learning patterns of JI as a terrorist group can help counterterrorist analysts identify how JI is changing and adapting. Such insights can also be useful in developing counterterrorism strategies to ensure that JI remains off balance and can be more effectively dealt with as a terrorist threat to the United States and its Southeast Asian allies.

References

Abuza, Zachary, "Funding Terrorism in Southeast Asia: The Financial Network of Al Qaeda and Jemaah Islamiya," *Contemporary Southeast Asia*, Vol. 25, 2003a, pp. 169–199.

___, *Militant Islam in Southeast Asia*, Boulder, CO: Lynne Rienner Publishers, 2003b.

Aglionby, John, "Police Find Embassy Bomb Clue," *The Guardian*, September 14, 2004.

"Al-Qaeda Program to Make WMD Halted by Afghan War," *USA Today*, January 26, 2004.

Andreoni, Alessandro, and Charles D. Ferguson, "Radioactive Cesium Seizure in Thailand: Riddled with Uncertainties," Center for Nonproliferation Studies, Monterey Institute of International Studies, July 17, 2003, available at http://cns.miis.edu/ (last accessed September 25, 2004).

Australian Federal Police, "Operation Alliance Investigating the Bali Bombing of 12 October 2002," available at http://www.afp.gov.au/afp/page/News/OperationAlliance.htm (last accessed May 23, 2004).

___, "Bali Bombing Trials, Reports of the Court Proceedings, Family Liaison Briefings, 2003," available at http://www.afp.gov.au/page.asp?ref=/News/BaliTrials/CourtReports/Home.xml (last accessed May 29, 2004).

"Australian Trained by al-Qaeda," BBC News (World Edition), May 17, 2004.

"Azahari's Tracks," *TEMPO Magazine*, September 8, 2003, p. 15.

"Bali Bomb 'Failed to Fully Explode, '" BBC News (World Edition), October 1, 2003.

BBC Monitoring Asia Pacific, "Indonesia: Amrozi Admits Role in Bombing of Philippine Envoy's House," translated from Indonesian Deikcom web site, September 2, 2003, available at LexisNexis.

Benjamin, Daniel, and Steven Simon, *The Age of Sacred Terror: Radical Islam's War Against America*, New York: Random House, 2003.

Black, J. Cofer, "Al-Qaeda: The Threat to the United States and Its Allies," testimony before the House International Relations Committee, April 1, 2004 (available at http://www.house.gov/international_relations).

Burnham, Gracia, with Dean Merrill, *In the Presence of My Enemies*, Wheaton, IL: Tyndale House Publishers, Inc., 2003.

"Carnage at Kuningan," *TEMPO Magazine*, September 14–20, 2004, available at http://www.tempointeractive.com/majalah/free/edl-list-e.html (last accessed December 21, 2004).

Cragin, Kim, and Sara Daly, *The Dynamic Terrorist Threat*, Santa Monica, CA: RAND Corporation, MR-1782-AF, 2004.

Davis, Anthony, "Southeast Asia Awaits JI's Next Move," *Jane's Intelligence Review*, September 27–29, 2004.

Greenlees, Donald, and John McBeth, "Terrorists' New Tactic: Assassination," *Far Eastern Economic Review*, June 17, 2004.

Gunaratna, Rohan, *Inside Al Qaeda: Global Network of Terror*, New York: Columbia University Press, 2002.

___, "Understanding Al Qaeda and Its Network in Southeast Asia," in Kumar Ramakrishna and See Seng Tan (eds.), *After Bali: The Threat of Terrorism in Southeast Asia*, Singapore: Institute of Defense and Strategic Studies, Nanyang Technological University, 2004, pp. 117–132.

"Hambali 'Eyed Bangkok Embassies,'" BBC News (UK Edition), August 22, 2003.

"Indonesia Sentences JI Leader," BBC News (World Edition), February 25, 2004.

"Indonesian Cleric to Be Charged," BBC News (UK Edition), September 24, 2004.

International Crisis Group (ICG), *Indonesia Briefing: Al-Qaeda in Southeast Asia: The Case of the "Ngruki Network" in Indonesia*, August 8, 2002a.

___, *Indonesia Backgrounder: How the Jemaah Islamiyah Terrorist Network Operates*, Asia Report No. 43, December 11, 2002b.

___, *Jemaah Islamiyah in South East Asia: Damaged but Still Dangerous*, Asia Report No. 63, August 26, 2003.

___, *Indonesia Backgrounder: Jihad in Central Sulawesi*, Asia Report No. 74, February 3, 2004a.

___, *Southern Philippines Backgrounder: Terrorism and the Peace Process*, ICG Asia Report No. 80, July 13, 2004b.

Jones, David Martin, Michael L. R. Smith, and Mark Weeding, "Looking for the Pattern: Al Qaeda in Southeast Asia—The Genealogy of a Terror Network," *Studies in Conflict & Terrorism*, Vol. 26, 2003, pp. 443–457.

Jones, Sidney, "What Indonesia Must Explain," *Far Eastern Economic Review*, September 23, 2004.

Manggut, Wenseslaus, and Bobby Gunawan, "A Careful Bomber," *TEMPO Magazine*, November 17, 2003, p. 20.

McBeth, John, "Bombs, the Army and Suharto," *Far Eastern Economic Review*, February 1, 2001.

___, "Terrorism: Fuel for Indonesian Anger," *Far Eastern Economic Review*, September 23, 2004.

___, et al., "Terrorism: Time to Get Tough," *Far Eastern Economic Review*, August 13, 2003.

National Commission on Terrorist Attacks Upon the United States, *The 9/11 Commission Report: Final Report of the National Commission on Terrorist Attacks Upon the United States*, New York: W.W. Norton, 2004.

"Police Identify Driver of Van Used in Jakarta Bombing," September 10, 2004, available at http://www.indonesia-oslo.no/news100.htm (last accessed September 10, 2004).

Rabasa, Angel M., *Political Islam in Southeast Asia: Moderates, Radicals and Terrorists*, London: International Institute for Strategic Studies, Adelphi Paper No. 358, May 2003.

___, "Southeast Asia: Moderate Tradition and Radical Challenge," in Angel M. Rabasa et al., *The Muslim World After 9/11*, Santa Monica, CA: RAND Corporation, MG-246-AF, 2004, pp. 367–412.

Ramakrishna, Kumar, "'Constructing' the Jemaah Islamiyah Terrorist: A Preliminary Inquiry," Singapore: Institute of Defense and Strategic Studies, Nanyang Technological University, Working Paper #71, October 2004, available athttp://www.ntu.edu.sg/idss/research_04.htm (last accessed October 21, 2004).

___, "U.S. Strategy in Southeast Asia: Counter-Terrorist or Counter-Terrorism?" in Kumar Ramakrishna and See Seng Tan (eds.), *After Bali: The Threat of Terrorism in Southeast Asia*, Singapore: Institute of Defense and Strategic Studies, Nanyang Technological University, 2003, pp. 305–337.

Ratnsar, Romesh, "Confessions of an al-Qaeda Terrorist," *Time*, September 23, 2002, pp. 35–41.

Report of the Inquiry into the Australian Intelligence Agencies, July 2004, available at Australian Government, Department of Defense site, http://www.dsd.gov.au/lib/pdf_doc/Intelligence_Report.pdf (last accessed September 24, 2004).

Ressa, Maria, "Jihad Rules in Islamic School," CNN.com, February 26, 2004.

___, *Seeds of Terror: An Eyewitness Account of Al-Qaeda's Newest Center of Operations in Southeast Asia*, New York: Free Press, 2003.

Sageman, Marc, *Understanding Terrorist Networks*, Philadelphia, PA: University of Pennsylvania Press, 2004.

Tan, Andrew, "The Indigenous Roots of Conflict in Southeast Asia: The Case of Mindanao," in Kumar Ramakrishna and See Seng Tan (eds.), *After Bali: The Threat of Terrorism in Southeast Asia*, Singapore: Institute of Defense and Strategic Studies, Nanyang Technological University, 2003, pp. 97–115.

Tarabay, Jamie, "Trial Shows Links Between Terror Groups," Associated Press, May 28, 2004, available at LexisNexis.

Turnbull, Wayne, *A Tangled Web of Southeast Asian Islamic Terrorism: The Jemaah Islamiyah Terrorist Network*, Monterey, CA: Monterey Institute of International Studies, July 31, 2003, available at http://www.terrorismcentral.com/Library/terroristgroups/JemaahIslamiyah/JITerror/JIContents.html (last accessed July 6, 2004).

U.S. Department of State, "Designation of Two Terrorists," Washington, DC: Department of State, press statement, January 24, 2003a.

___, *Patterns of Global Terrorism, 2002*, Washington, DC: Department of State, April 2003b.

White Paper, *The Jemaah Islamiyah Arrests and the Threat of Terrorism*, Singapore: Ministry of Home Affairs, January 7, 2003.

Wiljayanta, Hanibal W. Y., "Fireballs from Soap Bars," *TEMPO Magazine*, November 17, 2003, pp. 16–19.

Yusuf, Zulkarnaen, "Explosives, Bombs, Terror," *TEMPO Magazine*, September 8, 2003, p. 16.

CHAPTER FIVE

Provisional Irish Republican Army

Brian A. Jackson

Introduction

Even a cursory examination of the operational history of the Provisional Irish Republican Army (PIRA) reveals ample evidence of organizational change and evolution. Through its nearly 30-year history, the group has altered its tactics, manufactured new weapons, modified its targeting practices, and significantly changed its own structure to improve its security. PIRA has also devoted significant effort to circumventing or defeating systems and technologies deployed by security forces in their counterterrorism efforts.

PIRA stands out from other terrorist organizations in both the quality and scope of its learning capabilities. Hogan and Taylor note that "the remarkable evolution of this organisation has been characterized by internal learning, an exceptional ability to adapt, reorganize, and restructure, and the impressive development of a highly efficient and multi-dimensional support apparatus" (Horgan and Taylor, 1997, p. 27). Other assessments, however, paint a more complex, if not contradictory, picture. J. Bowyer Bell, a researcher who spent many years studying the group, raised serious questions about PIRA's ability to learn and its desire to change its modes of operation. Bell saw the group as constrained by past assumptions, and as a result, "[PIRA spent little time] in consideration of strategic options or tactical initiatives. . . . The Army Council or the individual volunteer . . . rarely [contemplated] the appropriate means to achieve the organizational goals" (Bell, 1993, pp. 26–27). Such an assessment seems to suggest a PIRA that barely thought, much less learned.

This chapter examines organizational learning within PIRA in a variety of areas, including

- Operations and tactics
- Training
- Logistics
- Intelligence and operational security

This analysis is intended to develop a better understanding of the group's learning efforts, including the areas in which it chose to learn, the results of its attempts do so, and, where possible, the processes through which it carried out its learning efforts. It directly confronts the apparent contradiction noted above. As the discussion will show, PIRA's level of success at learning and innovation varied; though in most areas it was extremely successful, some of its efforts were more mixed. As a result, the two viewpoints should be viewed as complementary, rather than contradictory. And the apparent conflict between them should be seen as a demonstration of the difficulty of making broad statements about an organization's capacity to learn across all areas, subjects, and technologies.

Background

Violent conflict over British involvement in Ireland has a history that reaches back decades. Even as the political landscape shifted—e.g., the British withdrew from the majority of the island in 1921 (the part that became the independent Republic of Ireland in 1948), and the island was geographically partitioned to form Northern Ireland—violent conflict persisted at varied levels of intensity. Conflict in Northern Ireland between Loyalists (supporters of continued English involvement) and Republicans (opponents of English involvement who desire unification of Northern Ireland with the Irish Republic) claimed many lives throughout the years of violence. Complicating the political elements, the conflict is also a religious one. The division between Loyalists and Republicans is also a division between Protestants and Catholics, making much of the violence as much about brutal sectarianism as about the political goals of the opposing sides (Coogan, 1993, pp. 3–28; Drake, 1991, pp. 43–44).

PIRA came into being in 1969, splintering from the rest of the Republican movement due to differences in political and military strategy (Bell, 1998b, pp. 367–368; Drake, 1991, p. 44). It operated as an insurgent terrorist organization until the late 1990s, carrying out operations and support activities in Northern Ireland, in the Irish Republic, on the British mainland, and in other areas, including continental Europe and the United States.[1] Since PIRA agreed to a ceasefire in 1997 as part of the regional peace process (Jane's World Insurgency and Terrorism, 2004), more-limited terrorist operations have been continued by splinter groups such as Real IRA and Continuity IRA.

---

[1] The vast majority of PIRA terrorist operations were carried out in Northern Ireland and on the British mainland.

Goals and Strategy

PIRA's goals and strategy were defined by the long history and philosophy of the Irish Republican movement. In a 1981 interview, a spokesman related PIRA's goals to events that occurred more than 60 years earlier: "Our aim [is] to force a British withdrawal from Ireland and to establish a Democratic Socialist Republic based on the Easter Proclamation of 1916" ("IRA Interview: Iris Talks to a Member of the IRA's General Headquarters Staff," 1981, p. 42). As it pursued these goals, the group sought to maintain the allegiance of the Catholic population in Northern Ireland and the Republic, its primary support community. PIRA also strove to maintain an image as a potent military force (Crenshaw, 1984; Silke, 2003), drawing on Republican traditions that called for physical force as the means through which the goal of Irish unification should be pursued (Smith, 1997, pp. 14–19).

Understanding that it lacked the capability to directly confront the British militarily, PIRA opted for terrorism and insurgent violence. The group's implementation of this strategy is articulated in *The Green Book*, a PIRA policy and training manual:[2]

1. A war of attrition against enemy personnel which is aimed at causing as many casualties and deaths as possible so as to create a demand from their people at home for their withdrawal.
2. A bombing campaign aimed at making the enemy's financial interest in our country unprofitable while at the same time curbing long term financial investment in our country.
3. To make the Six Counties as at present and for the past several years ungovernable except by colonial military rule.
4. To sustain the war and gain support for its ends by National and International propaganda and publicity campaigns.
5. By defending the war of liberation by punishing criminals, collaborators and informers (quoted in Coogan, 1993, p. 420).

An alleged PIRA leader summarized the group's strategy rather more succinctly as "blattering on until the Brits leave" (Drake, 1991, p. 45).

Organizational Structure

In order to act, a terrorist organization must be able to organize people and resources, gather information about its environment and adversaries, shape a strategic direction for actions of its members, and choose tactics, techniques, and procedures for achieving strategic ends. PIRA addressed these requirements through a multilevel management structure. The highest level of decisionmaking was the General Army

---

[2] "The Green Book listed the duties and responsibilities of Volunteers, as well as explaining the history of the movement, the rules of military engagement, and anti-interrogation techniques" (Collins and McGovern, 1998, p. 66).

Convention, "an organised meeting of delegates . . . [drawn] from other structures within the organisation" (Horgan and Taylor, 1997, p. 4). The Convention elected the 12-member Army Executive, which elected the seven-member Army Council. The Army Council was in charge of defining the organization's strategic and tactical direction. From its seven members, the Army Council chose a chairperson, a secretary, and a chief of staff. The chief of staff was the primary authority within PIRA.

The decisions of the Army Council and its chief of staff were implemented by the General Headquarters (GHQ) and two operational divisions, the Northern Command and the Southern Command, which controlled operations in Northern Ireland and in the Republic, respectively. The GHQ, based in Dublin in the Republic of Ireland, was divided into ten departments, as shown in Figure 5.1. Over time, the structure of PIRA's operational units changed in response to the group's external security environment. Initially, PIRA was built as a quasi-military organization consisting of battalions and brigades. As long as PIRA controlled areas with sympathetic populations, these components operated openly, but such openness could not be maintained under pressure from security forces and was discarded later in the group's

Figure 5.1
Organizational Structure of the Provisional Irish Republican Army

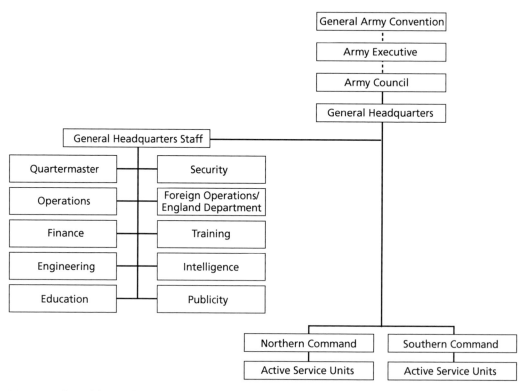

SOURCE: Adapted from information in Horgan and Taylor, 1997.
RAND MG332-5.1

career. In this structural transition, which will be discussed in more detail below, the quasi-military organization was replaced by a compartmented, cellular structure.

Operations and Tactics

Although PIRA split off from the already operational Irish Republican Army (which continued to exist alongside PIRA as the "Official IRA"), the group's initial capabilities were quite limited: "Initially, the principal military activity of the [PIRA] was stone-throwing and sometimes petrol bombing" (Coogan, 1993, p. 281). But as weapons became more available and the group evolved, PIRA's repertoire expanded; within months, it included firearms (Coogan, 1993, p. 282), and it progressed toward what would eventually become significant explosives expertise. In time, PIRA branched well beyond guns and bombs to become known for the variety of tactics and weapons it used effectively. Building operational and tactical capabilities required that the group make advances in weapons technology and usage as well as in the planning and execution of operations.

Weapons Technologies and Usage

At different points in its history, PIRA faced different constraints on its ability to acquire and use weapons technologies. When it began terrorist operations, its arms were limited: "It is literally true, for instance, that in August 1969, the only weapons known to be available to [PIRA] were ten guns" (Coogan, 1993, pp. 278–279). This void was gradually filled though infusions of funds from abroad, notably from the United States; interactions with sources in the Middle East, particularly Libya; and the international arms market (Bell, 1987, pp. 56, 256). The organization's access to arms was, however, limited by a lack of expertise in a decidedly nonmilitary area: the knowledge required to execute deals in the international arms market and to successfully get the weapons through the international shipping system. As noted by Bell, "The GHQ lacked foreign contacts and foreign allies, had little knowledge of the nature and problems of illegal arms traffic nor the diplomatic resources to purchase 'legally' what was needed. As a result, a string of failures and abortive plots occurred—and in some cases received wide publicity" (Bell, 1998b, p. 373).[3]

Counterterrorism officials interviewed for this study indicated that by the later stages of its operational career, PIRA had more than 30 varieties of weapons—including mortars and rockets—as well as numerous methods to lay and detonate explosives, advanced sniper tactics, etc., that it could draw on to mount opera-

---

[3] In some of these failures, the group's lack of expertise may have been exacerbated by direct intervention of the security forces: "It would appear in several cases the [supposed] arms source was, in fact, British Intelligence or agents thereof" (Bell, 1998b, p. 392).

tions.[4] This was partially the result of improvements in the group's ability to obtain weapons through procurement, including stocks of sophisticated weapons such as the Armalite rifles that the group made a *de facto* trademark of its military activities, advanced explosive devices, and powerful military-grade machine guns. When the group could not gain access to desired weapons, it turned to manufacturing them internally, producing its own explosives when stocks ran short, engineering and constructing its own mortars, and even seeking to manufacture its own antiaircraft missiles (Bell, 1998b, p. 438).

Although PIRA has used a wide variety of innovative attack forms, three types of weapons illustrate the group's learning activities particularly clearly:

- Explosives
- Grenade launchers
- Surface-to-air missiles

These are discussed in turn below. The discussion examines the circumstances that drove PIRA innovation in each type of weapon, the group's organizational learning efforts, and, to the extent possible, measures of the group's success.

Explosives: Continuous Improvement to Improve Device Safety and Competitive Learning to Maintain Group Capabilities

PIRA developed a reputation for its capabilities with explosives and the application of advanced technologies in the construction and use of bombs, mines, and other devices. These capabilities developed over time as a result of an intense learning process within the group.

Drivers of Innovation. In the early 1970s, PIRA bombs were basic, unstable, and almost as dangerous to the group itself as they were to its targets. One account of a member active at the time emphasized how the fatality rate from the devices affected group members' willingness to use them: "People who volunteered to work with explosives were regarded either as 'nutty professors' or as stark, raving mad because explosives, commercial and home-made, were dangerous and unpredictable and had cost [PIRA] persons their lives. Result—not many people wanted to work with explosives" (O'Doherty, 1993, p. 69).

The losses went beyond simply reducing the willingness of volunteers to plant bombs. Occasionally, the accidents claimed the lives of experienced veterans, such as Jack McCabe, who "was mixing ingredients for a home-made bomb in December 1971, using a metal shovel on a concrete garage floor. The predictable result was

---

[4] Personal interview with law enforcement officials, England, March 2004.

a spark and a premature explosion" (Geraghty, 2000, p. 205).[5] Later, PIRA lost Brendan Burns, one of its most experienced bomb-makers (Collins and McGovern, 1998, p. 172), and reportedly nearly lost Seamus Twomey, a leader in the Belfast PIRA, "due to a small misunderstanding about where and when the bomb would be laid" (Geraghty, 2000, p. 67).

The explosives failures were caused by the nature of the designs as well as the level of expertise of the individuals involved in manufacturing them. First-person accounts of PIRA explosives operations describe a range of errors, including forgetting to set the timer before arming the device (O'Doherty, 1993, p. 155), failures to test circuitry, problems with static electricity, and failures of volunteers to follow safety practices "in the name of expedience or out of ignorance" (Bell, 1998b, p. 392).[6] The result of the shortcomings in technology and technique was a toll on the organization that "was worse than [that] inflicted by the British Army during the height of bombing operations" (Bell, 1998b, p. 392).

As the group improved its skills, the price it paid in fatalities from premature detonation dropped from 31 in 1973 and 17 in 1974 to two or fewer a year by 1978. Even after adjusting the figures for the approximate level of the bombing operations occurring each year, the drop in yearly fatality rates remains (data from Sutton, 2004, and Police Service of Northern Ireland, n.d.). In fact, by 1993, such fatalities had become so rare that when a PIRA bomber was killed in an operationally botched bombing of a fish shop on the Shankill Road, there were initial speculations that his death must have been deliberate (Silke, 2003).

Fatalities caused by premature detonation were only one of the drivers of innovation for PIRA. The other primary driver was the need to respond to changes in the security and countermeasures of the group's adversaries. Both the British Army and law enforcement organizations devoted considerable resources to developing and deploying new technology to defeat PIRA's activities. These deployments seriously degraded the effectiveness of the group's operations by limiting the effectiveness of its explosive devices. Key efforts were focused on interfering with PIRA's capacity to use particular detonation mechanisms (discussed in detail below). Responding to these changes, therefore, was a major focus of PIRA explosives innovation.

Explosives Innovation. As its operations expanded, PIRA had to learn what was required to meet its need for basic explosives materials. In some areas, the group could steal what it needed from construction, mining, or other industrial sites

---

[5] In a morbid example of organizational learning, McCabe reportedly passed on the details of what had happened from his deathbed, to prevent other group members from repeating his mistake (Coogan, 1993, p. 279).

[6] "It was commonplace to work at bombs with bare hands instead of wearing rubber gloves and a lot of the young married Volunteers wore gold wedding rings; we later discovered that these sometimes made a contact where the two wires crossed the ring, completing the circuit and detonating the bomb" (O'Callaghan, 1999, pp. 82–83).

(O'Callaghan, 1999, p. 58). However, those sources could not sustain the group indefinitely, so by 1972, PIRA had extensive explosives manufacturing operations in place (Foreign and Commonwealth Office: Republic of Ireland Department, 1972a).

Some PIRA units specialized in explosives manufacture, supplying larger portions of the organization. One bomb factory, staffed by three people, was tasked to produce "two tons of fertilizer-based explosives every week . . . [to supply] the Mid-Ulster Brigade of the [PIRA]: South Derry, East Tyrone, South Fermanagh, North Antrim, North Armagh and West Fermanagh" (O'Callaghan, 1999, p. 89). Such an industrial approach allowed the group to adopt large, vehicle-based explosive devices as a central tactic. When PIRA received significant quantities of the plastic explosive Semtex from Libya in the mid-1980s, the materiel constraints on its operations shifted again. With less need to work on its ability to make explosives, the group could increase the range of devices it constructed (Harnden, 2000, pp. 242–243).[7,8]

PIRA is more broadly known for innovation in the design of explosive *devices*, rather than explosives materials themselves. Initially, the group used comparatively unsophisticated gasoline and nail bombs to attack security forces. Although it continued to use such hand-thrown devices—"coffee jar" bombs combining a small amount of explosives and shrapnel were a constant component of its arsenal[9]—these devices had disadvantages. In particular, thrown explosives require the thrower to be close to the target and expose him to considerable risk.

To protect volunteers and increase the chances of operational success, PIRA adopted two technologies that could separate the terrorist from the detonation of the explosive device in distance, time, or both:

1. **Remote manual detonation.** The bomb is set off by an individual, but technology moves the bomber away from the bomb.
2. **Automatic detonation.** The bomb does not require intervention to be detonated.

Remote Manual Detonation. One of the earliest detonation mechanisms adopted by PIRA was the use of long command wires, usually buried to avoid detection, which allowed a bomber to set off a bomb from some distance away. Frequently used for mines planted under roads to attack security force vehicles, long command wires sometimes took advantage of the border between Northern Ireland and the Republic to prevent security-force pursuit.

---

[7] It should be noted that PIRA made a number of innovations in the formulation of explosives materials themselves, both to match the materials they had available and to improve the properties of explosives for their operations. In the interests of space and to avoid the inclusion of certain types of restricted information in this report, innovation in that area will not be discussed here.

[8] Personal interview with a former security forces member, England, March 2004.

[9] Personal interview with law enforcement officials, Northern Ireland, March 2004.

Although command wires separate a bomber from the bomb, they still provide a tangible link between the two and limit their separation distance. The buried wire could also be detected, potentially compromising an operation. This drove PIRA to explore remote detonation, beginning with remote-controlled or radio systems.[10] Its first detonation of a remote-controlled bomb reportedly occurred in 1972 (Geraghty, 2000, p. 208; Urban, 1992). PIRA's first transmitters were based on a commercial unit designed for model airplanes or boats. To counter this new tactic, security forces began transmitting jamming signals on the transmitter frequencies, preventing detonation or prematurely detonating PIRA bombs (Harnden, 2000, p. 363; Urban, 1992, p. 112). PIRA answered this innovation by adopting more-sophisticated electronic switches (Geraghty, 2000, p. 208).

The back-and-forth innovation/countermeasure developments led to a "chase" across the radio spectrum. Once the security forces jammed a frequency, PIRA had to seek out a new area of the spectrum to reconstitute its capabilities.[11] First-person narratives describe how PIRA tested new technologies to ensure that their signals could penetrate the security forces' protective countermeasures (Collins and McGovern, 1998, pp. 155–156). For these innovation efforts, PIRA drew on expertise within the commercial sector (Bell, 1998a, p. 198) and on experts from abroad and within the military (McKinley, 1984). An American engineer, Richard Johnson, developed "the ingenious idea of using the Weather Alert Radio frequency to trigger [PIRA] bombs. The [system] . . . was unique to North America. Its frequency of 162.55 MHz was not in use in Europe and was therefore a clear channel for the [PIRA]" (Geraghty, 2000, p. 208; Harnden, 2000, p. 356).

However, as PIRA's devices became more sophisticated and used increasingly specialized components, they also provided ways for the authorities to track down the group's activities and link its outside consultants to terrorism (Harnden, 2000, p. 356; Neuffer, 1990).[12] The increasing specificity and sophistication of the devices also increased the risk to the group's capabilities, since the security forces could study PIRA bombs that failed to detonate. Intricate firing sequences and transmission technologies might make it possible to circumvent countermeasures, but if PIRA's technology was compromised, the countermeasures could be quickly updated: "Once a [PIRA] radio-bomb had failed to detonate, the army could retrieve the weapon and identify the radio code on the receiver, thus neutralizing all bombs using the same

---

[10] Triggering remotely controlled devices involves some expertise in timing when the target is positioned near the explosive. PIRA reportedly adopted some other auxiliary technologies, such as baby-monitor transmitters, to assist in detonating bombs even when they lacked a line of sight to the target (Geraghty, 2000, p. 208).

[11] Personal interview with a former security forces member, England, March 2004. The interviewee pointed out that this sequential "chase" from frequency to frequency was bounded by the availability of electronics components at the time.

[12] Personal interviews with law enforcement officials, England, March 2004.

signal. When this occurred the [PIRA] could spend more than a year trying to find a new signal which would break through the shield" (Collins and McGovern, 1998, pp. 155–156, 169). To protect its capabilities, PIRA had to learn how to prevent this from happening. To prevent security forces from gathering such evidence, therefore, some bombs were outfitted with self-destruct mechanisms to insure against their failing to detonate (Harnden, 2000, p. 20).

Paradoxically, as the bombs got more and more advanced, PIRA's overall capability became less robust—a single device failure could result in security forces hobbling the group's capabilities for an extended period. Because of these potential vulnerabilities, PIRA sought to broaden its repertoire of remote detonation technologies, exploring alternative options such as the use of radar detectors and police radar guns, photographic units triggered by flashes of light, infrared transmitters from garage-door openers, and even "projectile detonation," i.e., shooting two metal plates together to complete a firing circuit and set off a bomb (Geraghty, 2000, pp. 209–210).[13]

Even as detonation technologies became more and more advanced, PIRA retained older technologies for use when needed. As a result, while different transmitter methods were being used, command wires were being used as well. This allowed the group to cycle through both old and new as its latest-generation methods were penetrated and rendered ineffective (Urban, 1992, p. 113).[14]

Automatic Detonation. To enable bombers to escape, PIRA also used timing devices to delay detonation. Beginning with clocks and watches (O'Callaghan, 1999, pp. 82–83) and simple chemical delay mechanisms (Geraghty, 2000, p. 207), PIRA shifted to much more accurate timers taken from other devices or developed from scratch. The group built timers that could delay detonation for weeks or months, technology used in an attempt on Queen Elizabeth in 1977 (Glover, 1978) and a 1984 attack on Prime Minister Margaret Thatcher at a Party conference in Brighton.

---

[13] PIRA also explored alternative ways of separating the volunteer delivering the bomb from the attack itself. Letter bombs, although effective, produced a significantly negative response from the group's constituencies and were therefore seldom used (Crenshaw, 1984; Foreign and Commonwealth Office: Republic of Ireland Department, 1973a). The group also modified vehicles to deliver bombs in ways that did not require PIRA members' direct involvement. In one instance, a van was modified to travel on its own along rail lines (Harnden, 2000, p. 262, 264). In others, PIRA used guidance mechanisms that relied on human intervention. The group also used "proxy bombs"—stolen civilian vehicles that PIRA filled with explosives and forced their owners to drive them to their targets (Coogan, 1993, p. 285; Drake, 1991, p. 50). The group made an effort to use "human bombs," unwilling suicide bombers, but it rapidly gave up the practice (Bell, 1998b, p. 615). There are also reports of PIRA experimenting with building vehicles either guided by remote control (Harnden, 2000, p. 208) or using the global positioning satellite (GPS) navigation system, "somewhat like a pilotless cruise missile" (Geraghty, 2000, p. 212). This technology was cited as an example of convergence between PIRA and other groups, such as Basque Fatherland and Liberty (ETA) and the Revolutionary Armed Forces of Colombia (FARC), which reportedly have also experimented with and used such devices (personal interview with a former security forces member, England, March 2004).

[14] Personal interview with a former security forces member, England, March 2004.

PIRA also adopted movement-triggered devices to detonate bombs placed under cars, targeting the individuals who owned the vehicles. These devices were reportedly improved with assistance from other Irish terrorist groups, which may have obtained the technology from groups outside the region (Drake, 1991, p. 48; O'Ballance, 1981, p. 237).

A key development in PIRA timer technology was the adoption of the Memopark timer, a small pocket timer marketed to help people track the time remaining on their meter when they parked their car. The timers were very accurate, and the group acquired a large number of them.[15] Because of the suitability and availability of the Memopark timers, PIRA relied on them for an extended period and was not forced to innovate as dramatically in timer technology.[16]

Just as PIRA had specific cells producing explosives materials, it also institutionalized production of the bombs' electronic components. It developed nearly standardized timing and power units that the military cells could use as off-the-shelf components in their operations. This level of stability allowed the group to incorporate standard safety devices into its bombs, such as indicator lights to assure that the bomb was properly set before arming, and to use secondary timers that would arm the bomb after a set amount of time had passed.[17] The stability of device construction also enabled continuous improvement in the devices over time, since the same individuals were building many generations of explosive devices.[18]

Although security forces indicated that there were few barriers to expanding production of the units within the group—"only comparatively simple skills are needed [to manufacture the devices], . . . we would not expect PIRA to have great difficulty in expanding production and we expect this to happen" (Glover, 1978)—such expansion was not observed. Discussions with law enforcement and former security forces members indicated that signatures of individual bomb-makers could be tracked through much of the conflict. This suggests that PIRA decided it was more effective to diffuse these specialists' knowledge through the organization in the form of the devices they built, rather than broadly teaching many group members to make bombs for themselves.

Although the use of timers and delays before detonation improved the safety of volunteers, it also provided security forces with the ability to locate and defuse the

---

[15] Ibid.

[16] Personal interviews with a former security forces member and a law enforcement official, England, March 2004.

[17] These safety-to-arm devices were incorporated into manually detonated bombs as well to help ensure the safety of the volunteers planting them (personal interview with a law enforcement official, England, March 2004).

[18] Centralized manufacturing of the devices allowed the security forces to build up information on individual bomb-makers based on the characteristics of their devices. Glover states: "The devices used so far bear the stamp of being made by one man or under the supervision of one man" (Glover, 1978). Comments by interviewees suggested that this continued throughout the group's career.

devices (Jenkins and Gersten, 2001, p. 19). This required additional learning by PIRA and led to another area of technological competition between it and the security forces, i.e., building in tamper-resistance or "booby trapping" devices to prevent bombs from being defused. The innovations reportedly included the use of light-sensitive devices in detonators (O'Ballance, 1981, p. 169) and electromagnetic traps that would set off the bomb if a metal detector was used to try to locate its hiding place (Geraghty, 2000, p. 208).

Building Expertise. PIRA's long operational history and the ability of its bomb-makers to maintain their freedom and increase their expertise were critical to the organization's learning capability. "The mature terrorists, including for instance the leading bomb-makers, are usually sufficiently cunning to avoid arrest. They are continually learning from mistakes and developing their expertise. We can therefore expect to see increased professionalism and the greater exploitation of modern technology for terrorist purposes" (Glover, 1978). The ability of these individuals to operate in the comparative safety of the Republic of Ireland for a significant portion of the group's career was also important. Interviewees indicated that the group used test-firing ranges in the Republic and that there were frequent reports to local authorities of unexplained explosions in the middle of the night. It would only be much later that the crater that resulted from an experiment would be discovered in a remote forest or beach.[19] Tests were also reportedly carried out in the border counties where security forces' control was weaker—"South Armagh's strategic position on the border and the formidable strength of armed republicanism there have meant that it has long been the place where new weapons and prototype bombs have been tested after being produced by the [PIRA]'s Dublin based engineering department" (Harnden, 2000, p. 19).

The organization also instituted processes to investigate failures, which enabled it to learn from its mistakes. Though not all such investigations produced results (O'Doherty, 1993, pp. 151–152), the learning processes were a route for the group to understand and adapt to security forces' changes and innovations (Collins and McGovern, 1998, pp. 162–163).

Measures of Learning in the Use of Explosives. A number of measures could be used to gauge group learning in explosives. PIRA successfully carried out several significant technological changes, adopting new detonation mechanisms and techniques. Smaller modifications in the construction of devices, such as the incorporation of safety devices into timing and power units over time, are also an indicator of

---

[19] Personal interviews with former security forces members, England, March 2004.

learning. However, the real impact of individual changes to devices on their effectiveness or the effectiveness of the group overall is not always easy to understand.[20]

The overall decrease in PIRA fatalities caused by their own devices is a clear indicator of increased expertise in explosives use, but such an indicator, while relevant, is "inward looking" with respect to the group itself; it does describe a capability to effectively carry out terrorist operations.

Whether explosive devices worked as intended can also be used as a measure of group learning. Analyses of portions of PIRA's activities show that, even as significant changes were made in the way devices were detonated, many of them did not work at all: "Of the 81 explosive devices that were placed at transport targets [on the British mainland], 79 were hand-placed time bombs. Fifty percent of them did not work as intended" (Jenkins and Gersten, 2001, p. 12). Other analyses reach similar conclusions: "PIRA admitted that out of eighteen bombing missions carried out between February and May 1983, eight had to be aborted either because the bombs failed to detonate properly or because they were located by the security forces" (Smith, 1997, p. 177). Limitations in available data make it difficult to perform such analyses for more-comprehensive or representative samples of the group's operations.[21]

To develop better outcome measures of learning, analysts need information on group intentions for specific attacks. For example, numbers of casualties caused by bombings may or may not be appropriate measures of group improvement.[22] For some categories of targets, PIRA sought to cause significant numbers of casualties. However, because of the backlash generally associated with large numbers of civilian casualties, the group made at least some efforts to minimize them.

Economic damages could be used to assess the effectiveness of bombing operations, given that inflicting such damages were a stated part of PIRA's strategy (Bell, 1998b). But while estimates of direct damages from the campaign were available for some attacks, such assessments understate the economic impacts of the response to terrorist actions, e.g., the changes forced on security and police forces (Harnden, 2000, p. 19) or the costs of fortifying potential targets to deter or prevent attack.[23]

---

[20] Interviewees noted that there was no clear reason for some changes in the construction of devices or obvious impacts on performance (personal interviews with a law enforcement official and a former security forces member, England, March 2004.)

[21] It should be noted that some failures may have been due to actions of security forces, rather than mistakes on the part of the group. It has been suggested that counterterrorist forces sometimes disabled weapons in terrorist weapons caches so they would not work (interviews) or rigged them to fail catastrophically, taking the volunteer with them (Geraghty, 2000, pp. 133–134).

[22] Such measures of "lethal efficiency" reportedly led to increases in the intensity of security force actions in the mid-1980s, however: "The trend was not a marked one, but security chiefs were alarmed at the improved efficiency of the attacks, say those involved in policy-making at the time. The [PIRA] was, in effect, able to kill more people in each of its attacks" (Urban, 1992, p. 165).

[23] Personal interview with a law enforcement official, Northern Ireland, March 2004.

Grenade Launchers: From Outside-Sourced to Internally Built Capabilities

The rocket-propelled grenade (RPG) was a prestige weapon for PIRA. Often featured in photographs in PIRA publications, it was a weapon that reinforced the image of the group as a military organization. Because of the potential potency of RPGs against a range of targets, especially vehicles, their use significantly affected the tactics of security forces operating in Northern Ireland.[24] PIRA received its first shipments of RPGs in 1972; at the time, this "meant that in some respects the PIRA were more heavily armed than the British Army (though the inexperience of the Volunteers largely negated this)" (Drake, 1991, p. 45).[25] The impact of the group's early attacks with the weapon was reportedly significantly reduced by this lack of experience (Bell, 1998b, p. 396; O'Callaghan, 1999, p. 70).

Although there are reports of attempts to train members in the use of RPGs as early as 1972, the difficulty PIRA had in carrying out systematic live-fire training (because of the attention attracted by the noise) suggests that most, if not all, of this training did not involve actual firing of the weapons (O'Callaghan, 1999, p. 80). Similarly, PIRA was constrained by the number of the weapons it had available (Glover, 1978):

> Once the level of weapon sophistication is increased this problem of competence becomes more serious. . . . To anyone with an exposure to the military, a bazooka or [antitank rocket] is quite a simple weapon used for obvious purposes. The [PIRA] had never been trained to use a launcher. The GHQ was not about to practice with the few rockets available. Instead the RPG-7 was used for [PIRA] purposes rather than in the way the maker had intended. Fired into military and police posts the armor-piercing rocket zapped in one side and out the other. The entire exercise proved futile for the [PIRA] (Bell, 1987, pp. 53–54).

Problems with the storage of the weapons also limited their effectiveness for the organization: "Poor storage facilities . . . often had a detrimental effect on the weapons' batteries and firing pack. It was typical of the [PIRA]'s inefficiency during this time" (O'Callaghan, 1999, p. 70).

Incidents in which RPGs missed their targets and struck particularly embarrassing targets sometimes resulted in very bad publicity for the group (e.g., "No One Hurt as Terrorist Grenade Hits Ulster Schoolroom," 1984). As was the case for other weapons technologies, inexperience had the potential to be deadly: "One of our contingent decided to fire an RPG-7 warhead but was quickly stopped: the blow-back

---

[24] Personal interviews with a law enforcement official, Northern Ireland, and a former security forces member, England, March 2004.

[25] The details of that first shipment of RPGs also demonstrate the shortcomings of the organization's arms acquisition prowess. The group planned for the plane delivering the weapons to land at a rural airport whose runway turned out to be too short for the landing, requiring a diversion to another airport on short notice (O'Callaghan, 1999, p. 69).

from it would have fried everyone in the confined space of the lorry" (O'Callaghan, 1999, p. 96). The need for volunteers to carry away the launcher portion of the RPG, which the group could not afford to leave behind, also made escape more difficult.[26] In spite of these drawbacks, PIRA continued to use RPGs, presumably because of their propaganda value.[27] However, group members did learn from their mistakes, changing tactics and using the weapon at shorter ranges to reduce the risk of mishaps.[28]

Even while it continued to use RPGs obtained from sources outside the group, PIRA began an internal learning effort to develop its own version of the weapon. In the mid-1980s, PIRA built its first homemade launcher, the improvised projected grenade (IPG). Like many such weapons, the initial version had shortcomings—including both a lack of safety features and the characteristic bruises that use of the weapon left on the firer's shoulder, which aided apprehension (Geraghty, 2000, pp. 195–196). But since the group controlled the supply,[29] the new launchers could be discarded after use.[30] In 1991, PIRA introduced a second-generation weapon, the projected recoilless improvised grenade (PRIG). The design of this weapon may have been based on diagrams of similar weapons in published reference books. It incorporated features that made it usable in enclosed spaces, and its warhead used a shaped-charge design that increased its penetration power (Geraghty, 2000, p. 197).

Measures of Learning in RPG Use. The magazine *Iris*, a publication linked to the Republican movement, published reports of PIRA attacks during an approximately ten-year period between May 1981 and March 1992. Because it was the most complete record of PIRA actions available during this research, it was used to assess the results of the group's learning of RPG use.

The numerical results of the analysis must be interpreted cautiously, with the shortcomings of the dataset in mind. First, it contains only a fraction of all incidents counted in aggregate statistical descriptions during that period. Second, there is reporting bias in the selection of incidents included in the dataset. Where possible, the *Iris* data were verified against and supplemented by incident reports from other datasets and news sources. Of six RPG incidents identified in that process, four were

---

[26] Personal interview with a law enforcement official, England, March 2004.

[27] Personal interview with a former security forces member, England, March 2004.

[28] Personal interview with a law enforcement official, Northern Ireland, March 2004.

[29] The efforts PIRA devoted to arms manufacture and development also made "any [counterterrorist] effort to achieve weapons-control a doomed enterprise" (Geraghty, 2000, p. 187). Efforts to locate and seize weapons from the group could not be effective when PIRA could "store" the knowledge of how to manufacture mortars or PRIGs and produce them as needed (personal interview with a former security forces member, England, March 2004). The group's ability to manufacture and modify its own weapon systems also increased its flexibility, and this injected additional uncertainty into efforts to predict its capabilities. As a result, while learning and innovation by security forces limited PIRA, PIRA's learning bounded the effectiveness of counterterrorist actions as well.

[30] Personal interview with a law enforcement official, England, March 2004.

categorized as catastrophic failures in PIRA's use of RPGs—i.e., the missile not only did not function as intended, it hit another target and/or injured or killed civilians. Third, the time period of the data does not include PIRA's full operational career. Since the dataset starts with 1981, it does not contain any examples of PIRA's early use of RPGs, which, as discussed above, was apparently not particularly effective. Similarly, incidents after March 1992 are also excluded. We located a few incidents of RPG use after that date, most of which would be considered very successful, in other databases. However, they were not included in the analysis, since this would introduce other biases into the dataset. In particular, their inclusion would complicate measurement of attack rates during the different time periods.

Available data suggest that PIRA's efforts to develop and deploy its own RPGs did increase its operational capabilities (Figure 5.2), though the changes in the group's performance with the weapons were not uniformly positive across all potential measures of learning. Most dramatically, after the introduction of the new weapons, the absolute number of attacks and the rate of those attacks increased significantly. Though they are not included in Figure 5.2, single attacks using multiple RPG units also became more prevalent. This increase in operational tempo and tactical flexibility increased the group's range of possible attack modes.

Figure 5.2 includes several additional measures for assessing the results of the attacks themselves. The first and second measures address whether the attack did or did not result in casualties. Although casualties are not a perfect measure of an attack's success, in most instances PIRA targeted security force patrols, vehicles, or bases, with the intent of killing or injuring members of counterterrorist and law enforcement organizations. As a result, from the group's perspective, attacks resulting in casualties could reasonably be judged more successful than attacks that did not.[31] On the basis of this measure, adoption of the new weapons did not result in improved outcomes—a smaller fraction of attacks with both generations of the improvised weapons resulted in casualties, compared with attacks using externally sourced RPG systems.[32]

The third measure, catastrophic failure, is the percentage of attacks that not only did not hit the intended target, but also struck an unintended target, causing significant damage, injury, or death. As the new weapons were introduced, the occurrence of such catastrophic failures declined, suggesting that the weapons or their use by the group was improving.

---

[31] The language used to describe attacks in *Iris* supports this assessment.

[32] The limited data available on attacks after the introduction of the PRIG must be borne in mind when weighing this conclusion.

Figure 5.2
Results of PIRA Use of RPGs, IPGs, and PRIGs, May 1981–March 1992

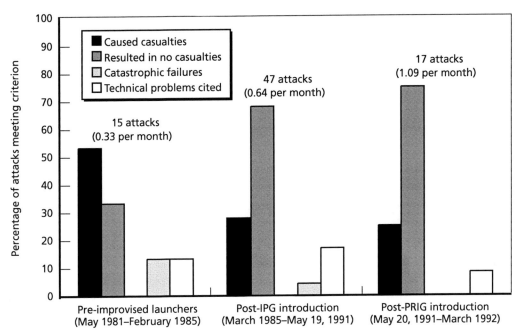

NOTE: IPG = improvised projected grenade, PIRA's first-generation homemade RPG system. PRIG = projected recoilless improvised grenade, PIRA's second-generation system. For the analysis, the total time period was broken into three phases; the second and third phases begin with the introduction of the IPG and the PRIG, respectively. A mixture of commercial and improvised RPG systems was used throughout all three phases. "Caused casualties" refers to attacks that resulted in at least one death or injury; "resulted in no casualties" refers to incidents that resulted in no deaths or injuries. Percentages of the "caused casualties " and "resulted in no casualties" categories add to 100. Additional categories describe attacks included in one of those two categories: "catastrophic failure" refers to incidents where, in addition to missing its intended target, the grenade struck an unintended target causing significant damage, injury, or death; "technical problem cited" refers to incidents where available information indicated that at least one grenade did not detonate or deflected from its target before detonating. In all cases, coding of incidents was based on available information in incident descriptions.

RAND *MG332-5.2*

In a number of instances, attacks with both externally sourced and PIRA-manufactured RPGs were affected by specific technical problems that caused the warhead either to deflect before detonating or to not detonate at all. As might be expected with the introduction of a new weapon, the percentage of attacks affected by such problems increased with the introduction of the IPG. However, the percentage later decreased after introduction of the PRIG. It should be noted that such problems may be underreported in the dataset.

Surface-to-Air Missiles: An Unsuccessful Search for Control of Airspace

In response to PIRA actions in which bombs and mines made ground transport very difficult in some areas, the security forces made extensive use of helicopters for transport and counterterrorist activities. The transition to use of the air caused PIRA to undertake an extensive and prolonged effort to obtain weapons that would give the group control of the airspace ("IRA Interview: *Iris* Talks to a Member of the IRA's General Headquarters Staff," 1981).

PIRA used various components of its arsenal to attack security forces helicopters: "PIRA's attacks on aircraft have been few and ineffective. Small arms fire and the RPG-7 have been the main methods. The M60 machine gun is a potentially useful weapon against helicopters given a suitable mounting or specially constructed fire position. We believe that it has been used in this role but so far without effect" (Glover, 1978). The group, particularly its unit in South Armagh, later had some success using firearms to attack aircraft (Urban, 1992, pp. 209–210). "According to Army records, since the beginning of the Troubles the [PIRA] has mounted some 23 helicopter attacks in South Armagh, bringing down three, compared with a handful in other areas of Northern Ireland" (Harnden, 2000, p. 358). However, PIRA judged that even the successes it had in shooting at helicopters with machine guns were not sufficient to give the group any real control over the airspace (Harnden, 2000, p. 362).

PIRA had received a small number of basic surface-to-air missiles, Russian-made SAM-7s, from Libya in the mid-1980s (Harnden, 2000, pp. 240–242). The group reportedly also received some training in the use of these missiles in Libya (Drake, 1991, p. 51). However, it was apparently not able to use the weapons effectively: "The only known deployment of a SAM-7 in Northern Ireland was against a Wessex [helicopter] at Kinawley on the County Fermanaugh border in July 1991; the missile failed to lock on to the helicopter and exploded on the ground" (Harnden, 2000, p. 371).[33]

Given its lack of success with externally sourced antiaircraft weapons, PIRA sought to develop and build its own. Its successes with other weapons technologies such as the RPG and improvised mortars made PIRA want to be able to control its own supply of antiaircraft weapons. One PIRA member emphasized that the group would "want to be able to manufacture" such weapons (Harnden, 2000, p. 366). To accelerate this effort, it called on the expertise of sympathetic individuals in the United States:

> In the early 1980's the [PIRA] developed a plan to design and produce its own anti-aircraft rockets in America. Developing an anti-aircraft missile is a multi-million pound undertaking, and even though the [PIRA] intended to cut the costs, it would still take years of effort. The project showed the degree to which highly qualified sympathizers were prepared to get involved with republican terrorism (Urban, 1992, p. 128).

---

[33] Later, in 2001, an expired chemical battery from a SAM-7 missile was found in a field in County Tyrone, but no information is available about how it got there or why (Jane's Terrorism and Insurgency Centre, 2003).

The individuals involved[34] were eventually arrested by the FBI, but the effort reached the prototype stage, including experimental test-firing in the Appalachian mountains (Harnden, 2000, pp. 362–372).

Operational Planning

The threat posed by a terrorist group is not a function simply of the acquisition of weapons and the group's ability to use them. A group's effectiveness also depends on how it uses its available operational resources. No matter how great its technical capacity is, a group that is unable to learn what it needs to plan operations effectively will be unable to achieve its aims. The following sections address operational planning in PIRA at both the tactical and the strategic level.

Tactical-Level Planning

The way a group plans individual operations is determined by judgments it makes about appropriate targets, its own capabilities, and the likelihood that it will be able to attack the targets successfully. Terrorists' initial choice of targets is largely defined by the group's ideology and the goals it is pursuing (Drake, 1998). Central targets for PIRA were security forces and individuals or sites that were allegedly contributing to British involvement in Northern Ireland. Practicalities make some ideologically acceptable targets inaccessible, however. While a group's tactical-level process for selecting the targets it believes it can successfully attack most likely consists of an implicit judgment on the part of the leadership or operatives, it can be diagrammed as a two-step process (shown in Figure 5.3) for the purpose of discussion. A basis for discussing that decision process is needed because it lays out a group's learning requirements for tactical-level planning.

Figure 5.3
Model of Tactical Decisionmaking by Terrorist Organizations

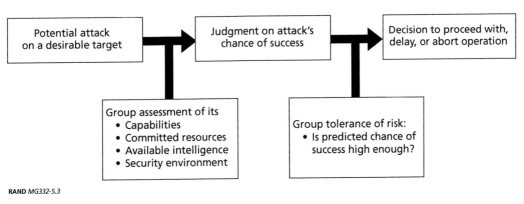

RAND *MG332-5.3*

---

[34] Including Richard Johnson, mentioned earlier in the discussion of remote-detonation-technology development.

The first of the two steps, the group's judgment of the likelihood an attack will be successful, is influenced by a number of factors:

- **Group capabilities.** The choices of tactics and the weapons the group has available significantly affect the probability of success. Certain targets may be judged inaccessible in the absence of particular attack modes.
- **Resources committed to the operation.** Particular attacks may be judged less likely to succeed if sufficient people and materials are not committed to the operation.
- **Available intelligence.** The amount a group knows about a target and its environment—including details of security arrangements, specific information on the target's vulnerability, etc.—affect its perception of its likelihood of success.
- **Security environment.** In the competition between terrorist groups and security forces, counterterrorist and antiterrorist activities affect a group's judgment about whether particular attacks will succeed.

A judgment based on these factors, in combination with the level of operational risk the group is willing to take, will determine whether a particular attack is deemed promising enough to go forward. As a result, for a given group at a particular time, there is a set of targets the group believes are accessible and can be attacked and a probably much larger set of targets that are not.

PIRA's Tactical-Success Criteria. Outside analysts and former PIRA members agree that the group evaluated potential operations against a relatively high standard before it went forward with an attack (Collins and McGovern, 1998; Horgan and Taylor, 1997; Silke, 2003). Such a statement has meaning, however, only if it is possible to infer what the group viewed as a successful operation.[35] Defining success is equally important for considering tactical-level learning, since learning is defined as change that makes the group more successful or more likely to succeed. Based on statements in publications such as *The Green Book* and statements by the group and former members, several factors can be identified that defined operational success over the course of PIRA's campaign:

- **Volunteer safety.** The ability of group members to survive and escape after an operation weighed heavily in operational planning: "During my meetings with [a PIRA intelligence officer] he had explained . . . that, regardless of whether an objective had been achieved successfully, if a volunteer were captured or killed

---

[35] What some groups would consider successful may or may not correspond to what an outside analyst would consider successful. Different criteria may also be more or less important to groups at different times, so the definition of success within a group may also not be stable.

in the process, then the operation was a failure" (Collins and McGovern, 1998, pp. 17–18).

- **Security force casualties.** Because of the focus of its actions in Northern Ireland, PIRA used the damage it inflicted on the security forces as a measure of success. Indeed, the group saw this as directly connected to its overall goal: "[Reportedly] . . . the Army Council set an initial target to kill thirty-six British soldiers because it was thought that this figure matched the number of troops killed in Aden and would supposedly impose enough pressure on the British to oblige them to negotiate" (Smith, 1997, p. 97).
- **Economic damage.** As part of a stated effort to undermine the governance of Northern Ireland, PIRA carried out many attacks aimed at causing direct economic damage and undermining investment in the region. The success of such attacks was discussed in monetary terms.
- **Publicity and public reaction.** Not unexpectedly, PIRA considered the likely level of publicity in both the location and scheduling of attacks: "Last year taught us that in publicity terms one bomb in Oxford Street is worth ten in Belfast" (PIRA spokesman quoted in Drake, 1991).
- **Minimization of civilian casualties.** Because PIRA wanted to appear to be a legitimate military organization, it had a stated goal of minimizing civilian casualties in its operations. PIRA's commitment to this as a criterion of success differed over the course of its operational history (Glover, 1978; Horgan and Taylor, 1997), however, and its actual (in contrast to verbal) commitment to it has been disputed. Use of this as a criterion also differed among PIRA's theaters of operation.

Depending on the specifics of a proposed operation and the conditions faced by the group or the individual cell planning it, a combination of judgments about these factors determined whether the operation went forward.

Learning in Tactical Planning. Organizational learning in tactical planning results in a group making changes to its decisionmaking and other processes to increase the chances that its operations will be successful. As shown in Figure 5.4, there are two distinct paths through which a group can improve its tactical planning. PIRA carried out learning activities along both paths.

The first path, *learning in target selection,* focuses on selecting a target and evaluating the chance that an attack against it will be successful (the light gray box in Figure 5.4). Learning in target selection takes group capabilities and environment as a given and focuses on improving the ability to select vulnerable targets and choose operations that are likely to succeed. It is, by definition, a learning process that focuses on continuously improving judgments about the activities that are within the group's reach.

Figure 5.4
Learning Processes in Tactical Planning

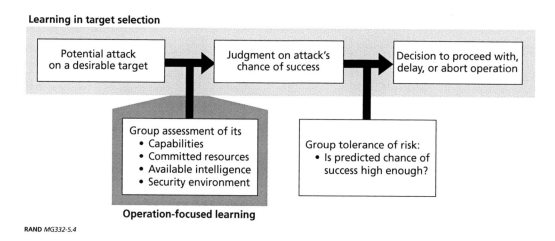

The second path, *operation-focused learning*, consists of the group developing better ways to marshal its capabilities or plan its operations to increase a given operation's chance of being successful (the dark gray box in the figure). In contrast to learning in target selection, operation-focused learning does not take group resources as a given, but instead is concerned with determining what resources are needed and how they should be applied to increase a desired operation's chances of success. One component of operation-focused learning is the group's seeking out new weapons, tactics, and intelligence. However, such learning also includes developing more-effective strategies for applying the group's capabilities.

Learning in Target Selection. According to a number of analysts, much of PIRA's tactical planning focused on selecting targets the group believed it could hit successfully, given its available capabilities:

> Political or strategic rationales did not dictate [PIRA] targets in England; operational considerations did. The [PIRA] did what was possible, using available resources. Capabilities in England were limited. Volunteers were its most precious commodity and had to be preserved. This dictated low-risk operations—targets had to be "soft" with few defenses and offering an easy escape (Jenkins and Gersten, 2001, p. 12).

PIRA's attack planning also focused on identifying accessible targets given current capabilities (Bell, 1998b, pp. 468–469, 638). While many of the assessment capabilities needed in this sort of planning are purely military—i.e., what targets are vulnerable to available weapons—others are quite different. For example, staging bombings that minimize civilian casualties requires understanding the precision of the timing devices used (Foreign and Commonwealth Office: Republic of Ireland Department, 1972b) and the systems that will act on advance warning that a bomb has been planted: "It's one thing to phone a warning, it's another to estimate how soon it will take effect" (Coogan, 1993, p. 289).

PIRA had learning mechanisms in place to improve tactical decisionmaking. Internal investigations were carried out after operations that went badly.[36] These investigations examined how operations were planned (O'Callaghan, 1999, p. 237) and how risk had been assessed before the decision was made to go forward: "As with Enniskillen, an investigation was begun into the operation and particularly into the question of how such a high-risk venture had been sanctioned by the Belfast leadership" (Silke, 2003, p. 52).[37] The results of such learning processes could be seen in changes in the group's targeting decisions. Over the group's operational lifetime, as targets became more difficult to strike (Drake, 1991) and security force activities made it more difficult to operate (O'Callaghan, 1999), PIRA shifted to carrying out attacks in different areas.

Operation-Focused Learning. Attacks that reflect PIRA's operation-focused learning activities include an attempt on the British Cabinet and Prime Minister Thatcher at Brighton, a mortar attack on 10 Downing Street, and the assassination of the Earl of Mountbatten. To focus the group's resources for these high-profile attacks, PIRA assembled specialized units (Bell, 1998b, p. 451). These units provided a mechanism for carrying out the unique learning requirements for operations and for organizing group resources in a way that increased their perceived chance of success. Such preparatory mechanisms included rehearsing operations before carrying them out (Bell, 1998b, p. 451) and addressing specific intelligence-gathering or preparation requirements. The special teams were frequently controlled directly by the GHQ, in contrast with the local control of most other PIRA operations (Bell, 1993, p. 109).

Operations aimed at specific targets or well-defended security force patrols also drove PIRA to adopt increasingly complex operational designs, a process that could be supported only by significant capability in operational planning. Over time, PIRA improved its ability to stage multipart and coordinated operations, sometimes to terrible effect. Their use of trap bombings—secondary devices targeting security forces example (Bell, 1998b; Harnden, 2000). Such complex operations relied on PIRA's

---

[36] Personal interview with a law enforcement official, Northern Ireland, March 2004.

[37] However, Bell has reported that the way decisions were made within PIRA made it difficult to learn from such approaches: "There is . . . in most cases no neat trail from first intelligence through authorization, command and operational control to retrospective analysis" (Bell, 1993, p. 99).

ability to collect intelligence on security forces tactics so that their procedures and reactions could be predicted and addressed. The group's planning and coordination ability also enabled it to stage coordinated simultaneous operations and to effectively use complex tactics involving many individual operatives (Drake, 1991; Urban, 1992).

Operation-focused learning is particularly important when a group carries out operations outside its traditional theater of conflict. PIRA stands out among ethnic terrorist groups for the number and scale of operations it staged outside its traditional operational area, Northern Ireland. According to the Canadian Security Intelligence Service, which analyzed these out-of-theater operations in the later phases of PIRA's operational career,

> Irish Republican terrorists committed 120 incidents in Great Britain from 1980–1993. In addition there were 53 acts of Irish Republican out-of-theatre terrorism during 1970–1990, in places as diverse as Washington, D.C. and Kinshasa, Zaire. However, the overwhelming majority of these acts have occurred in Western Europe (CSIS, 1994).

Data maintained by law enforcement organizations, which includes incidents and attempted incidents not broadly reported, puts the number of PIRA operations in Great Britain throughout its operational career more than five times higher.[38] To support these activities, PIRA had a designated department (the Foreign Operations, or England Department, shown in Figure 5.1) to manage these activities.

To execute out-of-theater operations successfully, a number of operation-focused learning requirements must be met. Groups must be able to gather intelligence on appropriate targets, obtain or produce the resources needed to stage the attacks, develop the operational plans to do so, train the individuals needed, and successfully infiltrate those individuals into the targeted areas. Tactics must be appropriately matched to the logistical and other complications of operating in a foreign environment where there are fewer opportunities for safe haven for the terrorist. Many of PIRA's operations on the British mainland involved bombings—letter bombs, timer-detonated bombs, and incendiaries—in contrast to the large number of shootings the group conducted in Northern Ireland. An early 1973, now-declassified British Government analysis of PIRA's early activities in Great Britain specifically highlighted the constraints: "Having no safe bases in Britain (unlike the predominantly Catholic areas which provide refuge and cover in Northern Ireland) it is unlikely that the [PIRA] will engage in sniping attacks on individual members of the police or armed forces in Britain." The analysis concluded that PIRA's out-of-theater

---

[38] Personal interview with a law enforcement official, England, March 2004.

attacks would continue to focus on bombing operations (Foreign and Common-wealth Office: Republic of Ireland Department, 1973b).

PIRA used multiple strategies to produce the weapons needed to carry out its out-of-theater operations. For some large operations, the weapons were organized in Northern Ireland and then exported to the foreign target area (e.g., Harnden, 1999); for smaller-scale operations, materials were sent to the foreign theater, where the operatives then built the bombs and devices themselves (O'Callaghan, 1999). In some cases, PIRA transferred full manufacturing capabilities of particular weapons outside of Northern Ireland: In December 1988, a bomb factory was uncovered in South London that included items related to the manufacture of the PIRA's Mark 10 mortar (Geraghty, 2000, p. 192). Whichever strategy was used, foreign operations, which involve infiltration into and activities within a more challenging and less hospitable environment, have significantly different learning requirements than attacks within a group's primary theater.

Strategic-Level Planning

Even if a group can plan effectively at the tactical level, tactical effectiveness is not sufficient for group success: "In any conflict the tactical efficiency with which military operations are executed will be meaningless unless they form part of a coordinated plan to achieve political ends, because the success of a strategy can only be judged with reference to attainment of the overall political objective" (Smith, 1997, p. 102).[39] Managing progress at this level requires the learning and analytical capability to frame realistic strategic goals, match tactical activities to those goals, evaluate progress, and alter behavior as a result. Analysts have questioned PIRA's capabilities over its operational career in a number of these areas.

The Physical-Force Tradition and Strategic-Learning Disability. In the Republican ideology, physical force was the most, and perhaps the only, appropriate approach for pursuing the goal of Irish reunification (Smith, 1997, pp. 219–220). This focus on one type of activity significantly limited PIRA's ability to gather and inter-

---

[39] Measures of tactical efficiency and capability may not be coupled at all to particular strategic goals. For PIRA, the desire to maintain a level of attacks—an operational tempo—was just such a goal. Wishing to both strengthen its image as an operational and potent group and keep constant pressure on the security forces in Northern Ireland (Bell, 1998b, p. 626), PIRA tried to stage attacks on an ongoing basis and to avoid long periods of apparent inactivity (Collins and McGovern, 1998; Smith, 1997). The fact that the group valued operational tempo as part of its overall strategy can be seen in the attacks reported in *Iris*, many of which would be considered failed operations by many measures—bombs that were defused or in which only the detonator exploded, rockets that missed their targets, and so on. As a result, it must be assumed that the group valued even failed attacks as evidence of the number of operations it was running and therefore reported them anyway. A focus on operational tempo as a strategic measure complicated the group's shift to a cell-based system, which inevitably would result in fewer operations. To prepare its "audiences" for the shift, the group announced that the numbers of operations would drop after the transition (Smith, 1997, p. 160). A desire to keep up the numbers of attacks during certain parts of its campaign also forced the group to involve less-experienced and less-reliable members in operations, resulting in damage to overall group security (Collins and McGovern, 1998, p. 84).

pret information about its actions, their impact on the group's progress, and potential alternative approaches to pursuing its goals. The primacy of military activities meant that there was frequently a focus on tactical rather than strategic concerns and, in fact, an absence of clear linkages between the group's tactical activities and any strategic plan (Bell, 1993).

Tactical success, measured in terms of damage or casualties inflicted, directly contributes to strategic success only if the damage can actually change the balance of forces in the conflict. While this might be the case in a conventional war, it is frequently not applicable in a conflict between a substate group and a state's military forces: "The fact that PIRA's attacks often resulted in the deaths of security force personnel or the destruction of buildings and so on did not mean that such attacks automatically related to the attainment of the strategic goal because individual operations were not aimed at the equalization of power with Britain" (Smith, 1997, p. 127).

The focus on physical force similarly blinded PIRA to situations where its military activities had created political opportunities (Alonso, 2001; Smith, 1997) and hamstrung group efforts to analyze its actions in light of strategic goals, leading it to "persist . . . in a particular strategy even though it [had] exhausted its potential" (Smith, 1997, p. 220). "Analysis" was focused on rationalization for armed actions that were taken, rather than on forward-looking strategic planning (Bell, 1993, p. 128; Smith, 1997, p. 140).

Incompatible Strategic Goals. Planning with respect to strategic goals is further complicated when a group has multiple, not necessarily compatible, goals. PIRA sought to maintain an image as both the defender of the Catholic population in Northern Ireland and a legitimate military, rather than terrorist, organization. Thus, the group sought to insulate itself from charges that it carried out sectarian attacks on Protestant individuals or sites. Beyond any sectarian motivations of PIRA members themselves, Loyalist attacks on Catholic targets made it difficult for the group to pursue both goals simultaneously. As a result, "in spite of what PIRA's leadership said, it was clear that, from mid-1972 onwards, Provisional units were killing Protestants in the same indiscriminate fashion [as the Loyalist groups]" (Smith, 1997, pp. 119–120). The PIRA attack on the Shankill Road fish shop in 1993, an attempted assassination of the leadership of the Loyalist Ulster Defense Association, is an example of the conflict between group strategic goals. Driven by PIRA's desire to be seen as defending the Catholic population, the failure of the attack significantly damaged the group's efforts aimed at other strategic goals (Silke, 2003). One way the group sought to have it both ways was to leave sectarian attacks unclaimed or to claim them in the names of cover groups (Smith, 1997, pp. 119–120).

PIRA Strategic Learning. For much of PIRA's operational career, the privileged position of physical force within the Republican tradition created barriers to strategic learning. As long as military activities were valued as the only appropriate tactic rather than being seen as one element of an overall strategy, it was difficult to shape group activities to effectively pursue any strategic goal. That would require a level of political control over the violence that was essentially absent early in the campaign. This led to very different interpretations of activities by the political side of the Republican movement (the overt political party, Sinn Fein) and PIRA:

> PIRA was inclined to see operations which went wrong and killed civilians as technical mistakes, resulting from faulty equipment, inadequate warning times and so on. [Sinn Fein], on the other hand, saw such actions as conceptually flawed, believing that operations should never be carried out in areas, such as towns, where there was a high risk to civilians (Smith, 1997, p. 178).

Later in PIRA's operational history, the balance of power between its political and military wings shifted, allowing somewhat more political influence over its actions. This in turn allowed a shift to a more "total strategy" where "the military instrument [could] be governed by calculations of its efficacy rather than ideological tradition" (Smith, 1997, p. 157). Such calculation was necessary to allow organizational learning to occur at the strategic level. One of the key factors that enabled this shift was a change in the leadership of PIRA and of important units and commands within it. Replacement of the initial leadership of the group, largely older and drawn from the south, by younger leaders from Northern Ireland opened up the group's thinking to new strategic options and was reportedly a key catalyst for the shift in strategy and the improvement in strategic learning capability (Drake, 1991, p. 46; O'Callaghan, 1999, p. 119; Smith, 1997, p. 154).

Training

PIRA used both general and specialized training programs to distribute knowledge among its membership and increase its operational effectiveness. Within its organizational structure, PIRA maintained training and education departments to run these programs (Figure 5.1). Training deficiencies can be costly: "The result of a lack of training is a high attrition rate and a considerable degree of inefficiency. Volunteers detonate their bombs too early, kill themselves, kill the crowd, ruin the operation" (Bell, 1998a, p. 137). However, the constraints of secrecy impose limits on the amount and level of training an underground organization can give its recruits. Unlike a national army, which devotes a significant fraction of its time to ongoing training, an underground organization must train in secret and for short periods. Training can be dangerous in itself, as it can attract the attention of security services (O'Doherty, 1993, pp. 167–168) or even result in the death of organization members through accidents (O'Callaghan, 1999, p. 59). While its overall membership would probably never have been considered well trained in conventional military

terms (Bell, 1987, p. 51), PIRA pursued a number of strategies to increase its capabilities, including links to other terrorist organizations, collecting and codifying
knowledge, organizational training programs, and internal knowledge transfer.

International Links

The literature on PIRA indicates that the group obtained technology and training
from a range of international sources. Such interactions may even predate the group's
founding: "During the 1950's, those members of the IRA who were destined to form
the core of the Provisional IRA in the 1970's, were imprisoned in England with
members of the Greek Cypriot terrorist group EOKA. By their own account they
learned from them" (Drake, 1998, p. 76).[40]

Another terrorist group, Basque Fatherland and Liberty (ETA), is frequently
linked to PIRA. Public acknowledgments of "good relations" between the organizations go back to 1974 (Coogan, 1993, p. 330), and first-person accounts by former
PIRA members confirm the relationship: "The links between ETA and the [PIRA]
run deep; the two organizations have often cooperated and pooled ideas, technology
and training. As far back as 1972, ETA supplied the [PIRA] with weapons. The
accounts of what was supplied differ but not the fact of it" (O'Callaghan, 1999,
p. 196). Training relationships between the groups reportedly go both ways over the
course of both groups' operational careers (Drake, 1991, p. 53; Geraghty, 2000,
p. 178; O'Callaghan, 1999, p. 196).

PIRA reportedly developed relationships with various groups and nations in the
Middle East, including Al-Fatah in Jordon (Foreign and Commonwealth Office: Republic of Ireland Department, 1972a), the Popular Front for the Liberation of Palestine (PFLP), the Palestine Liberation Organization (PLO) (Bell, 1998b, p. 438;
McKinley, 1984, p. 17), and the government of Libya. These relationships were
sought for both training purposes and weapons procurement.

The importance of the linkages between PIRA and other terrorist groups have
been questioned, however. Glover characterized the links as "elusive" and stated that
"there are no signs that PIRA has either the intention or ability deliberately to foster
them" (Glover, 1978). Others have suggested that it is "unclear how useful these
links are in operational terms" (Drake, 1991, p. 53); one PIRA member trivialized
the contribution the training in Libya made to the group: "Don't mind that talk
about Libya. The Libyans were trained in conventional warfare. They couldn't teach
us anything" (Coogan, 1993, p. 363).[41]

---

[40] Prison time has also been highlighted as a route for transfer of knowledge inside PIRA—with prisons serving as
"universities of terror"—later in its career as well (Geraghty, 2000, p. xxxi).

[41] Today, with PIRA on an extended ceasefire, concerns focus on transmission of the knowledge it developed to
other terrorist groups, including the splinter Real IRA and Continuity IRA. Former PIRA members may also be

Collecting and Codifying Knowledge

The initial step in any training program is the collection of relevant knowledge to pass on. Beyond its international connections, PIRA both sought out and developed its own knowledge sources. At first, it drew on available print and expert sources for bomb making and other information:

> I was surprised to find out how much information was available in the local library. I also studied the old IRA and British Army training manuals. . . . I was also active in Sinn Fein and sold the [PIRA] newspaper door-to-door. . . . One of my regular customers turned out to be a former British Army sapper. . . . I would go to his house during the day and over a cup of tea or two he would draw sketches of different booby traps, explaining the properties of different explosives. Updated [PIRA] training manuals were now available; I would show these to him and he would scribble notes and make comments on any errors or deficiencies (O'Callaghan, 1999, p. 55).

In addition to the explicit knowledge available in print, such expert sources provided the group with access to tacit information critical to success in dangerous activities such as working with explosives. First-person accounts by former PIRA members cite seeking out experts ranging from former members of the British Royal Marines Special Boat Squadron (Collins and McGovern, 1998, p. 237) to an individual who had survived an extended hunger and thirst strike to inform PIRA decisionmaking (Coogan, 1993, p. 377). PIRA also developed its own in-house experts. In 1970, the group persuaded a technically talented recruit to stay in school rather than joining PIRA immediately, so that he could gain the electronics and other skills needed to construct bombs (Harnden, 2000, p. 333).[42]

To facilitate broader training of its members, PIRA devoted significant effort to preparing written documents containing training information. Along with the bomb-making manual described above, the group had field manuals for particular weapons("Five Days in an IRA Training Camp," 1983, p. 39).[43] As part of its counterintelligence efforts, the group prepared manuals that taught ways to counter law enforcement actions: "The [PIRA], with customary thoroughness, debriefed Volunteers who had gone through the process of detection and trial and produced a 9,000 word document whose title could have been 'How Not to Incriminate Yourself'" (Geraghty, 2000, p. 83).[44]

---

interacting with organizations outside Ireland, such as the FARC in Colombia (McDermott, 2002) and Palestinian groups in the Middle East ("IRA Bomb Expert Arrested in West Bank," 2003).

[42] Later in its history, PIRA developed its own staff of in-house lawyers by supporting potential members while they were in law school (Geraghty, 2000, pp. 91–92).

[43] Personal interview with a law enforcement official, England, March 2004.

[44] Unlike al Qaeda, which prepared and disseminated a comprehensive manual that covered all components required for operations, PIRA had no "master instruction book." Because it had a support community and the

The Green Book was one of PIRA's best-known manuals. In addition to articulating the basis for the movement, it contained basic military information for new volunteers (Coogan, 1993, p. 369). "The Green Book listed the duties and responsibilities of Volunteers, as well as explaining the history of the movement, the rules of military engagement, and anti-interrogation techniques" (Collins and McGovern, 1998, p. 66). Lectures covering the content of *The Green Book* were a central element of initial training for potential recruits to PIRA.

Organizational Training

To provide a common basis for all of its members, PIRA ran a training program that taught certain basic skills and information that recruits would need as volunteers. In addition to presenting the content of *The Green Book*, the training covered a range of military skills, including some live-fire weapons training.

Early descriptions of the PIRA training curriculum indicate that the main focus was on the characteristics and use of weapons: "The majority of recruits undergo a week's training at one of the camps in Eire, during which they are instructed in small arms handling, target practice, demolition techniques and field craft" (Foreign and Commonwealth Office: Republic of Ireland Department, 1972a). More-experienced members taught the recruits to strip down, clean,[45] and load weapons, along with basic firearms safety (O'Callaghan, 1999, p. 50). Live firing focused on lighter weapons, "as the likelihood of discovery in such a remote area using the quieter .22 calibre ammunition was negligible, and this type of ammunition was cheap and easily available. Such freedom gave us a great opportunity to monitor development and to correct bad habits. Only those we felt had reached the required standard were allowed a short firing session with heavier weapons at a location deeper in the mountains" (O'Callaghan, 1999, p. 82).

Training programs later in the group's operational career are described as being similar to the early programs, though with an increasing focus on sighting and aiming of weapons ("Five Days in an IRA Training Camp," 1983). Later camps reportedly covered operational planning and intelligence techniques ("Five Days in an IRA Training Camp," 1983, p. 45), as well as the strengths and vulnerabilities of security forces: "The Brits and the RUC . . . introduced a new flak jacket . . . so Volunteers are now trained not to bother attempting body shots on uniformed enemy personnel . . . [in addition, training covers] what parts of an armoured vehicle to aim at, how to

---

ability to train people face to face, it did not have the same need for such a book (personal interview with a law enforcement official, England, March 2004).

[45] One account of PIRA training points out that the group did not sufficiently emphasize the importance of seemingly mundane tasks such as cleaning firearms in their training: "One of the most frequent causes of a gun jamming is dirt and excess oil and I was always amazed by how little the IRA cared about this" (O'Callaghan, 1999, p. 82).

fire most effectively in teams, and where and how to fire constructively after the all-important first aimed shot" ("Five Days in an IRA Training Camp," 1983, p. 41).

PIRA took advantage of the relative safety of the Republic of Ireland to carry out its training (Foreign and Commonwealth Office: Republic of Ireland Department, 1972a). Security of training camps was always an issue, however. Not only were the types of weapons recruits could use restricted, new members were also generally kept ignorant of the exact location where they were training (O'Callaghan, 1999, p. 51), and camps were placed to minimize the impact of the noise caused by firearms, e.g., in areas where the noise would not carry far ("Five Days in an IRA Training Camp," 1983) or where it would be covered by other similar noises, such as that from a nearby Irish Army Territorials rifle range (O'Callaghan, 1999, p. 52).

Despite this extensive training effort, serious questions have been raised about its impact on the capability of the organization. Bell argues that within such organizations, the real focus of training is "maintaining the creed"—passing on the philosophy of the organization—rather than "instilling the techniques of war" (Bell, 1998a, p. 136). Contemporary assessments of the quality of the PIRA training were critical of its military content as well:

> The training carried out is, except in explosives, fairly basic. The standard of recruit is poor and with a maximum of ten days training, only the basic handling of one, or perhaps two, weapons can be covered. . . . Thus while training standards and results in bomb-making and handling are good, general weapon training is poor and achieves standards far inferior to those of a trained soldier. On the other hand, the standard required of a guerrilla . . . are not those required of a professional soldier. . . . The [PIRA] standard is probably adequate for the operations they envisage (Foreign and Commonwealth Office: Republic of Ireland Department, 1972a).

Even training participants were critical of the training, especially early in PIRA's operational career. Some described it as "very rudimentary [in] nature" (O'Callaghan, 1999, p. 52) and indicated that it was more appropriate to rural operations than to the urban areas where a majority of PIRA's actions were conducted (O'Doherty, 1993, pp. 85–86).

Specialized Training

The capabilities and expertise of individual volunteers or units were not uniform across the organization. "As the [PIRA] became more organized, Volunteers began to specialize in areas such as sniping, explosives, logistics, or intelligence" (Harnden, 2000, p. 53). Such efforts were driven in part by effectiveness concerns. Specialization made it possible for some units to improve their capabilities in a particular area (O'Callaghan, 1999, p. 151), and certain weapons or tactics were more appropriate for operations in particular parts of the group's operational area.[46] It also provided PIRA with a range of human resources that could be allocated for different operations: Advanced members could carry out particularly sensitive operations, while less-trained volunteers could participate in less-risky "day-to-day" attacks (Jenkins and Gersten, 2001). Specialization was supported by advanced courses of training for particular operational areas and ongoing refresher training for people with particular talents.[47]

Differences among PIRA units produced differences and specialization within the group. Although these differences partially reflected the characteristics of the people in the units,[48] many arose from the way individual units trained their members. Early on, some units grouped volunteers carrying out similar activities to enable more effective learning (O'Doherty, 1993, p. 157). Other units went through rotation processes to teach volunteers the skills they needed and to spread knowledge and training capabilities among units (O'Callaghan, 1999, pp. 77–78).[49] The PIRA cell in South Armagh focused on training within the unit, a practice credited with that group's effectiveness:

> [South Armagh] had taken a number of people and they had worked with them over a period of years, gradually acclimatising them to the type of warfare they were going to be involved in, rather than putting them in at the deep end quickly, which is what happens in the urban areas. South Armagh developed a slow process of training the volunteer. They would have taken raw recruits and put them in with skilled people and took them on. They didn't push them too hard. And they got them used to what they were going to be faced with. This system meant that there were fewer mistakes and therefore fewer arrests in South Armagh than in any other [PIRA] Brigade area (Harnden, 2000, p. 46).

Other units made different choices. The Newry PIRA unit, as a result of past mistakes, chose to segregate its subunits by the quality of the volunteers: "There were now two units: one was known as the 'elite unit' and was staffed by four experienced and effective men. The other was a relatively new group of three novices, all in their early twenties" (Collins and McGovern, 1998, p. 66). Although such a choice might

---

[46] Personal interview with a former security forces member, England, March 2004.

[47] Personal interview with a law enforcement official, Northern Ireland, March 2004.

[48] For example, the unit in South Armagh was made up of the same people for almost the entire history of the conflict, enabling the unit to build up high levels of expertise in many areas (Harnden, 2000, p. 43).

[49] After PIRA's reorganization to a cell structure in the late 1970s, such internal rotations were less relevant as knowledge transfer mechanisms. However, even then, there was some exchange of individuals among units that allowed "mentoring on the job" by more-experienced operatives. Whether such mentoring could compensate for reductions in technology transfer across the group overall depended strongly on the way individual units structured themselves and managed their members (personal interview with a law enforcement official, Northern Ireland, March 2004).

address the short-term goal of minimizing the risk of compromise and loss of elite group members, it does not provide the organizational learning benefits that a mixed structure does.

Staging terrorist operations outside a group's traditional theaters of activity (discussed above in the context of operation-focused learning) imposes unique training requirements on a group. Because of the number and scope of PIRA's activities both on the British mainland and in other locations, units had to be appropriately prepared to conduct operations outside their home area. The training they received included instruction in how to gather intelligence on targets in the area of the operation and how to blend into the environment, as well as defensive behaviors, such as how to evade surveillance practices used in the target nation (Harnden, 2000, p. 326).

Logistics

The effectiveness of any organization depends on the logistical system it has to support its activities. PIRA's material and financial management practices have evolved over the years, and evidence of major changes in its arms procurement and storage practices is readily available in the published literature. The group's success in connecting with Libyan arms sources and the discovery of "sometimes remarkable underground facilities" used for storing and working on arms (Horgan and Taylor, 1997, p. 8) imply that it devoted significant effort to improving its logistical capabilities. However, comparatively little data are available on the learning processes that supported these changes.

Somewhat more information is available regarding PIRA's learning practices relating to finance. Originally relying on support from Irish expatriate communities, PIRA eventually diversified its financial operations into many areas, including alcohol and gambling and criminal activities such as robbery, fraud, smuggling, and extortion (Harnden, 2000; Horgan and Taylor, 1999, 2003; O'Callaghan, 1999). Like a legitimate business, PIRA used relatively simple profit-and-loss measures to guide its learning efforts. The effectiveness of logistical operations was assessed by whether they were producing the expected levels of resources: "At that time the level of operational effectiveness in the Southern Command [where many logistical functions were managed] was poor. In August 1981, two small armed robberies had taken place during the annual Rose of Tralee International Festival. At that time of the year both targets—a hotel and a restaurant—would have been awash with cash. In each case, however, an inexperienced [PIRA] team had done the job, leaving behind large amounts of undiscovered money" (O'Callaghan, 1999, p. 151).

Individual components of PIRA were judged on the basis of whether they were generating their share of the required resources (O'Callaghan, 1999, pp. 226–227).

Actions taken to improve performance included the development of specific active service units "tasked with carrying out armed robberies" (O'Callaghan, 1999, p. 151) and increasing the "'professionalization' of the [PIRA's] handling of its finances, to the point where the [PIRA] in Northern Ireland now [in 1998] employs its own homegrown lawyers, accountants and computer experts" (O'Callaghan, 1999, p. 228).

Intelligence and Operational Security

Counterintelligence and operational security were sufficiently important to merit extensive discussion in *The Green Book*. New volunteers were instructed to avoid activities that would identify them as Republican sympathizers, warned them of the dangers of drink-induced talk, and provided methods to help them withstand interrogation (Coogan, 1993, p. 413).[50] Intelligence collection was also included in recruit training:

> Recruits are educated and informed of ways in which they are expected to both evaluate information and report it. Recruits are advised that any information may hold potential value to the organisation as "intelligence" which may facilitate or determine the tactics, pace and conduct of operational activities. . . . PIRA recruits are reminded that they are not just "soldiers" but the "eyes and ears" for their own comrades (Horgan and Taylor, 1997, p. 15).

The manual describes in detail good intelligence practices such as verification of sources, control of information on a need-to-know basis, and categorization of information to be passed upward in the group (Horgan and Taylor, 1997, pp. 15–17). PIRA sought to build both offensive and defensive intelligence capabilities to support its operations and protect itself from counterterrorist efforts.

Offensive Intelligence

PIRA relied on first-person reports and individuals placed within government offices to identify targets that met their targeting criteria, i.e., individuals connected with the security services or law enforcement organizations (Collins and McGovern, 1998). Inside sources such as sympathetic members already within those organizations could provide dividends beyond targeting information. For example, presumably with inside assistance, "In early 1979 [PIRA] brought off a coup which really displayed arcane knowledge, taking from the English mails a top-secret British military assessment . . . in which the British concluded, among a number of other judgments, that

---

[50] The explicit lessons were reinforced with simulated interrogations to familiarize members with what to expect (Coogan, 1993, p. 422).

the [PIRA] could not be defeated—an incredible morale booster to receive from an enemy" (Coogan, 1993, p. 283).[51]

Once a potential target was identified, PIRA operatives used standard surveillance methods to identify locations where they would have the opportunity to attack and escape routes for the attackers (Collins and McGovern, 1998; Drake, 1998, p. 63). For operations in rural areas, intelligence collection followed a military model: "Every attack is carefully planned. The operating pattern of the Army is studied in detail. Secure firing positions, fields of fire and killing zones are worked out, and escape routes well thought out" (Harnden, 2000, p. 77).

PIRA was limited in carrying out these offensive intelligence operations by the quality of its information sources. Individual reports could be wrong, resulting in the wrong people being attacked or the selection of targets that were not actually acceptable given the group's stated targeting criteria (Collins and McGovern, 1998). PIRA's operations in Europe have been singled out as examples of failures in offensive intelligence gathering: "Overseas [PIRA] actions were not as impressive. . . . From January 1988 to June 1990, there were seventeen [PIRA] attacks. Nine used Semtex to construct bombs that generally proved ineffectual. The other eight were a series of shooting incidents that tended to focus on the wrong target or hit an innocent transient" (Bell, 1998b, p. 614).[52]

PIRA used public information sources such as "Who's Who" to select targets for assassination in England (O'Doherty, 1993, p. 140). Such sources could be obsolete, however, a fact PIRA discovered when it set off a bomb at the *former* address of former Conservative Party Treasurer Lord McAlpine in June 1990 (Drake, 1998, p. 59). In addition, constraints imposed on the organization by both secrecy and communication security meant that intelligence often could not be utilized (Bell, 1993, p. 5).

Comparatively little information is available on PIRA efforts to improve its offensive intelligence capability. Intelligence gathering was included in the members' training, and a few descriptions of individuals' efforts to improve collection in their areas can be found in the literature. The first-person report of Eamon Collins, a PIRA intelligence officer for many years, describes his efforts to systematize one unit's intelligence capability:

> I convinced myself that the [PIRA] had become dependant on hit-and-miss information and gossip from unreliable sources. What the organization needed was a network of sources ranging from local people, who could provide low-grade,

---

[51] This document, written by J. M. Glover, has been quoted throughout this chapter.

[52] European countries in which PIRA carried out operations included Belgium, The Netherlands, Gibraltar, and West Germany.

every-day intelligence, to people inside the apparatus of the state, who could provide a lot more (Collins and McGovern, 1998, pp. 16–17).

Because "intelligence officers tend to have a longer operational life than gunmen or
guerrillas and so over time accumulate trade experience" (Bell, 1998a, p. 198), such
individuals may have a high degree of intelligence expertise. However, the need for
secrecy to protect sources provides a disincentive to sharing intelligence-collection
information or to creating records that would assist others in carrying out intelligence
activities (Bell, 1994, p. 134).

Keeping intelligence collection at the individual level limits a group's capabilities and, importantly, means that those capabilities are never truly organizational. In
Bell's words, "The rebel world of intelligence . . . seldom evinces elegance or grace,
much less institutionalized competence" (Bell, 1994, p. 119). The lack of institution-
alization means that those capabilities may be lost if key individuals are captured or
killed:

> On March 20, 1979, the key GHQ operational officer Brian Keenan had been
> arrested . . . . Whatever his virtues, Keenan was not a tidy administrator nor very
> forthcoming. Much of what he knew went into prison with him. Some did
> not—he had kept an address book that fascinated the authorities. As for the
> [PIRA] both his talents and his contacts—not to mention the address
> book—were gone (Bell, 1998b, p. 472).

Demonstrating the value of such key individuals to the organization, PIRA attempted unsuccessfully to break Keenan out of prison. As a group evolves, it may also
move away from focusing primarily on secrecy, thereby weakening the forces that
work against activities like record-keeping and allowing more institutionalized intelligence activities (Bell, 1994, p. 135; Horgan and Taylor, 1997, p. 15).

Defensive Intelligence

A covert organization requires significant intelligence efforts to protect itself from
infiltration, apprehension, or harm from security services. Some of these efforts are
quite basic—in its early years, PIRA had sympathizers announce the presence of
security patrols by "banging dust-bin lids and blowing whistles" (Foreign and Commonwealth Office: Republic of Ireland Department, 1972b).

Defensive efforts gradually shifted to "more subtle forms of communication.
Telephones were used to pass cryptic messages. Sympathizers living in tall blocks of
flats would spot patrols with binoculars and then hang a towel on their balcony or
open a window. These warning posts made it safer for the [PIRA] to stage attacks or
move weapons and, in turn, forced an increase in undercover surveillance by the security forces" (Urban, 1992, pp. 113–114). This competition gradually shifted to
higher-technology arenas, with PIRA monitoring security services' communications

with the use of "military-style transmitters, specialized monitors, and position-fixing devices" (Bell, 1998a, pp. 197–198). The group also tapped telephones serving key security service members, providing access to information on counterterrorism activities and on potential PIRA targets (Bell, 1998a, pp. 197–198; Urban, 1992, p. 114).

PIRA also reportedly relied on its internal assets and contacts for defensive intelligence information. "For instance, in 1969 they learned of internment in advance so instead of being a crushing blow, it proved a launching pad. . . . They learned that British Intelligence was operating behind the cover of at least one seemingly ordinary business and brutally crippled this endeavor" (Coogan, 1993, p. 283). Infiltration of law enforcement organizations reportedly also provided PIRA with information it used to protect its activities and operatives (Harnden, 2000, p. 237; Taylor and Quayle, 1994, p. 63).

Organizational Reorganization for Improved Security

In the late 1970s, PIRA made major organizational changes to increase security. The organization's comparatively open, military-style structure had been effective early on, but it was vulnerable to penetration. During the ceasefire that held through much of 1975, counterterrorist forces penetrated many parts of the organization, and the operations it tried to carry out subsequently were largely compromised (Smith, 1997, p. 133). PIRA therefore reorganized its operational components into a cell-based structure built on individual service units:

> These would comprise four or five Volunteers working in a tight "family" group. There would be a quartermaster with responsibility for weapons and explosives, an intelligence officer, and at least two operators capable of carrying out shootings and bombings (Collins and McGovern, 1998, pp. 82–83).

The reorganization was described in a document seized from PIRA Chief of Staff Seamus Twomey when he was arrested in 1977 (Coogan, 1993, pp. 354–355). Communication between individual units was theoretically only on a need-to-know basis (Horgan and Taylor, 1997, p. 20). Units were also supposed to broaden their use of disguise and operate outside their home areas to reduce the effectiveness of police surveillance.

In designing its new structure, PIRA reportedly undertook a "careful study of the several international terrorist groups that had been obtaining universal publicity for their exploits, such as the Palestinian ones, the Baader-Meinhof Gang, and the Basque ETA" (O'Ballance, 1981, p. 226). In addition, Republican prisoners, insulated from the day-to-day pressures of being in the underground, were reportedly key in developing the new structure and strategy (Davies and Dolamore, forthcoming).

Because of different demands in rural and urban areas, PIRA's reorganization into a cell system was not uniformly implemented across the group (Coogan, 1993, pp. 354–355), and some exchange of individuals among cells still occurred.[53] However, the effort was effective as assessed by a range of measures. "The system was successful in stopping the haemorrhage of arrests. In 1978, there were 465 fewer charges for paramilitary offenses than the previous year. As part of the restructuring process, the organization was slimmed down to a core of 300 or so activists" (Smith, 1997, p. 145).

Though the cellular structure did increase security of the organization, a price was paid in terms of the organization's subsequent ability to learn. A key goal of such a structure is the compartmentalization of information, which reduces an organization's overall ability to use and apply information and capabilities.[54] A former PIRA member cited his inability to use any established contacts when he came into a new area to operate: "I knew the engineering department spent a lot of time in Waterford and obviously had reliable contacts but these were not available to Ferris or me" (O'Callaghan, 1999, p. 220).[55]

The concentration of knowledge and capability into smaller cells, while protecting the organization overall from large-scale penetration, increased individual components' vulnerability:

> The reduction in the number of PIRA activists made it far easier for the security forces to concentrate their resources against known operatives. . . . Between 1978 and 1988, some thirty PIRA members were killed in [Special Air Services] operations. . . . The damage was felt not just in numerical terms but also in the loss of experience and seniority. For example, in May 1987 one of PIRA's most hardened units, the East Tyrone Brigade, was all but wiped out when eight of its men were killed in an SAS ambush during an attack on an RUC station at Loughall, Co. Armagh. The move to the cell system thus made even modest losses hard to bear (Smith, 1997, p. 188).

Although it increased the survivability of the group overall, focusing resources in individual cells reduced the robustness of particular capabilities and units within the organization.

---

[53] Personal interview with a law enforcement official, Northern Ireland, March 2004.

[54] Bell points out, however, that there were barriers to knowledge transfer in PIRA's initial structure as well: "In the case of the IRA in Belfast . . . the very strength of operating on home turf among neighbours had often meant isolation from other IRA units (the Turf Lodge Provos not only knew little of South Armagh—much less Dublin—but also cared little for Andersonstown)" (Bell, 1998b, p. 437). As a result, the transition may not have increased barriers to information exchange as much as might be assumed.

[55] Former volunteers also cited situations where compartmentalization could create security problems: "I was sufficiently concerned about my own safety and that of the people who worked with me to want to know if any operations were planned for areas where I had flats containing explosives and other materials" (O'Doherty, 1993, p. 164). Thus, security responses to one unit's attack could compromise the logistical base of another.

Counter-Law Enforcement and Counter-Forensic Activities

Throughout its campaign, PIRA maintained a keen awareness of the capabilities of law enforcement and the techniques the authorities brought to bear in investigating and prosecuting terrorist offenses.[56] As the security forces applied advanced forensic science techniques to PIRA-initiated events, the organization had to devote resources to learning how to thwart them (Horgan and Taylor, 1997, p. 23). PIRA developed manuals and training materials to teach its members how to defeat forensic science, to help the volunteer "break the forensic link to incriminating chemical [and other] residue" (Geraghty, 2000, p. 86) tying him or her to an attack. The documents describe evidence-collection procedures that should concern a volunteer in operational planning. They include

- Collection of incriminating evidence in hair, a problem accentuated by use of hair spray or gel
- Gunpowder residues associated with the use of firearms (the manuals include recommendations to wear overgarments and to avoid capture until they are washed)
- Contamination during explosives manufacture
- Garment fibers (the manuals include recommendations on clothing selection to limit fiber evidence)
- Particle contamination from smashed glass or paint
- DNA evidence and identification
- Footprint analysis
- Document analysis (Geraghty, 2000, pp. 81–90)

PIRA developed standard practices, such as wearing rubber gloves and the group's iconic balaclava facemasks, to reduce members' vulnerability to many forensic techniques (Urban, 1992, p. 115). To circumvent computer systems for tracking car license plates and registrations, PIRA falsified car identification numbers so that its vehicles would appear to be similar cars owned by innocent civilians (Urban, 1992, p. 115).[57] The level of "forensic threat" led PIRA to use incendiary devices to destroy evidence (Bell, 1998b, p. 624) and even to directly attack the central forensic sciences facility in Northern Ireland on two occasions (Geraghty, 2000, p. 90).

PIRA reportedly built a keen understanding of the capabilities and constraints of law enforcement practices, including how interviews with suspects were recorded or monitored and the procedures through which prisoners were processed.[58] It also

---

[56] Personal interview with a law enforcement official, Northern Ireland, March 2004.

[57] Personal interview with a university researcher, Northern Ireland, March 2004.

[58] Personal interview with a law enforcement official, Northern Ireland, March 2004.

built up knowledge on the ways security forces observed and areas in which PIRA members could and could not be seen, and it kept track of which volunteers the security forces had identified as PIRA members.[59] This allowed the group to blunt the effectiveness of police surveillance by using individuals who were not known to security forces for high-value operations (Silke, 2003, p. 50).[60] To circumvent the constraints this put on some activities, PIRA sought to take advantage of occasions when forensic science was unable to identify the victims of bombings: By announcing the deaths of high-value members under such circumstances, the group could "resurrect" them later for "specialised operations under a cloak of anonymity" (Coogan, 1993, p. 294).

The main mechanism PIRA used to build its knowledge of law enforcement practices was debriefing and interrogation of members who had been arrested and members suspected of being informants for the security services.[61] The internal security unit that performed this function applied interrogation techniques learned from, among other sources, their own interrogations by the security services (Collins and McGovern, 1998, p. 241). These debriefings occurred whenever anyone was arrested, an operation was penetrated, or events during an action did not go as planned.[62]

PIRA was willing to invest a considerable amount of time and effort in these internal investigations, demonstrating the value it ascribed to this learning activity. When law enforcement penetrated its training department in the Republic, compromising subsequent PIRA operations there, it "was almost a year before the training department was able to resume normal business" (O'Callaghan, 1999, pp. 144–145) after a rigorous investigation was completed. Investigations of failures and compromises in other areas also dampened PIRA activities for considerable periods (Harnden, 2000, p. 414; O'Callaghan, 1999, p. 243).

As a complement to its internal investigations, PIRA eventually exploited court proceedings to gain information on law enforcement practices. Early on, captured PIRA members refused to put up a defense in court as part of their effort to impugn the legitimacy of English governance and judicial structures. This allowed the prosecution to simply summarize its evidence to obtain a conviction. Later in the campaign, the group altered its approach and by pleading not guilty forced law enforce-

---

[59] As described in Harnden, "An IRA volunteer told the author that the organisation had made detailed 'dead ground studies' of South Armagh and worked out exactly where they could and could not be seen [from watchtowers]; he estimated the towers could see no more than 35 percent of the land area and this could be reduced dramatically in certain weather conditions" (Harnden, 2000, p. 259).

[60] This sometimes imposed a price on the organization, requiring it to use less-experienced volunteers.

[61] Personal interview with a law enforcement official, Northern Ireland, March 2004.

[62] Ibid.

ment to fully describe all the evidence and the methods through which it was obtained.[63]

Conclusions

Much of a terrorist group's learning can be understood by looking at specific elements of its operations. However, focusing only on individual parts of such operations risks missing important cross-cutting issues that affect learning in many areas and, as such, could be particularly relevant in the design of counterterrorism policies. The following sections address four such issues:

- The potential role of key individuals in group learning
- Tradeoffs between group control and individual-unit initiative in strategic and tactical learning
- The impact of group leadership on innovation
- The importance of safe havens for group learning activities

Key Individuals

Innovation—in particular, discontinuous learning—frequently comes from individuals with ideas and the motivation to pursue them. Therefore, the presence, roles, and tenure of such individuals can affect an organization's ability to learn in all areas. Because of the nature of terrorist organizations, there is no guarantee that a group will attract the type of people needed to drive innovation. Analysts have been particularly dismissive of PIRA's members in this respect:

> The Provisional IRA . . . revealed a very special personnel profile. . . . if open to all, only a special segment of society volunteered. . . . Very few had educational qualifications, few had skills . . . The skills necessary to run a modern underground—those of the banker, electrical engineer, computer expert, political pollster, military technician, those of the traveled and sophisticated and well-read were almost completely lacking (Bell, 1998b, p. 463).

The importance of identifying and utilizing the right individuals can be seen in the group's strategies in pursuit of surface-to-air missiles, the development of mortar technology, and the manufacture of bomb components. The fact that PIRA did not succeed in acquiring missile technology after the American engineer anchoring the effort was captured highlights the potential vulnerability that results when expertise is concentrated in specific individuals.

---

[63] Personal interview with a law enforcement official, England, March 2004.

Not all technical capabilities are so vulnerable, however. Gabriel Cleary, PIRA director of engineering and "the man most responsible for its range of very effective homemade weaponry—from mortars to sophisticated long delay timing devices" (O'Callaghan, 1999, p. 305)—was captured during a failed arms importation attempt in 1987. Arms development capability was clearly held more broadly than by Cleary alone, however, and in the five years he was in prison (Mac Dermott, 1998), the organization continued to introduce new generations of increasingly effective mortars (Geraghty, 2000).

Group Control Versus Individual Initiative

In a group the size of PIRA, the level of central control over the activities of individual units can vary considerably. The vast majority of PIRA activities were carried out without direct intervention or control by the GHQ leadership (Bell, 1993, p. 19). Individual PIRA units had significant operational freedom even before the group reorganized into a cell-based structure in the 1970s (Foreign Office: Western Department and Foreign and Commonwealth Office, 1971), although the reorganization further strengthened that independence. Because of the variation it introduces in group activities, such autonomy has both positive and negative impacts on a group's ability to learn in a variety of areas.

Sources of Unit Autonomy

A central reason for the autonomy of individual units within PIRA was simply practical. PIRA tried to maintain control over operations by controlling the means to carry them out (Collins and McGovern, 1998, p. 220), but this was not always possible: "The leadership has always tried to exercise tight control . . . over the allocation of weapons and funds. Thus detailed instructions [illegible word] have to be passed through several links both within the Republic and in the Province" (Glover, 1978). Those detailed instructions and approval processes were vulnerable to penetration and compromise (Geraghty, 2000, p. 154). As the security forces got more skillful at penetrating communications processes, the group was forced to become more decentralized—minimizing the level of communications was a way to reduce security risks (Horgan and Taylor, 1997, p. 23).

In addition to allowing individual units considerable freedom, central PIRA leaders reportedly seldom criticized actions taken by the units:

> The Provos are aware that punishing enthusiasm, no matter how misguided and counterproductive to movement aims, leads to schism or to dissent. Certain targets can be denied to the Volunteers and certain efficiencies advocated, but the [PIRA] center must make do with existing assets (Bell, 1993, p. 116).

Beyond simply reserving criticism, GHQ frequently acted after the fact to justify local actions that would never have been approved had the leadership been given prior notice (Drake, 1998, p. 29).

Tradeoffs Between Tactical and Strategic Learning

Allowing significant freedom to individual units results in mixed outcomes from the perspective of organizational learning. It generates significant opportunity for tactical learning in that it allows units to experiment with new weapons and tactics that might otherwise be seen as too risky or speculative. The hesitancy of PIRA's central leadership to punish mistakes reduced the perceived cost of failure, while competition for status among different units provided an incentive for innovation (O'Doherty, 1993). A number of units tried experimental tactics ranging from attacking and sinking British coal ships while they were under way to attempts at aerial bombing of security force targets ("War News," 1981, p. 51; Bell, 1998b, p. 404). Some of these experiments were repeated, others were not.

Autonomy of individual units can be much more problematic with respect to strategic learning. Freedom and experimentation activities mean that units will make "mistakes"—in targeting, planning, and action—that complicate progress toward strategic goals (Bell, 1993, p. 109). As noted by Bell, "the Army Council and often the GHQ were engaged in oversight, not command. Operational matters were often controlled by those close to the target. . . . This operational freedom often meant blunders, innocent people killed, incompetents sent in harm's way, bombs detonated when quiet was needed" (Bell, 1998b, pp. 468–469). Differences in the assumptions of the central leadership and those of units could therefore undermine the group's overall strategy:

> After twenty years the [PIRA] could not murder with competence and could not take care to protect the innocent. . . . the [PIRA] GHQ had made it clear that great care would be taken henceforth in target selection and timing. This apparently consisted of simply asking the local units to be cautious. Local units are not in the business of caution and must often rely on Volunteers ideologically sound but without wit or experience or skill to plan and carry out operations (Bell, 1998b, p. 591).

Beyond making mistakes, some units "simply went their own way and made their own rules" (Bell, 1998b, p. 406), taking actions that were sometimes highly sectarian (Bell, 1998b, p. 610; Smith, 1997, p. 122) and that undermined the group's attempt to be viewed as a legitimate military organization.

Leadership

The characteristics of an organization's leadership almost invariably affect its level of innovation. Leadership of some PIRA units, such as the South Armagh unit, made organizational learning activities a priority. In other cases and at other points in the organization's history, individual leaders were impediments to innovation:

> Throughout the early months of 1973 it was becoming clear that a large number of [PIRA] men in Kerry were unhappy with the conservatism and caution of the local leadership. They had joined looking for action and were getting precious little of it. The leadership had been in charge, almost unchanged, for many years and was very set in its ways. The leaders had also become arrogant and were intolerant and dismissive of criticism (O'Callaghan, 1999, p. 71).

In addition to limiting organizational learning within a unit, such a perspective can reduce the organization's success in recruiting new members, thereby restricting the flow of new ideas and limiting the human resources available for learning activities (O'Callaghan, 1999, pp. 101–102).

Safe Havens

The level of pressure on an organization, while frequently providing an incentive to learn, can make carrying out learning activities more difficult:

> Getting arms, or explosives or planning anything is the same for us as for anyone, the [army] or the [police], except we don't have recourse to back-room "boffins" with resources, science and so on to bear down on any problem. Our back rooms can be raided or under surveillance at any time, but still we do analyse any situation we come to, though it takes us longer than our enemies. The analysis and adaption goes on all the time. Sometimes people think the [PIRA] is on the run. The truth is the [PIRA] is always on the run, and always learning (Coogan, 1993, p. 364).

The need to relieve that pressure and provide a location for group learning activities such as the training of recruits drives a search for safe havens, where members can carry out experiments, test new weapons, and assess the contribution new tactics or techniques could make to group operations. Early in its operational history, PIRA effectively controlled parts of Northern Ireland, where it established a base for training and other learning activities and for launching operations (Bell, 1998b, p. 382). PIRA also maintained considerable freedom within South Armagh throughout the conflict, contributing to that cell's ability to experiment with new weapons and carry out other learning activities (Harnden, 2000, p. 18).

For many years, the Republic of Ireland provided PIRA with its most important safe haven:

> The headquarters of the Provisionals is in the Republic. The South also provides a safe mounting base for cross border operations and secure training areas. PIRA's logistic support flows through the Republic where arms and munition [sic] are received from overseas. Improvised weapons, bombs and explosives, are manufac-

tured there. Terrorists can live there without fear of extradition for crimes in the North. *In short, the Republic provides many of the facilities of the classic safe haven so essential to any successful terrorist movement* (Glover, 1978, emphasis added).

Sanctuary in the Republic for the GHQ, including the engineering department, which was primarily responsible for the group's weapons development, insulated those parts of the organization from counterterrorist pressure (Horgan and Taylor, 1997). The Republic was also a refuge for group members who were known to or actively fleeing from security forces and "a place where meetings could be held away from the prying eyes and ears of the British security forces" (Harnden, 2000, p. 75).

Having the PIRA headquarters in the relative safety of the Republic of Ireland not only facilitated difficult-to-conceal learning activities such as the testing of explosives, it also facilitated less-dramatic organizational learning activities. It is difficult for an organization to carry out strategic planning or to assess ways to exploit new tactics or technologies under the pressures of being underground. By insulating the PIRA members from these pressures, the Republic provided a haven in which this sort of "bigger picture" thinking and learning could be done more effectively.

Although incarceration would not generally be considered a form of safe haven for terrorist group members, prison did insulate individuals from the day-to-day pressures of clandestine operations, which reportedly also contributed to PIRA's learning efforts. Republican prisoners made significant contributions to the planning for the group's reorganization in the 1970s. Prisoners similarly contributed to deliberations about group strategy and efforts by the leadership to make PIRA more potent politically: "Away from the heady mixture of action and conspiracy they [the prisoners] were able to reflect on the problems . . . afflicting the movement" (Smith, 1997, pp. 145–146).

Concluding Remarks

PIRA was an innovative group in many ways. It made significant investments in resources and efforts in organizational learning, ranging from maintaining an engineering department to building training facilities for new recruits. PIRA effectively carried out continuous improvement efforts, such as stepwise improvements in explosive devices to increase volunteer safety or avoid countermeasures, and discontinuous changes, such as the deployment of novel weapons systems. Over time, PIRA greatly expanded and improved its repertoire of tactics and weapons, designing and manufacturing much of the required materiel within the group itself.

Although it is easy to generalize about PIRA's overall level of innovation, examination of specific group learning practices in some cases reveals more diversity than commonality in the reasons, processes, and outcomes of its learning efforts. In some areas, PIRA innovation was driven strongly by the need to respond to security force action; in others, the group pursued new tactics and technologies independent of outside drivers. While many parts of the group selected targets mainly on the basis of their vulnerability to immediately available weapons, other parts meticulously planned and carried out operations requiring extensive intelligence gathering, specialized teams, and specific preparation. PIRA sought to make some of its knowledge fully organizational by encoding it in manuals and training courses available to large numbers of volunteers; other knowledge was restricted to specialists such as bomb and weapons manufacturers, who were kept apart, sharing only their creations with the rest of the organization.[64]

Although PIRA built a reputation as an innovative and effective terrorist group, not all of its learning efforts were successful. The same group that developed generation after generation of new radio detonators to circumvent security force countermeasures could not put off-the-shelf surface-to-air missiles to productive use. The same group that learned so effectively at the tactical level, under the influence of its deeply held assumptions about violent strategy, learned much less effectively at the strategic level.

While many of PIRA's operations developed and were executed as planned, the group did not accomplish everything it set out to do: Logistics teams failed to deliver critical weapons, bombs failed to go off, targets' routines shifted, operations failed for any number of other reasons of chance or insufficiency (Bell, 1998b, p. 450). But for a group that carried out many hundreds of operations every year, envisioned each action as part of an ongoing campaign, and amassed the resources to mount another operation tomorrow if today's failed, individual failures were not very important. Having taken measures to ensure that it could do so, PIRA learned from one day's failures and applied that knowledge to the operations it carried out the next.

References

Alonso, Rogelio, "The Modernization in Irish Republican Thinking Toward the Utility of Violence," *Studies in Conflict and Terrorism,* Vol. 24, 2001, pp. 131–144.

Bell, J. Bowyer, *The Gun in Politics: An Analysis of Irish Political Conflict, 1916–1986,* New Brunswick, NJ: Transaction Books, 1987.

____, *IRA: Tactics and Targets,* Swords, Ireland: Poolbeg, 1993.

____, "The Armed Struggle and Underground Intelligence: An Overview," *Studies in Conflict and Terrorism,* Vol. 17, 1994, pp. 115–150.

____, *The Dynamics of the Armed Struggle,* London, UK: Frank Cass, 1998a.

____, *The Secret Army: The IRA,* Dublin, Ireland: Poolbeg, 1998b.

---

[64] Personal interview with a former security forces member, England, March 2004.

Canadian Security Intelligence Service (CSIS), *Irish Nationalist Terrorism Outside Ireland: Out-of-Theatre Operations 1972–1993*, Commentary No. 40, February 1994, available at http://www.csis-scrs.gc.ca/eng/comment/com40_e.html (last accessed January 6, 2005).

Collins, Eamon, and Mick McGovern, *Killing Rage*, London, UK: Granta Books, 1998.

Coogan, Tim Pat, *The IRA: A History*, Niwot, CO: Roberts Rinehart Publishers, 1993.

Crenshaw, Martha, "The Persistence of IRA Terrorism," in Yonah Alexander and Alan O'Day (eds.), *Terrorism in Ireland*, London, UK: Croomhelm, 1984, pp. 246–271.

Davies, Roger, and Michael Dolamore, "IRA 'Playing with Fire,'" in John Parachini (ed.), *Motives, Means, and Mayhem*, Santa Monica, CA: RAND Corporation, forthcoming.

Drake, C.J.M., "The Provisional IRA: A Case Study," *Terrorism and Political Violence*, Vol. 3, No. 2, 1991, pp. 43–60.

___, *Terrorists' Target Selection*, New York: St. Martin's Press, 1998.

"Five Days in an IRA Training Camp," *Iris*, No. 7, November 1983, pp. 39–45.

Foreign and Commonwealth Office: Republic of Ireland Department, *H. H. Tucker—The IRA in Eire*, FCO 87-3, British National Archives, 1972a.

___, *IRA Tactics in Northern Ireland*, FCO 87-1, British National Archives, 1972b.

___, *Robert Carr—The Possible Pattern of IRA Activities in Great Britain, Memorandum to the Prime Minister, 23 March 1973*, FCO 87-177, British National Archives, 1973a.

___, *British Embassy Memorandum, Washington, DC*, FCO 87-178, British National Archives, 1973b.

Foreign Office: Western Department and Foreign and Commonwealth Office, *Diplomatic Report No. 157/71—Sinn Fein and the IRA*, FCO 33-1593/4, British National Archives, 1971.

Geraghty, Tony, *The Irish War: The Hidden Conflict Between the IRA and British Intelligence*, Baltimore, MD: The Johns Hopkins University Press, 2000.

Glover, J. M., *"Northern Ireland Terrorist Trends,"* London, UK: Ministry of Defence, British Government, 1978.

Harnden, Toby, *Bandit Country: The IRA and South Armagh*, London, UK: Coronet Books, LIR, 2000.

Horgan, John, and Max Taylor, "The Provisional Irish Republican Army: Command and Functional Structure," *Terrorism and Political Violence*, Vol. 9, No. 3, 1997, pp. 1–32.

___, "Playing the 'Green Card'—Financing the Provisional IRA: Part 1," *Terrorism and Political Violence*, Vol. 11, No. 2, 1999, pp. 1–38.

___, "Playing the 'Green Card'—Financing the Provisional IRA: Part 2," *Terrorism and Political Violence*, Vol. 15, No. 2, 2003, pp. 1–60.

"IRA Bomb Expert Arrested in West Bank," 2003, available at http://www.foxnews.com/story/0,2933,91788,00.html (last accessed June 24, 2004).

"IRA Interview: Iris Talks to a Member of the IRA's General Headquarters Staff," *Iris,* Vol. 1, No. 1, April 1981, pp. 42–48.

Jane's Terrorism and Insurgency Centre, "JTIC Exclusive: Proliferation of MANPADS and the Threat to Civil Aviation," 2003, available at http://www.janes.com (last accessed April 14, 2004).

Jane's World Insurgency and Terrorism, "Provisional Irish Republican Army (PIRA)," 2004, available at http://www.janes.com (last accessed July 2, 2004).

Jenkins, Brian Michael, and Larry N. Gersten, *Protecting Public Surface Transportation Against Terrorism and Serious Crime: Continuing Research on Best Security Practices,* San Jose, CA: Mineta Transportation Institute, 2001.

Mac Dermott, Diarmaid, "Three Get 20 Years on Bomb Factory Charges," *Irish News*, February 1, 1998, available at http://archives.tcm.ie/irishexaminer/1998/02/14/ihead.htm.

McDermott, Jeremy, "Colombian Attacks 'Have Hallmark of IRA,'" 2002, available at http://news.bbc.co.uk/2/hi/americas/2186244.stm (last accessed April 14, 2004).

McKinley, Michael, "The International Dimensions of Irish Terrorism," in Yonah Alexander and Alan O'Day (eds.), *Terrorism in Ireland,* London, UK: Croomhelm, 1984, pp. 3–31.

Neuffer, Elizabeth, "Tapes Key to IRA High-Tech Trial," *The Boston Globe*, May 1, 1990, p. 17.

"No One Hurt as Terrorist Grenade Hits Ulster Schoolroom," *The Washington Post*, February 11, 1984, p. 14.

O'Ballance, Edgar, *Terror in Ireland: The Heritage of Hate*, Novato, CA: Presidio Press, 1981.

O'Callaghan, Sean, *The Informer*, London, UK: Corgi Books, 1999.

O'Doherty, Shane, *The Volunteer: A Former IRA Man's True Story*, London, UK: Fount, 1993.

Police Service of Northern Ireland, "Security-Related Incidents 1969–2004," available at http://www.psni.police.uk/security_related_incidents_cy-10.doc.

Silke, Andrew, "Beyond Horror: Terrorist Atrocity and the Search for Understanding—The Case of the Shankill Bombing," *Studies in Conflict and Terrorism,* Vol. 26, 2003, pp. 37–60.

Smith, M.L.R., *Fighting for Ireland? The Military Strategy of the Irish Republican Movement*, London, UK: Routledge, 1997.

Sutton, Malcolm, "An Index of Deaths from the Conflict in Ireland," available at http://cain.ulst.ac.uk/sutton/chron/index.html (last accessed February 2004).

Taylor, Maxwell, and Ethel Quayle, *Terrorist Lives*, London, UK: Brassey's, 1994.

Urban, Mark, *Big Boys' Rules: The Secret Struggle Against the IRA*, London, UK: Faber & Faber, 1992.

"War News," *Iris,* Vol. 1, No. 1, April 1981, pp. 49–52.

CHAPTER SIX

The Radical Environmentalist Movement

Horacio R. Trujillo

Introduction

The Earth Liberation Front (ELF), the Animal Liberation Front (ALF), and other elements of the radical environmentalist movement[1] are considered by the U.S. Federal Bureau of Investigation (FBI) to be the nation's top domestic terrorism threat (Lewis, 2004). While the prominence of radical environmentalist organizations on the FBI watch list is reason in itself to be concerned with how these organizations learn and evolve, this concern is even more pressing in light of the increasing pace and destructiveness of attacks attributed to them each year.

Understanding organizational learning among the ELF, the ALF, and other radical environmentalist elements is also critical because of the unique organizational structure of the movement. By examining collectively the components of this movement, we can see how an appreciation of organizational learning is critical to understanding and anticipating the evolution of capabilities not only of formally structured terrorist groups but also of more loosely integrated organizations and networks of organizations. One of the most important lessons learned from this particular case study is how an appreciation of discontinuous and transformational organizational learning could help law enforcement and counterterrorism agencies anticipate meaningful shifts in both the focus and tempo of activities by radical environmentalists or other terrorist organizations, even as they change little operationally or tactically.

To properly assess organizational learning within the radical environmentalist movement, it is important to recognize the unique character of the movement and the nature of the terrorism associated with it. Therefore, this discussion begins with a review of the significance and history of radical environmentalist terrorism in the

---

[1] For the purposes of this analysis, the ELF, the ALF, and other organizations with similar objectives and underlying motivations are referred to in this chapter as "radical environmentalists." While there are critical differences that distinguish these organizations from one another, and the label might seem at first to be especially inapplicable to the ALF, all of these organizations can nonetheless be considered part of the "radical environmental milieu" as defined by Bron Taylor, who has conducted extensive ethnographic studies of the radical environmentalist movement.

United States. It then examines how the structure of the radical environmentalist movement—a segmentary, polycentric, and integrated network of single-issue groups—both facilitates and impedes tactical and strategic learning within and among the component groups. We next consider how training, one of the most tangible manifestations of organizational learning, is distributed throughout the movement by the strong virtual and social integration of these groups. We then consider how these groups learn with regard to intelligence and operational security. The chapter concludes with a short discussion of how the lessons concerning organizational learning within the radical environmentalist movement might help law-enforcement and counterterrorism agencies anticipate and defend against ecoterrorism.

Background

The Significance of Radical Environmentalist Terrorism

Since 1976, 1,100 criminal acts have been committed in the United States by radical environmentalist groups, resulting in more than $110 million in property damage alone, a figure that does not include the significant additional costs associated with lost research, increased security, and dampened productivity (Phillipkoski, 2004).

The significance of ecoterrorism is not lost on the rest of the world either. Law enforcement agencies in Europe also now consider radical environmentalists a top security threat. In the year 2000 alone, more than 1,200 ecoterrorism incidents took place in the United Kingdom, resulting in a total of $3.7 million in damage (Bilouri, 2001). According to Paul Wilkinson, a terrorism researcher at St. Andrews University (Scotland), radical environmentalism, particularly in the form of animal liberation, now tops the list of causes that prompt violence throughout the United Kingdom (BBC News, 2000).

The placement of radical environmentalism at the top of security threat lists in the United States and Europe illustrates the growing significance of the movement and the importance of an assessment of the evolution of its capabilities. This assessment is even more important in light of the increasing pace and destructiveness of ecoterrorism attacks. By 1990, the rate of new damage being caused by radical environmentalists had risen to between $20 million and $25 million per year, with individual attacks also increasing in destructiveness (Bilouri and Makarenko, 2003).[2] Moreover, some observers of radical environmentalism contend that the rhetoric of

---

[2] The most destructive of all radical environmentalist actions in the United States was the 2003 arson of an apartment complex under construction in San Diego, California, which resulted in total damage of $50 million (or more). Prior to that attack, the most costly action was the 1998 arson of a ski lodge and ski lifts in Vail, Colorado, that caused total damage of $12 million.

certain individuals and organizations within the movement is becoming increasingly apocalyptic, suggesting that these activists could become more willing to effect as much destruction as possible as a means of influencing business practices, mobilizing public opinion, and motivating government policy regarding environmental protection (Philippon, 2002). Such an escalation in destructiveness would in fact represent a sea change for the movement, which has focused until now largely on property damage and has yet to produce any fatalities. Notably, however, to the extent that such a shift is possible, it is likely that explicitly militant or lethal activities would appeal to only a small extremist fringe of the movement.

Some Preliminary Definitions: The Radical Environmentalist Movement and Ecoterrorism

When applied to the radical environmentalist movement, the assessment of the organizational learning of terrorist groups demands a degree of attention to definitions that is unique among the cases in this volume.

First, unlike the other cases, radical environmentalism must be recognized as a social movement as much as, if not more than, a formal organization. That is, the other terrorist organizations discussed herein can be characterized as recognizably constituted groups, whose membership is at least in some sense formally defined. In comparison, the radical environmentalist movement lacks formal organizational structures and boundaries. That is, it is not at all clear who the members of the component organizations are, or even whether membership is a relevant concept. In fact, in some cases, these activists reject the very ideas of structured organization and "membership." Earth First!, one of the original radical environmentalist organizations, eschews the concept of membership in its organizing guidelines, noting that there are no "members" of Earth First!, only "Earth First!ers," who live in accord with the principles of the movement. In a similar fashion, the ELF considers any person who acts on behalf of the organization, so long as such actions are consistent with ELF guidelines, to be an "Elf," or agent of the organization, and any actions undertaken by Elves can be considered actions of the ELF as a whole.

This distinction has two important implications for the analysis of organizational learning within and among radical environmentalist organizations. First, because there is no formal membership, it is difficult to attribute the actions of individuals specifically to radical environmentalist organizations as collective entities and hence to argue that these actions can be interpreted as markers of organizational learning. Second, because of the ambiguous structure of these organizations, which their own supporters generally refer to as "movements," it is also difficult to describe how they can institutionalize knowledge management and distribute recall capabilities. Thus, the assessment of organizational learning in radical environmentalist organizations requires an appreciation of how such learning can be transmitted through informal social processes as well as formal bureaucratic ones.

Moreover, radical environmentalist organizations are part of a larger, general movement, and learning therefore occurs among as well as within them. Of course, some of the other groups discussed in this volume are also parts of broader social movements. What sets radical environmental organizations apart is the extent to which their successes and failures have led to the development of other more- or less-radical offshoots and the extent to which all of these organizations have continued to coexist and cross-fertilize each other after splintering. Because of this, while the ELF is the centerpiece of the assessment presented here, it is not possible to conduct such an analysis in a meaningful way without taking into account the history of its predecessor, Earth First!, its alliance with the ALF, and its relationships with other, less-prominent organizations. This approach accords with the view of various observers, including the FBI, that the activities of the radical environmentalist organizations are unquestionably linked with those of the ALF and other animal liberation organizations.

This line of analysis also coincides with Luther Gerlach's conceptualization of environmental activism as a segmentary, polycentric, and integrated network, or SPIN (Gerlach, 2001). Given this conceptualization, it is necessary to appreciate that organizational learning in the ELF and the rest of the radical environmentalist movement is not the product of any one organization alone, but the result of the interaction among them. Recognizing this interaction and the fact that this learning process is social—i.e., informal and unstructured—rather than formally structured, we focus the analysis on the evolution of the radical environmentalist movement as a whole, with the ELF/Earth First! at its center, and on how the movement has exhibited organizational learning, as well as a seemingly advantageous lack of learning, throughout its history.

Finally, in addition to a nuanced understanding of organizational learning, it is important to recognize the distinct character of the terrorism carried out by radical environmentalists. In general, radical environmentalist organizations advocate "direct action" against the property of persons and businesses that are engaged in activities considered harmful to the environment and to "animals, human and non-human." The most common direct actions are arson, vandalism, and theft, all of which fall clearly within the FBI's definition of terrorism—"the unlawful use of force or violence against persons or *property* to intimidate or coerce a government, the civilian population, or any segment thereof, in furtherance of political or social objectives" (emphasis added). For this reason, any assessment of organizational learning within terrorist groups must include the ELF and related radical environmentalist organizations.

Most of these organizations also explicitly call upon those who might take up their cause to avoid any actions that put human life at risk. In fact, the ELF's website (www.earthliberationfront.com) claims that members engage only in "non-violent activism" while conducting "economic sabotage against those who would profit from the destruction of the natural environment." The website also explicitly suggests that would-be ecoteurs should "make absolutely sure that no animals, human or otherwise, will be inadvertently injured or killed." In this way, all but the most radical environmentalist organizations avoid directly targeting violence at persons. This distinction is not meant to diminish in any way the threat posed by such organizations; it simply acknowledges that discussing terrorist organizations whose characteristics, goals, and activities differ greatly is problematic and that caution should be taken in applying conclusions based on the study of certain groups to others that differ in important ways.

In fact, radical environmentalists largely reject the label of terrorism (including the derivatives "ecoterrorism" and "environmental terrorism") to describe their direct actions and argue that it is the businesses that exploit the environment and the governments that do not stem such practices that are the ecoterrorists. This war of words is, of course, not unique to the debate over radical environmentalism but is endemic to any discussion of terrorism, as noted by Richard E. Rubenstein, who suggests that "to call an act of political violence terrorist is not merely to describe it but to judge it. . . . To the defenders of a particular regime or social order, any politically motivated disobedience (even mass resistance) smacks of terrorism. . . . And on the other hand, a regime in power is considered terrorist by those who deny its legitimacy even if they are but a handful and their opponents legions" (Rubenstein, 1988, cited in Eagan, 1996, p. 2).

The challenge is pressed all the more by radical environmentalists insisting that their direct actions against property cannot be appropriately termed "violent" in light of contradictory classifications of such acts in various criminal and civil laws. Bearing in mind, then, the political character of the terminology of terrorism, we attempt in the discussion that follows to present our analysis in a manner that does not unnecessarily engage in the contest surrounding the characterization of radical environmentalism as terrorism. Understanding that a large number of participants in the radical environmentalist movement do not engage in direct actions, we generally avoid referring to radical environmentalists as terrorists, even as we refer to their direct actions as terrorism.

"No Compromise": The Philosophy of Radical Environmentalism

To understand the organizational learning that characterizes the radical environmentalist movement, we begin with a brief discussion of the philosophy of radical environmentalism.[3] Radical environmentalists justify their activities by suggesting that

---

[3] This discussion of the history and philosophy draws particularly on Eagan (1996), as well as Taylor (1998), Carpenter (1990), and Lee (1995).

society's lack of progress in protecting the environment demands direct action. They draw on the philosophy of "deep ecology" that stems from the work of Norwegian philosopher Arne Naess. Deep ecology comprises two subordinate concepts—"biocentrism" and "restoration ecology." Biocentrism is the belief that the human being is but one member of the biological community and that "equal rights" should be applied to all creatures and, according to some strident deep ecologists, even to inanimate natural objects. The second concept, restoration ecology, calls for a rollback of human civilization and urban-industrial development in order to recreate wilderness as a means of restoring an ecological balance that is equally suitable for all animals, human and non-human. Eagan (1996) suggests that it is this philosophical underpinning of the radical environmentalist movement that has evolved into a millenarian social-justice orientation that provides individual activists with the motivation for engaging in low-level direct action.

Craig Rosebraugh, a former spokesman for both the ELF and the ALF,[4] in response to a reporter's question about how direct action could be justified, replied, "In the legal system there is a defense called the choice-of-evils defense, and what we are saying with these direct-action cases is that you have to ask the question: Is it greater evil to destroy this property of this corporation or to choose to allow this corporation to continue to destroy the environment, and I guess what the activists and what I am saying is that I guess it's a lesser evil to stop these corporations from destroying the planet" (Sullivan, 1998). Rosebraugh's remark illustrates how radical environmentalists view themselves as entrenched in a struggle for environmental and animal justice against the established social order and also captures two of the three characteristics that Eagan (1996, p. 2) identifies as common to all radical environmentalist organizations:

- An uncompromising position (epitomized by the slogan of EarthFirst!: "No compromise in defense of Mother Earth!")
- Direct action versus lobbying
- A grass-roots, non-hierarchical structure (Eagan, 1996, p. 2)

The belief in direct action rather than lobbying makes radical environmentalists unique among environmental activists. The objectives of these direct actions range from simply sabotaging corporate polluters to purposefully influencing government

---

[4] It is important to recognize the self-designated character of the role of "spokesperson" for the ELF and the ALF that Rosebraugh and others, such as Rodney Coronado and Leslie James Pickering, have played. Although the groups are largely devoid of official leaders or representatives, Rosebraugh declared himself their "unofficial" spokesperson after receiving without prior notice an announcement from an Elf claiming responsibility for a direct action and requesting that he distribute it to media outlets and otherwise disseminate it. Rosebraugh has maintained that he has not engaged in any direct actions himself, even though he is a committed supporter of the groups. Other ELF/ALF "spokespersons" have given similar explanations for their assumption of the role.

policy. The ELF's guidelines for its members illustrate how these objectives are framed within the movement:

> The Earth Liberation Front is an international underground movement whose members are advised by the leadership to abide by the following guidelines:
> - To inflict economic damage on those profiting from the destruction and exploitation of the natural environment.
> - To reveal and educate the public on the atrocities committed against the earth and all species that populate it.
> - To take all necessary precautions against harming any animal, human and non-human (Earth Liberation Front, n.d.).

As Eagan notes, these objectives correspond well with the targets of terrorism outlined by Alex Schmid in *Political Terrorism: A Research Guide to Concepts, Theories, Data Bases and Literature* (1983, cited in Eagan, 1996). According to Schmid, terrorism has four potential targets: (1) the direct victims of a terrorist act, (2) related parties who are threatened by the prospect of being victims of similar acts, (3) the wider audience of the terrorism, and (4) parties that could be secondary targets of demands by the terrorists. The ELF guidelines explicitly call for directly targeting victims and threatening related parties while indirectly making a wider audience aware of its concerns. In fact, it can be argued that the primary objective of radical environmentalists' direct actions is increasingly to influence public opinion and secondary parties, such as the government, upon whom demands can be made.

Many persons knowledgeable about the radical environmentalist movement, including Mike Roselle, one of the original founders of Earth First!, have explained how affecting public opinion shapes the agenda of radical environmentalists. Roselle notes that the problem of grasslands destruction may be a greater threat to the long-run health of the environment than logging is, but "no ecosystem looks more destroyed than a recently clear-cut old growth forest" (Eagan, 1996, p. 11). In summing up Earth First!'s position on the public-influence role of direct actions, Roselle refers directly to Schmid's fourth target of terrorism, parties from which secondary demands can be sought: "There are many ways to lobby more efficiently than hiring someone to go to Washington, DC" (Eagan, 1996, p. 11). According to U.S. Forest Service Special Agent James N. Damitio, who investigates radical environmentalist organizations, the public-influence role of direct actions is not simply a primary objective of radical environmentalists, but in fact motivates the evolution of the agendas of these organizations: "The objective of these people is to bring attention to their cause for change. And if they don't feel like they're getting that attention, they try something else" (Denson and Long, 1999). As discussed later in this chapter, the evolution of targets is one of the unique means of learning that characterize the radical environmentalist movement.

The Origins of Ecoterrorism: From Earth First! to the ELF-ALF Alliance

The first major wave of direct actions carried out by radical environmentalists in the United States occurred in 1970, following the first Earth Day celebration. The activists included the Arizona Phantom, who dismantled railroad tracks and disabled equipment in an attempt to stop construction of a coal mine in the desert highlands; the Eco-Raiders, a group of male college students who caused $500,000 in damage by burning billboards, disabling bulldozers, and vandalizing development projects in and around Tucson; the Fox, who plugged drainage pipes, capped factory smokestacks, and dumped industrial waste from a U.S. Steel plant into the Chicago offices of the company's CEO; the Billboard Bandits, who toppled roadside advertisements in Michigan; and the Bolt Weevils, a group of farmers in Minnesota who disabled 14 electrical towers that were to be used for a new power line across the prairie (Philippon, 2002).

In the decade that followed, a number of new environmental organizations dedicated to direct action were formed, setting the stage for the founding of the modern radical environmentalist movement. Greenpeace, founded in 1971, was one of these early direct action groups. A more radical splinter group, the Sea Shepherds/Orcaforce, spun off from Greenpeace in 1977. Possibly inspired by the Sea Shepherds, David Foreman and four others established Earth First! in 1980. In creating Earth First!, he explained, they were acting in the belief that there was "a need for a radical wing that would make the Sierra Club look moderate. Someone needs to say what needs to be said, and do what needs to be done, and take the strong actions to dramatize it" (Eagan, 1996, p. 6).

The specific events that motivated Foreman to form Earth First! were the U.S. Forest Service's 1979 Roadless Area Review Evaluation II (RARE II) and other policies that rolled back environmental protections during the following year. In reaction to the RARE II decision, which opened 36 million acres of wilderness to commercial development, set aside 11 million acres for potential development, and preserved only 15 million acres as protected wilderness, Foreman resigned from his post as the Wilderness Society's chief Washington lobbyist and returned to his previous position as the society's representative in the American Southwest (Lee, 1995, p. 112). After President Reagan further rolled back federal environmental protections, Foreman and his four colleagues struck out on a week-long camping trip to Mexico to consider how they might fight more strongly against the erosion of federal environmental protections. They decided to commit themselves to starting a movement modeled after the Monkey Wrench Gang, "the neo-Luddite rebels with an ecological cause who scoffed at the convoluted tactics of environmentalism and instead took direct action to protect the environment," idealized in Edward Abbey's 1975 novel, *The Monkey Wrench Gang* (Eagan, 1996, p. 6). Upon returning from Mexico, Foreman and the others quit their jobs and established Earth First!.

Earth First!'s first action was a peaceful demonstration by more than 70 persons at Glen Canyon Dam at Lake Powell, Arizona, in 1981. In 1984, the organization began to engage in more destructive direct action, driving long metal spikes into trees on public lands that had been scheduled for harvesting. Tree spikes can cause logging saws to shatter into shrapnel-like pieces upon contact and are thus potentially dangerous to persons cutting the trees or operating lumber mill machinery. According to radical environmentalists, tree-spiking is intended to deter logging but not to actually cause any harm to "any animal, human [or] non-human." In defending this practice, the environmentalists contend that the spikes do not actually harm the trees themselves and that tree-spikers usually make publicly known the areas that have been spiked so that logging operations can avoid them.

Earth First!'s use of tree-spiking almost immediately spawned a number of copycat incidents, including the largest-ever tree-spiking incident, in which the Hardesty Avengers spiked hundreds of trees in the Hardesty Mountain portion of the Willamette National Forest, Oregon (Eagan, 1996, p. 6). It is worth noting that Earth First! was not the first modern environmentalist organization to engage in tree-spiking in the United States; it adopted the technique from other smaller organizations. Nor was Earth First! the first organization to directly confront U.S. Forest Service personnel over a land-use issue. At least one previous incident of direct confrontation with public authorities is documented: On May 4, 1980, about 100 persons, including some armed with knives or clubs and others throwing rocks and garbage, confronted a 14-person U.S. Forest Service crew, sheriff's deputies, and U.S. Forest Service law enforcement personnel, forcing the local district ranger to sign an agreement not to spray herbicide in the area near Takilma, Oregon, for one year. Soon after the confrontation, and bowing to growing public opposition, the U.S. Forest Service revised its guidelines to severely restrict the use of 2-4D herbicide in the Northwest (Long and Denson, 1999a). These early uses of direct-action strategies by other radical environmentalists indicate that since the earliest days of the modern radical environmentalist movement, organizations have been learning vicariously by observing each other, even if the exact routes of learning (e.g., general media coverage, movement-specific publications, exchange of personnel) are not clear.

Influencing public opinion, rather than inflicting injury, appears to have been the major rationale for tree-spiking and other forms of direct action undertaken by the early activists. According to one of the Earth First! activists, "The major result of ecotage has been to raise the stakes and raise the issues that were being ignored, and in a sense, sensationalizing issues in a way the media would pay attention to." Another Earth First! member stated that "the bottom line is that as a result of all this unfavorable coverage regarding spiking, people in the West Coast are acutely aware of the crisis that exists with our forest, and our role in trying to prevent it" (Elsbach and Sutton, 1992, cited in Eagan, 1996, p. 10). These activists strongly believed that the attention had the desired effect of mobilizing support for their cause.

The early radical environmentalists showed a proclivity for organizational learning in their adaptations to thwart the counterterrorism efforts of timber companies. For example, the Earth First!ers and other radical environmentalists responded to loggers' use of metal detectors by using ceramic and stone nails in their tree-spiking actions. It is not easy to draw lines of learning from one organization to another, but regardless of where this adaptation originated, it spread through the movement.

Early successes for Earth First!, however, came at a price. By 1987, largely due to the success of the movement's campaigns, the composition of its membership began to change. Prior to the California and Oregon campaigns, the majority of Earth First!ers were over the age of 30, shared a common background as conservation activists, lived in the American Southwest, and were generally committed to biocentrism, which also meant that they were committed to "monkeywrenching." The new Earth First!ers, in contrast, were younger West Coast career activists who were involved in many political causes and less at ease with the concept of biocentric equality. Their involvement in legitimate political activity and commitment to other causes involving human welfare also made them less willing to undertake risks that might threaten their ability to carry out their activities or lead others to question the legitimacy of their causes. Not surprisingly, then, they were more comfortable with civil disobedience than direct action. By 1987, Foreman and the biocentric old guard of Earth First!, who were becoming increasingly frustrated with their relative lack of success in achieving their grander goals and impatient with the humanistic leanings of the newer members, developed an increasingly apocalyptic view of the Earth First! movement and its role in the world.

The split among Earth First! members finally came to a head in 1990, when Foreman and four others were convicted for the attempted sabotage of the Palo Verde nuclear power plant in Arizona, one of the most dangerous and potentially catastrophic direct actions of the American radical environmentalist movement. The Palo Verde attack was also only one part of the so-called "Evan Mecham Eco-Terrorist International Conspiracy" which included plans to bomb the Diablo Canyon nuclear power plant in California and the Rocky Flats nuclear weapons plant in California (Eagan, 1996, p. 7). After their claims of entrapment were denied, the five defendants pled guilty, with Foreman, who was not directly involved in the Palo Verde incident, facing only a charge of providing instructional material to the perpetrators of the attack.[5] Although Foreman's sentence was delayed for five years and was ultimately limited to probation, it represented the death knell of his active participation in and leadership of EarthFirst! Also during 1990, Judi Bari, one of the

---

[5] Foreman was one of two defendants who were not actually involved in the attempted cutting of the power lines at Palo Verde. He did, however, give two copies of *Ecodefense* to the three persons who staged the attack and provided some financial support for the event (Lee, 1995, p. 122).

leaders of the West Coast faction, presumptively on behalf of Earth First! issued a public renunciation of the tactic of tree-spiking. By this time, Foreman and most of the biocentrists had abandoned Earth First!, claiming that it had been "infiltrated by leftists" and "had abandoned biocentrism in favor of humanism" (Lee, 1995, p. 122). Following Foreman's departure, the humanist faction of Earth First! gained control over the group, and as a result, the movement strayed even further from the idea of biocentric equality.

This takeover of Earth First! had the unforeseen consequence of radicalizing the environmental movement, as a number of more-militant environmentalist organizations splintered from Earth First! and continued to engage in violent direct actions ("Eco-Terrorists Abandon Spikes," 1990; Bilouri and Makarenko, 2003). Notably, while the majority of the more-temperate Earth First! activists of the time might have condemned the violent attacks of the splinter organizations as immoral and counterproductive, many of them still supported these exploits. Among the supporters was Judi Bari, who herself had fought against pro-violence rhetoric in the *Earth First! Journal* but had suggested that the movement could potentially be better served by dividing strategically, based on attitudes toward violence: "I think we need a split, like the Weather Underground and SDS [Students for a Democratic Society] so those who want to do such tactics can do so without any official connection to Earth First!" (Taylor, 1998, p. 11). This lenient, "big-tent" thinking about the need for co-operation between more- and less-radical environmentalist organizations as well as with other activist organizations was institutionalized in the *Earth First! Journal*, which not only continued to publish articles about ecotage after 1990 but also began to include articles about animal liberation and direct action by other non-environmentally focused organizations.

Today's most prominent radical environmentalist organization, the ELF, is a direct heir of this history. The ELF, one of the early militant organizations that splintered from Earth First!, is now the most prominent organization within the movement. The ELF emerged initially in England in 1992 and quickly spread to the United States, where it is now more active than it is in the United Kingdom. The ELF claimed its first direct action in the United States on October 31, 1996, the burning of the Oakridge Ranger Station in Oregon. Only the failure of a timed fire-bomb to ignite saved a second ranger station in Detroit, some 70 miles away, from also being burned down that night. The rapid pace of activity for the ELF did not stop with its own actions; by 1997, the group had formalized an alliance with the ALF, declaring in a letter to the supervisor of the Willamette National Forest that "solidarity between the two groups was the worst nightmare of those who would abuse the Earth and its citizens. Leave the forests alone, and no one gets hurt" (Denson and Long, 1999).

Table 6.1
Significant Events in the Evolution of the Radical Environmentalist Movement

1970	The first Earth Day celebration is followed by direct actions undertaken by various groups to protest environmental destruction, including attacks by the "Arizona Phantom" and the "Eco-Raiders" (Arizona), the "Billboard Bandits" (Michigan), and the "Bolt Weevils" (Minnesota).
1971	Greenpeace is founded in Vancouver, Canada.
1976	The Animal Liberation Front (ALF) is founded in England by Ronnie Lee.
1977	Sea Shepherds/Orcaforce is founded by Paul Watson (co-founder of Greenpeace).
1979	Earth First! is founded by David Foreman and others.
1980	In Takilma, Oregon, environmental activists confront U.S. Forest Service officials over the use of herbicides on public lands.
1981	Earth First!ers protest at the Glen Canyon Dam, Arizona.
1984	The "Hardesty Avengers" spike hundreds of trees in the Willamette National Forest, Oregon.
1990	David Foreman and other Earth First!ers are arrested for their involvement in the attempted sabotage of Palo Verde nuclear power plant in Arizona.
	Judi Bari, a prominent Earth First!er, renounces tree-spiking, catalyzing the effective split of the more-radical environmentalists from Earth First! and the emergence of a "big-tent" Earth First! which inclued articles on animal liberation and other non-environmentally focused direct actions in the *Earth First! Journal*.
1992	The Earth Liberation Front (ELF) claims its first direct action in the United States, the arson of the Oakridge Ranger Station, Oregon.
1997	The ELF and the ALF declare their solidarity in a letter to the supervisor of the Willamette National Forest.

This evolution of radical environmentalism, from the 1970 Earth Day protests to the 1997 declaration of solidarity between the ELF and the ALF, is summarized in Table 6.1.

Having surveyed the philosophy of radical environmentalism and the origin of today's radical environmentalist movement, we now examine how radical environmentalist organizations, particularly the ELF, operate, as well as how they institutionalize and manage knowledge.

Operations and Tactics

In terms of general operations, the ELF and other radical environmentalist organizations are significant examples of what Gerlach (2001), as noted above, refers to as segmentary, polycentric, integrated networks, or SPINs. This section addresses how such an operational arrangement both benefits and hinders the nature of learning in these organizations.

Segmentation is the most obvious characteristic of the ELF and related radical environmentalist organizations. These organizations function as highly decentralized associations of activists, a relatively small number of whom actually engage in direct actions; the majority of the activists do not participate in direct actions but are largely sympathetic to them. Those who do engage in direct actions tend to operate alone or in small cells that communicate very little with other cells. Thus, the radical environmentalist movement can justifiably be characterized as a "leaderless resistance" movement, albeit with some qualification, as some members are suspected of playing more central roles within the organization.[6] The ELF, the ALF, and the other organizations largely operate independently, although it is believed that a subpopulation of activists carry out attacks on behalf of more than one organization. This segmentation would seem to pose a significant challenge to organizational learning within the movement.

Tactical-Level Learning

Despite the segmentation of the movement, operational learning has been facilitated by the notable integration of this network of organizations. Of particular importance has been the movement's use of published material, first in print and now via the Internet, to disseminate and store knowledge. Beginning in 1982, the Earth First! newsletter semi-regularly published a column entitled "Dear Ned Ludd," which offered guidance for individuals interested in direct action. In 1985, in the spirit of *Ecotage!*, published in 1972 by Sam Love and D. Obst, David Foreman compiled much of this information and published it in *Ecodefense: A Field Guide to Monkeywrenching*. The Ned Ludd column still exists and is now published on the Earth First! website along with a disclaimer that Earth First! does not formally endorse any of the practices explained therein.

Advances in information technology, particularly the Internet, have significantly increased the reach of these organizations' materials and have provided the ELF with the ability to disseminate training and logistics information (Chalk, 2001b). Radical environmentalists frequently use chat rooms and electronic mail to exchange information and plan strategies. Not surprisingly, this technology permits the movement to operate even "more as a networked entity than as a concrete group" (Chalk, 2001a). A particularly interesting by-product of this decentralized-yet-networked character is that while decentralization might be thought of as hindering the movement's ability to learn and adapt strategically, in reality, it seems to have enabled the movement to respond more fluidly and dynamically by being able to distribute new information and share the task of interpreting it.[7]

---

[6] Peter Chalk (2001b) explains how significant the radical environmentalist movement's adoption of leaderless resistance is in the evolution of terrorism in the United States: "The adoption of these amorphous and largely ephemeral structures marks a significant development in terrorist organization dynamics, setting groups such as the ELF and US militia movement apart from the more established organizations of the past."

[7] Chalk (2001a) explains this paradox more fully: "The main aim is to base a group on so-called phantom cell networks or 'autonomous leadership units' (ALUs) that operate completely independently of one another, but which are able, through the combined force of their actions, to precipitate a chain reaction that eventually leads to a national revolution. Integral to the concept is information technology (IT), which is used to facilitate communication between like-minded individuals and as a means for circulating and distributing propaganda and information. Of particular importance are mediums such as the internet, e-mail and the world wide web. These cyber-

The dramatic increase in capacity for knowledge management and distribution that the Internet has provided to these organizations cannot be overstated. According to Wilkinson, radical animal rights organizations have acquired bomb-making expertise from manuals and the Internet (BBC, 2000). And Bilouri (2001) reported that European law officials believe separate cells of radical environmental organizations are increasingly using the Internet to coordinate activities, with the likely aim of orchestrating larger-scale attacks. In fact, in 2003 the ELF emphasized the singular importance of the website to its operations by eliminating virtually all contact with the media and the wider world except for information disseminated through its website and requests for interviews delivered via electronic mail (Bilouri and Makarenko, 2003).

The Internet also permits the ELF network to reach many more potential sympathizers while operating with even greater anonymity than before. In fact, it is believed that ELF actions are now increasingly undertaken by random ideological sympathizers who are motivated and directed by the guidelines and how-to material available on the organization's website. While there is no typical ELF member, most who are known tend to be either young—in their 20s, often undergraduate or graduate students from middle- or upper-class backgrounds—or well-established and well-educated persons in their 30s, often with families and active in their communities (Chalk, 2001b; Bilouri and Makarenko, 2003). The older members appear to be drawn to ELF by concerns about the long-term implications of environmental destruction for future generations, and maintaining their anonymity is critical to allowing them to continue to be respected and active members of their communities and public advocates of pro-environmental and animal rights policies (Bilouri and Makarenko, 2003). What ties all of these activists together is the movement's ability to act more as a networked entity than as a concrete group, which both facilitates and depends upon the distributed management of knowledge.

Information technology has also transformed the direct actions of radical environmentalists by changing the way in which they claim responsibility for and debrief others about their actions and by allowing them to experiment increasingly with cybersabotage. Responsibility for these attacks can at least initially be frequently determined from messages spray-painted at the site, which typically include the name or acronym of the organization (e.g., "Save Our Bio Region ELF" or "ELF—Stop Sprawl") with which the perpetrators consider themselves affiliated. Beyond this, however, the method of choice for communicating the motivation for such attacks to the public at large now appears to be encrypted and rerouted e-mail to the North American ELF press office (NAELFPO), a legally registered news outlet (Chalk,

---

based mediums play a crucial role in ensuring that all individuals are kept fully abreast of events, allowing for planned responses and attacks but always on the basis of individual initiative. Used in this way, IT both overcomes the 'tyranny of distance' and obviates the necessity for orders and directives—thereby precluding the need for a physical group [or a centralized leadership]."

2001b). The advancement of encryption software and the ability to reroute e-mail through the Internet has enabled radical environmentalists to communicate with the public more freely and with less fear of being traced than was the case with mailed or faxed messages. While cybersabotage is still a relatively undeveloped tactic, some organizations—in particular, Stop Huntingdon Animal Cruelty (SHAC)—have attempted to use it. FBI indictments against seven persons allegedly associated with SHAC cite telephone and e-mail blitzes, fax blitzes, and Internet attacks against Huntingdon Life Sciences and its business partners (Jones, 2004; Dawdy, 2004).

While the radical environmentalist movement seems to have a fairly efficient system in place for disseminating best practices regarding direct action, there is very little discussion within the movement about learning from failed actions. However, John Curtin, a long-time animal liberation activist who was jailed for his participation in direct actions, did discuss in an interview in *Bite Back Magazine* (No. 1, n.d.) the lessons to be learned from the movement's failures. Several similar articles were also included in a special issue of *Bite Back* (No. 6, n.d.) on what went wrong. Nevertheless, the limited discussion of failed efforts is likely a significant constraint on the learning of these organizations.

Similarly, in spite of the notable integration of the movement via the Internet, radical environmentalists have generally been resistant to changing their tactics. This apparent lack of learning, however, could be paradoxically interpreted as a sign of learning if radical environmentalists have opted not to adapt their methods because they realized early on that low-tech methods are actually best for their intended activities. As a case in point, arson continues to be the method of choice for direct actions in the United States. An exhortation on the ELF website provides an explicit rationale for this emphasis: "On a pound-for-pound basis, incendiaries can do more damage than explosives against many type [sic] targets if properly used" (Barcott, 2002). Most arson fires attributed to radical environmentalists are started with simple firebombs—plastic jugs filled with gasoline lit by birthday candles attached to the handles—or with electrically timed firebombs (Bilouri and Makarenko, 2003). There is no indication that radical environmentalists are interested in using more-advanced technology, such as plastic explosives or dynamite (Jane's Consultancy, 2001).

While the avoidance of more-advanced technology could be attributed in some way to the neo-Luddite philosophy of the organization, leaving the issue at this would ignore the very real tactical benefits that this "lack of learning" offers. For one, low-tech methods are easier to replicate and less susceptible to failure due to errors in the design process. Also, the low-tech direct-action techniques match well with the organizations' methods for recruiting new activists. Asking sympathizers to undertake a complicated means of engaging in direct action could cause them to hesitate, whereas low-tech tactics are easy for newly inspired activists not only to conceptualize, but to actually put into play. A final and extremely important benefit of low-tech methods is that they employ substances that are more difficult for law enforcement to trace than more-powerful substances such as plastic explosives or dynamite are (Jane's Consultancy, 2001).

Nevertheless, despite the fact that radical environmentalists in the United States have shown fairly little interest in adopting new tactics, it should not be assumed that individuals within these organizations could not take it upon themselves to try new tactics. Given the international exchanges that are almost certainly taking place among radical environmentalists in this country and throughout Europe, tactics could migrate from one country to another. For example, in Europe, the most commonly used types of direct action are vandalism, ranging from graffiti and broken windows to disabled equipment and glued locks, and product contamination. Other tactics commonly used in Europe include direct intimidation of persons connected to environmental or animal rights abuses and letters carrying spring-loaded razor blades, often tipped with rat poison (Bilouri, 2001). A U.S. Department of Justice report on animal liberation organizations emphasizes that "animal rights extremism in the UK set the ideological stage for adherents in the United States and other countries over the years, but it also has established the example for violence and destruction" (Hendley and Wegelian, 1993, p. 25). The report goes on to reiterate that this multinational exchange of operational techniques is facilitated by the existence and proliferation of underground manuals and openly available publications (Hendley and Wegelian, 1993, p. 25).

Strategic-Level Learning

In contrast to this relatively low level of tactical learning in the modern radical environmentalist movement, however, the organizations within the movement have shown a significant capacity for learning at the strategic level, which has led to notable transformational shifts in the scope of their activities.

From Primary Targets to Secondary Targets

The first significant shift in strategy was that of the organization called Stop Huntingdon Animal Cruelty, or SHAC. SHAC originated in the United Kingdom with the goal of persuading Huntingdon Life Sciences (HLS), a research laboratory, to discontinue animal experimentation. After considerable direct action by SHAC, ranging from vandalism of the company's headquarters to the brutal beating of its president, HLS transferred most of its operations from the United Kingdom to New Jersey in 2001. While HLS hoped that this shift would put it beyond the reach of SHAC, the organization was able to mobilize activists in the United States and continue its intimidation.[8]

---

[8] While the way SHAC migrated to the United States is unclear, it is reasonable to assume that this expansion was significantly facilitated by the established relationships between animal liberationists in the United States and those in the United Kingdom. The U.S. Department of Justice (DOJ) Report to Congress on the Extent and

Having successfully followed HLS across the Atlantic, SHAC decided to target not just HLS itself, but also its suppliers and clients. Activists vandalized the homes of employees of Chiron, a pharmaceutical company based in Emeryville, California, and posted flyers around the neighborhoods in which the employees lived and worked, decrying them as "puppy killers." In August 2003, Chiron and Shaklee, a health- and beauty-products company with connections to HLS, were targeted by arsonists, and SHAC also claimed responsibility for vandalizing the homes of several managers of accounting firm Deloitte & Touche and hand-delivering death threats to the homes of managers of insurance broker Marsh & McLennan. SHAC claims that these efforts aimed at secondary targets related to HLS have had tremendous success, with more than 100 companies, including Deloitte & Touche, Marsh & McLennan, and both the Royal Bank of Scotland and the Stephens Group, which had held financial loans of HLS, opting to sever ties with HLS (Best and Kahn, 2004; Phillipkoski, 2004).

From the Forests to the Streets

Radical environmentalist organizations have also altered their strategy by refocusing their activities on suburban areas. The earliest ELF-attributed attacks, including the 1996 Oakridge incidents (which caused $9 million in damage), the 1997 arson of an animal slaughterhouse in Redmond, California ($1.3 million), the burning of two federal wildlife offices in Washington state ($1.9 million), and the 1999 arson of the Boise Cascade Corporation headquarters after the company announced its intention to build a strandboard manufacturing plant in Chile ($1 million), centered on targets related to wilderness protection and management (Chalk, 2001b). More recently, however, the ELF and other radical environmentalist organizations have increasingly shifted their focus to issues that are more salient to the general public.

In an April 2004 statement issued by the North American ELF Press Office (NAELFPO), a legally registered news service, the ELF claimed responsibility for the firebombing of several homes under construction in four different Washington state towns. The statement declared, "It is clear from past statements and recent actions of

---

Effects of Domestic and International Terrorism on Animal Enterprises makes little reference to the extent of this relationship, but other sources emphasize the depth of UK animal liberationists' involvement in motivating U.S. activities. According to the DOJ report, "It is not entirely clear whether the ALF took root in the United States as a transplanted organization or simply as a cause adopted and emulated by frustrated activists. . . . It has been observed, however, the [sic] some prominent activists within the animal rights movement in the United States are, or at one time were, British subjects. Some even suspect that ALF in the United Kingdom operates 'training camps' for activists from the United States and other countries. . . . Despite this apparent separation, however, it can be observed that ALF in the United States has followed organizational and operational patterns established in the United Kingdom, escalating quickly in both activity and technique, while maintaining the same central objective" (Hendley and Wegelian, 1993, p. 5). Best and Nocella (n.d.) stake out a stronger position on the strength of the relationship between U.S. and UK animal liberationists in their discussion of how the founder of the ALF, known legendarily only as Valerie, traveled to the United Kingdom to attend a "commando-style" camp to receive training before launching the U.S. branch.

the ELF that urban sprawl has become a central issue in the struggle to protect the earth" (Schwarzen, 2004). According to Rodney Coronado, a former spokesperson for both the ELF and the ALF, this shift can be seen as at least partly an admission of less-than-ideal results of the movement's focus on wilderness protection to date: "Unfortunately, we're taking a beating on forest protection. I think we've left that battlefield in defeat, and now we're fighting to protect what's in front of us. It's still the ELF, but it's morphing into a more urban environment" (Schwarzen, 2004). However, Coronado adds that this shift is still in keeping with the movement's objective of furthering social justice by financially hurting organizations and individuals that profit from environmental destruction—"there's a direct relation in the fact that environmental destruction in one's own community—urban sprawl and poor air quality—are becoming the largest issues. . . . So we're seeing less environmental focus on the wilderness and what's pristine, and we're working to protect the local communities that we live in" (Schwarzen, 2004). This overall shift is a striking example of how the strategy of a decentralized and integrated organization can emerge from the membership at large, which is particularly evident in the NAELFPO statement.

Other recent urban attacks attributed to the ELF include the following:

- The February 2004 destruction of equipment at the construction site of a mixed-use building in Charlottesville, Virginia
- The 2003 burning of a five-story apartment complex under construction in San Diego, California; homes under construction in the Sterling Oaks development in Chico, California; and two homes in the Willow Ridge development in Macomb County, Michigan
- The 2001 arson that destroyed the University of Washington's Center for Urban Horticulture
- The attacks in 2000 on luxury homes in Mount Sinai, New York

The turning point in the ELF's strategy was probably the 1998 Vail, Colorado, arson. Rick Scarce, author of *Eco-Warriors: Understanding the Radical Environmental Movement*, suggests that the Vail action signaled that "a whole different scale of sabotage had become acceptable. . . . The environmental movement has been radicalized permanently. I don't rule out the next step . . . that people will be killed" (Best, n.d.).

ELF-affiliated direct actions are increasingly taking place in more densely populated areas. Philip Celestini, FBI special agent in the Domestic Terrorism Operations Unit, has acknowledged that this trend is likely to continue and even worsen: "The spread of populated areas into previously undeveloped parts of the country is going to cause more and more conflicts between developers and those who want to preserve, which is why we've seen eco-terrorism rise to where it is now" (Schwarzen, 2004).

According to Coronado, this reality is the simple outcome of the progression of the radical environmentalist and animal liberationist movement. He notes that, "in the 1980s, any woman wearing a fur coat should have expected to get it spray-painted. Today, you build a luxury home, you can possibly expect it to be burned down" (Schwarzen, 2004).

From Environmentalism to Anticapitalist Anarchism

It is possible that the shift in the radical environmentalists' strategy was not solely the result of internal strategizing by the movement. Bruce Barcott (2002) notes that environmental radicals found a number of new allies during the 1999 World Trade Organization (WTO) protests in Seattle, Washington. There, radical environmentalists found themselves shoulder-to-shoulder with opponents of capitalism. Subsequent incidents demonstrated a blend of environmentalist, anticapitalist, and antiwar messages. In March 2004, several vehicles were burned and vandalized in related attacks in Edison, New Jersey, and at a Navy recruiting office in Montgomery, Alabama. The spray-painted messages left at the attack sites included claims of responsibility by the ELF and the Direct Action Front, a radical anticapitalist organization, and antiwar slogans such as "Leave Iraq" and "Stop Killing." One month later, similar attacks on three SUVs in Erie, Pennsylvania, and 60 SUVs and trucks in Santa Cruz, California, included vandalism declaring "No War," "SUVs Suck," and "No blood for oil" (Bilouri and Makarenko, 2003). And, so, similar to the shift of the radical environmental movement in the early 1990s from biocentrism to humanism, parts of the movement may have shifted again, this time to a broader even more anarchic agenda. It is unclear, however, whether this was truly an ideological shift or simply a new means of grabbing the public's attention for the environmentalist cause. Daniel Glick, who has written extensively about the ELF, notes, "There is a symbolic force to taking out a Hummer or 10,000 square-foot trophy home" (Schwarzen, 2004).

Statements by NAELFPO and sympathizers also seem to clearly illustrate the increased tendency of the radical environmentalist movement toward an increasingly anticapitalist and even anarchist bent. In February 2000, following a subpoena to testify before a grand jury, NAELFPO issued a press release declaring that both "the ELF and the ALF are clear representation of the people's struggle against the capitalist ideology and its horrifying effects on the planet and life. This struggle will not be stopped" (Schneider, 2003). NAELFPO's pamphlet of Frequently Asked Questions notes that "it is not enough to work solely on single, individual environmental issues but in addition the capitalist state and its symbols of propaganda must also be targeted. . . . The ELF ideology maintains that the social and political ideology in operation throughout the westernized countries is creating the various injustices on this planet and ultimately the destruction of life. That ideology is capitalism and the mindset that allows it to exist" (Ackerman, 2003b, p. 189).

Leslie James Pickering, a former spokesperson for the ELF, adds to these statements, saying, "I do not believe that the actions of the ELF are strictly environmental in their scope. It has probably already become clear that I recognize the actions of the ELF as acts of revolution, not reform. . . . The liberation of the Earth equals the liberation of everyone [sic] of us" (Ackerman, 2003a, p. 153). Finally, Steven Best, a professor of anthropology and a sympathetizer of the radical environmentalist and animal liberationist movements, observes, "If it is not already obvious, the struggle for animal rights is intimately connected to the struggle for human rights. . . . The animal rights community can no longer afford to be a single-issue movement, for now in order to fight for animal rights we have to fight for democracy. As different expressions of peace and justice struggles, progressive human and animal rights organizations need to identify important commonalities and for alliances against capitalism, militarization, patriarchy, state repression, and many other social pathologies that affect everyone, whatever their gender, sexual preference, class, race or species" (Best, n.d.).

In addition to influencing the radical environmentalist movement's choice of targets, anarcho-anticapitalists have also seemingly influenced the public relations and mobilization practices of radical environmentalism. For example, the first International Day of Action and Solidarity with Jeff "Free" Luers included events in more than ten U.S. cities and several foreign sites to protest the imprisonment of Luers, who is serving a 22-year sentence in Oregon for a 2000 arson at an auto dealership and an attempted arson at an oil company ("'Day of Action' Plans Trigger FBI Warning," 2004). Although the materials promoting the event (provided by Free's Defense Network (www.freefreenow.org)) included no call for direct action, the FBI nonetheless issued a general warning in its weekly intelligence bulletin distributed to some 18,000 law enforcement agencies cautioning that the events to be held on or around June 12, 2004, could include acts of ecoterrorism (Associated Press, 2004a). While there were few reports of such acts, the arson of Stock Building Supply, near Salt Lake City, Utah, which resulted in damages estimated at $1.5 million, was attributed to the ELF (Elsworth, 2004), and a letter with an ELF heading faxed to KSL, a local radio station, named four additional targets, including an SUV dealership and a lumberyard (Elsworth, 2004; Animal Liberation Front, n.d.).

In July 2004, the Total Liberation Tour sponsored various speakers and entertainers associated with radical protest groups, who appeared in ten cities throughout the United States. Once again, ecoterrorism events in Utah corresponded with this protest event. Ray Mey, a supervisor of the FBI's Joint Terrorism Task Force, stated that these ALF-attributed events, including an arson, the release of lab animals, and the destruction of aquarium experiments at Brigham Young University in Provo, were likely associated with the tour's passing through Salt Lake City (Associated Press, 2004b). These events, and particularly the affiliation with non-environmentalist protest groups, suggest that radical environmentalists have both learned from and allied themselves with broader radical protest movements, resulting in the further development of their operations.

Training

In spite of the segmented, cellular structure of radical environmentalist organizations, it is believed that formal efforts, apart from the dissemination of self-training materials via journals and websites, are being made within the movement to train activists. While there is little information suggesting that the ELF, per se, engages directly in coordinating radical environmentalist organizations, its relationship with the ALF gives reason to believe that a large number of those organizations are integrated through the ELF-ALF alliance. Evidence indicates that the ALF is an umbrella for a number of activist cells, including the Animal Rights Militia, the Animal Rights Action Foundation, and the Justice Department, each of which has claimed to be a separate and independent organization. The considerable similarity in aims and tactics among these organizations and the ALF leads many experts to conclude that the distinctions between them are false attempts to evade detection and create an image of a more forceful movement (Hendley and Wegelian, 1993, p. 7). In the United Kingdom, terrorism experts and law enforcement officials strongly believe that the ALF is at the center of a "web of British animal rights terror groups" (BBC News, 2000).

As has already been mentioned, the ELF and the ALF formally allied themselves as far back as 1997, and they had begun working together some years before that. It is also known that for some time, people such as Rodney Coronado and Craig Rosebraugh played active roles in both organizations. And until 2003, both organizations released official public statements through NAELFPO. However, these relationships are only a small indication of how integrated the two organizations and several others are thought to be. According to Philip Celestini, an FBI special agent in the Domestic Terrorism Operations Unit, "[radical environmentalism] is the most vexing and troublesome issue that the FBI investigates, [and] we don't think for a minute that these groups are entirely different sets of people" (Phillipkoski, 2004).

This integration has significant consequences for the operations of the organizations, including increasing their reach and effectiveness. In an investigative piece on radical environmentalism, James Long and Bryan Denson reported that "the mounting assault through the West has gained force since the late 1980s, as those fighting for wilderness joined with those fighting for animals, vandalizing or setting fire to research laboratories, logging sites and targeted businesses" (Long and Denson, 1999a).[9]

Moreover, it is widely believed that activities and training among radical environmentalist organizations from different countries are also widespread. There is considerable reason to believe that the ALF organization in the United Kingdom has made significant efforts to provide training to ALF branches throughout the world, including those in the United States, Canada, Germany, and Japan (BBC News, 2000).

Recent reports suggest that this learning runs in both directions. Bilouri (2001) notes that support European radical environmentalists received from their counterparts in the United States enabled them to conduct various attacks, including ten arsons against McDonald's restaurants in Genk, Belgium, in 1998, to protest the slaughtering of animals and the destruction of rainforests for cattle raising. Similarly, while Earth First! offshoots in Europe have not been as active as their U.S. counterparts, they have replicated many of the efforts of the U.S. radical environmentalists. SHAC organized a similar "training camp" for animal-liberationist organizations held in England in September 2004 (Bloomfield, 2004). Other organizations, including EarthFirst! and the Ruckus Society, hold regular events (annual gatherings and training camps) that include training in various direct-action techniques. These events are publicized on the Internet and open to activists from any related organization.

Finally, while the radical environmental movement is characterized by leaderless resistance or, at the least, polycentrism, reports in *Jane's Intelligence Review* contend that the ELF has a small, cohesive leadership core, which not only suggests targets to local cells but whose members also travel between countries to garner support and to increase the flexibility of the organization (Bilouri and Makarenko, 2003). Other reports assert that the 2003 attacks on SUVs and trucks in Pennsylvania and California were carried out by a "traveling circus" of ELF-affiliated activists moving across the country to spark direct actions and recruit new activists. Various law enforcement agencies in Europe share the belief that separate cells of radical environmental organizations began to coordinate their activities to stage strategically organized attacks as far back as 1990 (Bilouri, 2001).[10]

---

[9] Bron Taylor (1998, 2003) is an important dissenter in the otherwise nearly unanimous view that representatives of the ELF and the ALF cooperate very closely. Even Taylor, however, acknowledges the likelihood of significant cross-fertilization.

[10] We emphasize that polycentrism does not necessarily preclude strategic learning, although such learning could be impeded by the lack of a single consistent force moving an agenda forward. In fact, because of the increased capacity for interpretation and storage that characterizes an effectively integrated network, learning does not depend on any one individual and can therefore potentially be more efficient.

Intelligence and Operational Security

Radical environmentalists commonly follow several practices intended to provide operational security when engaging in direct actions. Most notably, their attacks are almost always carried out at night by a single person or a small ad hoc group of no more than six persons. Other operational security practices promoted via the movements' various websites include wearing large shoes to leave deceptive tracks, switching license places, borrowing cars that cannot be identified, and traveling across state borders to stymie law enforcement investigators (Long and Denson, 1999b; Chalk, 2001b). Once again, the most telling features of these tactics are their simplicity and their relative constancy throughout the history of modern ecoterrorism.

Radical environmentalists have demonstrated a significant capacity for operational planning and intelligence and for distributing this capacity throughout the movement. Stefan Leader and Peter Probst (2003) note that, according to the FBI, ELF activists often conduct pre-operation video and photographic surveillance and study industry and trade publications, as well as other open-source material, to understand their targets and to identify their prime vulnerabilities. ALF members, in particular, infiltrate their targets, sometimes by taking on low-level jobs within targeted organizations or by cultivating close contacts with employees, in order to collect information on the security practices of the targets and "evidence" of offending practices (Hendley and Wegelian, 1993, p. 6). John Curtin detailed the surveillance that he and others would undertake in preparation for an operation:

> That is a large part of all the raids I've ever known of—the surveillance beforehand. You really want to know the run of the place, you want to know what time the staff come in, what time do the rotators change, what time does the day staff change, when does the security make their rounds—and you want to know all of this like the back of your hand. . . . So for the few hours it takes to do the raid . . . it takes many, many weeks of 24/7 concentration on it in order for it to go well. There may be times when you could do something spur of the moment, but you don't want to rush into that intentionally. I would always want to know my enemy before I went there (*Bite Back Magazine*, n.d.).

Most important, however, are the various methods by which radical environmentalists are able to propagate these operational security skills throughout the movement, i.e., through written manuals or guidelines distributed in newsletters, magazines, and websites and direct-action training camps hosted by various organizations, most notably the Ruckus Society (www.ruckus.org).

Conclusions

Anticipating Radical Environmentalism

Together, these examples of learning in the radical environmentalist movement—both at an operational and tactical level by distributing knowledge via the Internet and at a more strategic level by shifting targets to achieve greater influence—offer law enforcement officials and counterterrorism researchers the opportunity to consider how the movement might evolve next. However, past examples of how or what the movement has learned must be accompanied by an appreciation of the motivations for and context of potential future learning and development. In this final section, we discuss briefly whether or not the radical environmentalist movement might be poised for an increase in the destructiveness of its activities to assist in assessing the risks associated with the movement's future evolution.

Is the Threat of Radical Environmentalist Terrorism Increasing?

Determining whether the radical environmentalist movement is likely to become increasingly violent is clearly a key priority for law enforcement. Certainly, some recent declarations of the ELF, the ALF, and related organizations signal an increased willingness to engage in more violent protest acts. Gary Ackerman of the Monterey Institute for International Studies notes that such a shift in propaganda is considered to be the key indicator of an increase in an organization's propensity to use violence (Ackerman, 2003a).

A notable example of such escalating rhetoric appeared in the ELF communiqué following the August 2002 fire at the U.S. Forest Service Northeast Research Station in Irvine, Pennsylvania. The message contained the following two sentences, which seem to indicate that the ELF is backing away from avoiding harm to any animal, human or non-human: "In pursuance of justice, freedom, and equal consideration for all innocent life across the board, segments of this global revolutionary movement are no longer limiting their revolutionary potential by adhering to a flawed, inconsistent, 'non-violent' ideology. While innocent life will never be harmed in any action we undertake, where it is necessary, we will no longer hesitate to pick up the gun to implement justice" (Knickerbocker, 2002). While the message states that "innocent life will never be harmed," the phrase itself may indicate a willingness to distinguish innocents from those guilty of abuses against the environment rather than a commitment to avoid harming any persons.

Two other recent messages from radical environmentalists also hint that these activists might be prone to greater violence in the future. A warning left by the Revolutionary Cells Animal Liberation Brigade after its September 2003 bombing of a California beauty-products company—"all customers and their families are considered legitimate targets"—stands out for its extension of the threat of violence beyond the company and its business partners to customers as well (Knickerbocker, 2003).

And on June 17, 2004, an InfoShop News reader, "pr," posted the following message in response to an interview with Anthony J. Nocella II, co-editor of *Terrorists or Freedom Fighters? Reflections on the Liberation of Animals*, that was published on the alternative news website: "Long live the bible free [sic], ALF, ELF and anarchist movements and long live netwar and all free beings everywhere. We do have a right to destroy those who would destroy us" (comment amended by Kahn, 2004). Interestingly, while "pr" is not an official spokesperson of the ELF, the ALF, or any other organization affiliated with the radical environmentalist movement, the message communicates the threat of violence very powerfully. In fact, the comment is potentially even more telling of the threat posed by the movement, in that this non-official reader not only sees the ELF and the ALF as being closely affiliated, but also sees them as closely affiliated to anarchists. The reference to netwar, along with the threat of destroying "those who would destroy us," makes the message particularly ominous. Similar comments from other contributors abound on radical environmentalist and alternative news websites.

Some observers have feared the threat of worsened violence since the convergence of the ELF and the ALF in 1997, largely because the tactic of violent attacks used by the ALF and related animal rights organizations might be adopted by the ELF and other less-animal-focused organizations. Some confirmation of this fear appeared within the first two years of the alliance, when attacks claimed by the ELF increased in number and scale. During this period, the ELF claimed responsibility for at least 12 major arson attacks, each causing $50,000 or more in damage and all potentially endangering human lives (Chalk, 2001b). This escalation continued through 2002 and 2003, each of which had more attacks than the previous year, in spite of the belief that such actions would decrease following the events of September 11, 2001.

Moreover, radical environmentalist organizations, particularly animal liberationists, have engaged in potentially lethal actions in the United Kingdom for years, and British police now fear that these organizations are moving toward "full blown urban terrorism" (BBC News, 2000). This fear increased following an attack in which nine bombs were planted on a fleet of refrigerated meat trucks. And although both the ELF and the ALF have avoided tactics that directly target individuals, e.g., letter-bombs, there is fear that other organizations such as the Justice Department, which advocates "removing any barriers between legal and illegal, violent and non-violent" means of challenging animal abuses, could influence less-violent organizations (Knickerbocker, 2002). As Mark Potok, editor of the *Intelligence Report of the Southern Poverty Law Center*, noted, "The evidence is indisputable that they're turning to more and more violence. When you start burning buildings it just seems to me obvious that, at some point, some night watchman is going to get burned up" (Knickerbocker, 2002). Several direct actions are also cited as signals of the movement's increasing willingness to inflict mass casualties. These actions include the

1989 plot to blow up the Palo Verde nuclear facility, the 1991 threats to inject rat poison into soft drinks to protest scientific and animal testing, and the 2000 planting of three jars of cyanide in downtown Minneapolis to protest animal genetic engineering.[11] Nonetheless, it is unclear whether riskier direct actions will actually be more violent.

There are also other reasons to believe that radical environmentalist organizations might move toward increasing violence. Gary Perlstein suggests that the ELF, the ALF, SHAC, and other radical activist organizations receive "a great deal of moral and perhaps even financial support" (2003, p. 171) from sympathetic academic communities. This support lends a legitimizing character to the movement, which could encourage more-violent activities. Perlstein points to Fresno State University's hosting of a conference billed as a dialogue about revolutionary environmentalism between academics and activists, to which only persons sympathetic to radical environmentalism were invited, and the Portland State University Faculty Senate's posting of a letter to law enforcement agencies requesting that they no longer refer to environmental activists as terrorists. But while Perlstein suggests that there is reason to believe that activists will increase their violent actions because "bombings, arsons and intimidations lead to praise and a feeling of importance" (2003, p. 171), he fails to illustrate exactly how displays of sympathy have encouraged further direct action.

Jean Rosenfeld, a senior researcher at the Center for Study of Religion at UCLA, has an alternative explanation for the radical environmentalists' potential inclination toward greater violence. According to Rosenfeld, "a group's perception of prosecution, combined with its perceived failure to meet its ultimate goals may result in an escalation of violent acts" (Knickerbocker, 2002). Leslie James Pickering makes this relationship even more clear:

> When they start coming down on people it's only going to radicalize people. When they come down on the ELF calling them terrorists, what that might spawn is, and I'm not saying this as a personal threat, but what that might spawn is a more radical more militant organization. When the oppressor rises so do the forces of the people—the forces of liberation. While it might have been okay to destroy property but not okay to harm individuals in one persons [sic] mind, if you beat that person down a little bit more they might change their mind (Ackerman, 2003a, pp. 154–155).

---

[11] The last two incidents in particular seem to illustrate the interorganizational connections previously discussed, as they closely resemble similar events that took place earlier in England. In 1984, the Animal Rights Militia (ARM), an offshoot of the ALF, reported to the media that it had poisoned Mars candy bars, forcing the company to recall its product from stores. While the ARM later acknowledged the threat as a hoax, Mars nonetheless ceased the tooth-decay experiments it had been conducting with animal test subjects (Bilouri, 2001). Similarly, in 1981, a group referring to itself as Operation Dark Harvest left buckets of plastic-sealed soil outside of public buildings in England to motivate the remediation of a remote stretch of Scotland that had been used by the government for anthrax testing (Eagan, 1996, p. 8).

This hypothesis could also help explain the ELF's recent foray into suburbia, which Coronado attributes to the organization's lack of success in protecting the wilderness.

Other comments by Rosenfeld, however, offer a more mixed message: "If a group is underground, as ELF is, considers itself an elite corps, and believes a higher law mandates violent acts in order to bring about what it considers to be salvation—for example, of the earth and all life—then it may have difficulty recruiting enough members and it may become more fanatical and violent over time" (Knickerbocker, 2002). While the ELF and other radical environmentalist organizations certainly consider themselves elite forces with a divine mission, the evidence does not indicate that they have had difficulty recruiting. Therefore, it is still unclear whether the recent shift in activities and rhetoric marks an increased tendency toward more violent tactics or simply a strategic change to put the movement's public agenda forward more effectively.

Other observers of the radical environmentalist movement, including Bron Taylor and David Helvarg, take a different view. Taylor, who has conducted probably the most extensive ethnographic study of the radical environmentalist movement, suggests that the movement is unlikely to become more violent. He contends that the violent rhetoric of radical environmentalists tends to be exactly that—rhetoric, rather than reality—and often is inappropriately taken out of context by the movement's opponents.[12]

Whether or not such rhetoric actually translates into action is another question, however. Extreme statements by radical environmentalists and related organizations are not new: John Davis, the original editor of the *Earth First! Journal*, once stated, "I suspect that eradicating smallpox was wrong. It played an important part in balancing ecosystems" (Carpenter, 1990). Critics also point to a 1987 *Earth First! Journal* article that suggested that AIDS could reduce the human population significantly enough that it would undermine industrialism and preserve wildlife and wilderness areas (Lee, 1995, p. 121). Similarly, Ronnie Lee said early in the ALF's history, "Animal liberation is a fierce struggle that demands total commitment. There will be injuries and possibly deaths on both sides. That is sad but certain" (Bilouri, 2001). Despite these extreme statements, there have yet to be any deaths linked to these organizations.

Ackerman also argues that conflating radical environmentalists with animal liberationists or other activists is highly problematic. While acknowledging the sometimes considerable working relationships between the two movements, Taylor argues

---

[12] In a response to Perlstein and Taylor, Ackerman (2003b) notes that he has identified at least 36 separate statements by more than a dozen distinct environmentalists that can be interpreted as encouraging the use of violence against human beings. While such comments seem to be becoming more frequent or more violent, at least upon a superficial review, it is still far from certain that this is the case. The comments may simply be reported more, particularly through alternative media outlets, and observers may be comparing the violence to the very broadly threatening discussion of biological warfare by early activists.

that the influence of animal liberationists on radical environmentalists will continue to be minimal, largely due to the incompatible philosophical underpinnings of the two movements.

In fact, Taylor suggests that if either organization is likely to be influenced by the other, the animal liberationists would be moderated by the radical environmentalists, suggesting that most radical environmentalists refuse to engage in direct action that carries an apparent risk of human injury. In a similar vein, Helvarg suggests that the most likely prospect for the future of the radical environmentalist movement will be a shift away from monkeywrenching toward greater nonviolent civil disobedience (Philippon, 2002).

Chalk (2001b) notes that the ability of radical environmentalists to engage in greater violence is, in reality, extremely limited. In particular, he contends that these organizations lack both the resources and the expertise needed to overcome the technical hurdles of using chemical, biological, or radiological weapons. And even if radical environmentalists were to attempt to use unconventional weapons, such actions would likely be small in scale and limited in scope, intended to galvanize public attention to a particular issue rather than to produce mass casualties.

Further supporting his argument against the likelihood of radical environmentalists becoming more violent, Taylor identifies several dynamics that could encourage or discourage the transmission of a proclivity to more-violent action. The dynamics that he identifies as potentially encouraging violence within the movement include the tendency for radical environmentalists to view their activities as defending sacred values and the potential for their opponents to demonize the movement to the point that it will attract only individuals who are predisposed to violence and repulse those who might be more moderating (Taylor, 1998, p. 10). His list of traits and dynamics discouraging violence is much longer:

- Radical environmentalists tend to temper their revolutionary rhetoric with a realistic or even exaggerated respect for state power; they thus recognize that serious contemplation of violent action when under intense scrutiny by law enforcement entails considerable risk (p. 12).
- Radical environmentalists generally do not sever ties with their natural families or communities; in fact, they sometimes rely on these relationships (p. 12).
- Except for the most underground and isolated, radical environmentalists commonly engage face-to-face with their adversaries, which can humanize their opponents and constrain the confrontation (p. 13).
- There is no dominant, charismatic leader within the egalitarian, anti-hierarchical movement, and any figure that might attempt to establish such a position would likely be blocked or deposed (p. 14).
- The anti-hierarchical character of the movement also provides a venue for debate that has a moderating effect (p. 14).

- Open lines of communication, particularly the Internet, reduce insularity (p. 14).
- General religious sentiments that the earth and all life are sacred present serious ideological constraints on the contemplated actions of even the most radical environmentalists (pp. 14–15).

Thus, Taylor concludes that the transmission of a tendency toward more violent direct actions is unlikely, and the converse, that the movement will tend to become more moderate, is actually probable. Making this case more dramatically, Lee Dessaux, an animal rights activist convicted for assaulting two bison hunters while protesting a hunt, has said, "It is a laugh to me when they call us violent or terrorist. I say, if we were, don't you think we'd have killed people by now?" (Taylor, 1998, pp. 6–7).

However, Taylor still admits that there is some threat that greater violence could come from the movement in the form of a "lone wolf assassin," a single individual who happens to become isolated from the movement and its moderating effects (Taylor, 1998, p. 11). Similarly, FBI official Kevin Favreau warns, "Ultimately, the type of thing we're trying to avoid is the lone guy who takes it to the furthest extreme" (Bilouri and Makarenko, 2003).[13]

Context Matters

Finally, while a consideration of organizational learning among radical environmentalists might help us to better understand how the movement could adapt and evolve, it is also critical to contextualize this information. One model particularly well suited for understanding this context is the J-curve theory of revolution, developed by James C. Davies.[14] According to this theory, revolution is most likely to occur within a particular social order when a prolonged period of social progress is followed by a short period of sharp reversal. Christopher Hewitt notes that it is but a small step to translate this theory to the realm of terrorism:

---

[13] While some observers, led by researcher Martha Lee and Center for the Defense of Free Enterprise spokesman Ron Arnold, have suggested that the Unabomber, Ted Kaczynski, exemplifies the risk of violence that radical environmentalists pose, this relationship is highly suspect. For a concise rebuttal of this hypothesis, see Taylor (1998, pp. 14–17, 26–30), who notes that while Kaczynski did at times expropriate language from the radical environmentalist movement and attempt to exploit contact with Earth First! (including sending a letter to the *Earth First! Journal* under the moniker "FC," posing as a group calling itself the Freedom Club, and attending one of the group's major gatherings), these actions hardly mark him as a product of the movement. Taylor notes that in fact there are critical disparities between the philosophy of the radical environmentalist movement and that espoused by Kaczynski, differences that allowed him to justify the use of violence against persons in a manner not defensible within the radical environmentalist movement.

[14] The idea of adapting Davies' J-curve theory to the analysis of the radical environmentalist movement was suggested by Bruce Barcott (2002).

When your hopes have been raised and you feel there's a chance for victory through legitimate political means, you'd be foolish to resort to terrorism. Terrorism is a high-cost option, a weapon of the weak, a tool of last resort. But if your movement suddenly collapses or suffers political reversals, then some activists will be tempted to go for terrorism (Barcott, 2002).

Barcott notes that the J-curve theory could help to explain the ELF's use of its first major firebomb in 1996, the year in which then-President Clinton signed the timber-salvage rider that made it easier for logging companies to harvest trees, potentially indicating a reversal of his administration's previous four years of progressive environmental protection. The theory might also help to explain the original formation of EarthFirst!—after three years of environmental promise under President Carter, the RARE II decision and the rollbacks under President Reagan spurred David Foreman and the other founders of Earth First! to turn to direct action. The J-curve theory could even help to explain the increase in direct actions following the 1999 WTO meetings in Seattle, which the movement seized upon as a symbol of commercial overrunning of environmental interests, as well as the increase in suburban direct-action activity beginning in 2001, the year in which President Bush took office and his administration began to advocate environmental rollbacks, from opening the Alaska National Wildlife Reserve to oil drilling and the U.S. pullout from the Kyoto Protocol.

Of course, the J-curve framework is not a complete explanatory theory unto itself; the factors influencing the radical environmentalist movement are far more complex and, as suggested, highly dependent upon the learning behavior of the movement and its participants. Still, the theory could be helpful in identifying when critical shifts in organizational adaptation might be most likely to occur and thus when greater interference in these processes by law enforcement might be most effective.[15]

Organizational Learning in a Movement

If the examination of the radical environmentalist movement can teach us anything about organizational learning within terrorist groups, the most valuable lesson would be that cross-fertilization among even loosely structured organizations is not only possible but potentially highly effective. While the ELF, the ALF, and other radical

---

[15] In particular, law enforcement officials should consider how the behavior of various factions within the movement might correspond to behavior suggested by the J-curve theory. Distinctive adaptations of different groups to changes in the societywide context of environmentalism could suggest different strategies for disrupting the learning and evolution of these groups. As Perlstein (2003, p. 172) notes in refuting Ackerman (2003a), local law officials are not likely to be capable of dealing with the threat posed by radical environmentalism, due to a relative lack of training and, even more important, to a lack of awareness of the nonlocal stimuli that might spur direct actions. Because of this, it is critical for national law enforcement officials to track and analyze how national or even international events might cause a shift in the path of environmental "progress." They could then advise local officials and warn them of potential upswings in direct actions at the local level.

environmentalist organizations have demonstrated relatively little interest in developing more-sophisticated means of executing their attacks, this does not mean that they have not demonstrated a significant penchant for learning. The most important facet of this learning has been the tremendous exploitation of information technology, particularly the Internet, as a means of readily distributing and effectively storing the movement's knowledge. This has allowed the movement to rely less upon tactical innovation and more on facilitating activists' acquisition of the relatively accessible knowledge and skills necessary to extend their activities. Similarly, while the Internet is a very valuable tool for promoting learning among activists, the movement's embrace of the technology is itself a notable example of rapid and effective learning.

The movement's exploitation of information technology is not the only or even the most critical example of its organizational learning. The movement has also learned to disseminate best practices in operational security, to develop new activists at direct-action training camps, to adopt mass organizing tactics utilized by other radical protest organizations, and to affiliate with those organizations. Most significant, however, is the movement's learning at a strategic level. It has shifted the targets of its terrorism from the wilderness to the suburbs not only to address changing priorities within the movement, but also to allow the movement to more effectively impress upon its public audience the weight of its actions. Considering that the object of terrorism, by most common definitions, is not only to cause damage by terrorist acts but to move a broader audience to action, this shift can be seen as a demonstration of exactly how effective the learning within the radical environmentalist movement has been in maintaining the movement's salience in the wider world.

Epilogue: On the Integration of the Radical Environmentalist Movement

This chapter began with a discussion of the interconnectedness of a wide variety of radical environmental organizations and the need for analyses of organizational learning to largely conflate these organizations, yet it is important that these organizations, or subcultures, not be presented as a monolithic and cohesive movement.[16] While Craig Rosebraugh and Leslie James Pickering, both former spokespersons for the ELF, left these roles to found Arissa, an anarchist social-revolution group that espouses greater violence to foment social change, "the extent to which Arissa can be construed as an offshoot of the ELF is debatable" (Ackerman, 2003a). Thus, while some might argue that Rosebraugh and Pickering's current work signals a leaning toward potentially greater violence within the radical environmentalist movement, this assertion must be questioned. Such a link is tenuous at best, as neither Rosebraugh nor Pickering was significantly involved in the movement before taking

---

[16] For a more complete discussion of the differences among the subcultures of the radical environmentalist movement, one should begin with Taylor (1998, 2003).

on self-designated roles as ELF spokespersons, and both were drawn to the ELF largely because "as anarchists if not anarcho-primitivists, they perceived fellow travelers behind the anti-industrial rhetoric of some ELF statements" (Taylor, 2003, p. 177). Taylor contends that Rosebraugh and Pickering's departures may actually signal the difference in the perspectives and strategies of these organizations, observing that, "[Rosebraugh and Pickering] left the movement because their primary identity and motivation is located in anarchism, not the environmental cause, although they believe if human freedom/anarchy can be achieved, environmental well-being will follow" (2003, p. 177).

Nonetheless, even though the various radical environmentalist subcultures undoubtedly face different constraints upon their behavior, this should not be interpreted to mean that learning among these organizations is completely impeded. From a theoretical perspective, this should be easy enough to recognize: Learning itself is not necessarily impeded by a difference in philosophy, although the interpretation and translation of that learning into behavior can certainly be constrained by different philosophical worldviews and objectives. Even Taylor, who argues convincingly against the conflation of the tactics and the potential for violence among the various organizations within the radical environmentalist milieu, acknowledges that "activists in one stream find certain ideas and tactics common within the other streams plausible or compelling. But when push comes to shove, the issues activists choose to prioritize, and the tactics they select in the struggle, signal which subcultural axiology and ideology has captured their primary allegiance" (Taylor, 2003, p. 176). And the fact also remains that there are considerable indicators of relational bridges between these organizations across which fragments of ideology, tactics, and occasionally even evident cooperation can flow: "One cannot deny, for example, that the Animal Liberation Front (ALF) served as an organizational template for the ELF or that anarchist ideas have not infused much of the ELF's ideology" (Ackerman, 2003b, p. 187).

References

Ackerman, Gary A., "Beyond Arson? A Threat Assessment of the Earth Liberation Front," *Terrorism and Political Violence*, Vol. 15, No. 4, Winter 2003a, pp. 143–170.

___, "My Reply to Perlstein and Taylor," *Terrorism and Political Violence*, Vol. 15, No. 4, Winter 2003b, pp. 183–189.

Animal Liberation Front, www.animalliberationfront.com.

Associated Press, "Police Watching for 'Green Terror,'" www.CBSnews.com, June 12, 2004a.

___, "FBI Worried Utah Ecoterrorism Becoming More Violent," www.KUTV.com, July 9, 2004b.

Barcott, Bruce, "From Tree-Hugger to Terrorist," *New York Times*, April 7, 2002.

BBC News, "Animal Rights, Terror Tactics," BBC News.com, August 30, 2000.

Best, Steven, "It's War! The Escalating Battle Between Activists and the Corporate-State Complex," available at http://utminers.utep.edu/best/papers/vegenvani/itswar.htm (last accessed June 14, 2004).

___, and Richard Kahn, "Trial by Fire: The SHAC7 and the Future of Democracy," available at InfoShop news at www.infoshop.org/inews/stories.php?story=04/04/28/1046873 (last accessed August 30, 2004).

___, and Anthony J. Nocella II, "Behind the Mask: Uncovering the Animal Liberation Front," available at http://www.animalliberationfront.com/ALFront/Behind_The_Mask.pdf (last accessed September 14, 2004).

Bilouri, Daphne, "Eco-Protest Develops More Militant Edge," *Jane's Intelligence Review*, October 1, 2001.

___, and Tamara Makarenko, "Earth Liberation Front Increases Actions Across the USA," *Jane's Intelligence Review*, September 1, 2003.

Bloomfield, Steve, "U.S. Animal Activists May Be Kept Out of UK," independent.co.uk, August 1, 2004.

Carpenter, Betsy, "Redwood Radicals," *U.S. News and World Report*, September 17, 1990, p. 50.

Chalk, Peter, "Leaderless Resistance," *Jane's Intelligence Review*, July 1, 2001a.

___, "U.S. Environmental Groups and 'Leaderless Resistance,'" *Jane's Intelligence Review*, October 1, 2001b.

Dawdy, Phillip, "A Suspect Roundup," *Missoula Independent*, June 24, 2004.

"'Day of Action' Plans Trigger FBI Warning," *Seattle Times*, June 12, 2004.

Denson, Bryan, and James Long, "Eco-terrorism Sweeps the American West," *The Oregonian*, September 26, 1999.

Eagan, Sean P., "From Spikes to Bombs: The Rise of Eco-terrorism," *Studies in Conflict and Terrorism*, Vol. 19, 1996, pp. 1–18.

Earth Liberation Front, "Meet the ELF," www.earthliberationfront.com (last accessed June 2004).

"Eco-Terrorists Abandon Spikes," *San Francisco Chronicle*, April 16, 1990, p. A26.

Elsbach, Kimberly D., and Robert I. Sutton, "Acquiring Organizational Legitimacy Through Illegitimate Actions: A Marriage of Institutional and Impression Management Theories," *Academy of Management Journal*, Vol. 35, 1992, pp. 699–738, cited in Sean P. Eagan, "From Spikes to Bombs: The Rise of Eco-terrorism," *Studies in Conflict and Terrorism*, Vol. 19, 1996, pp. 1–18.

Elsworth, Catherine, "Eco-terrorist Elves Are Blamed for Arson Attack," *The Telegraph*, www.news.telegraph.co.uk, June 18, 2004.

Gerlach, Luther P., "The Structure of Social Movements: Environmental Activism and Its Opponents," in J. Arquilla and D. Ronfeldt (eds.), *Networks and Netwars: The Future of Terror, Crime and Militancy*, Santa Monica, CA: RAND Corporation, 2001.

Hendley, Scott E., and Steve Wegelian, *Report to Congress on the Extent and Effects of Domestic and International Terrorism on Animal Enterprises*, Washington, DC: U.S. Department of Justice, 1993.

"Interview with John Curtin," *Bite Back Magazine #1*, available at http://www.directaction.info/library_jon.htm.

Jane's Consultancy, "Eco-terrorists Climb to Top of FBI's Domestic Threat Tree," *Jane's Terrorism and Security Monitor*, February 1, 2001.

Jones, Pattrice, "Attack of the Terrorist Fax," www.dissentvoice.org, June 17, 2004.

Kahn, Richard, "Interview with Anthony J. Nocella, II, Co-editor of Terrorists or Freedom Fighters? Reflections on the Liberation of Animals," *Infoshop News*, June 16, 2004.

Knickerbocker, Brad, "In U.S., a Rise of Violent Environmental Tactics," *Christian Science Monitor*, September 26, 2002.

___, "New Laws Target Increase in Acts of Ecoterrorism," *Christian Science Monitor*, November 26, 2003.

Leader, Stefan H., and Peter Probst, "The Earth Liberation Front and Environmental Terrorism," *Terrorism and Political Violence*, Vol. 15, No. 4, Winter 2003, pp. 37–58.

Lee, Martha F., "Violence and the Environment: The Case of 'Earth First!'" *Terrorism and Political Violence*, Vol. 7, No. 3, Autumn 1995.

Lewis, John E., "Testimony Before the United States Senate Committee on the Judiciary Hearings on Animal Rights: Activism vs. Criminality," May 18, 2004.

Long, James, and Bryan Denson, "Terrorist Acts Provoke Change in Research, Business, Society," *The Oregonian*, September 28, 1999a.

___, "Can Sabotage Have a Place in a Democratic Community?" *The Oregonian*, September 29, 1999b.

Perlstein, Gary, "Comments on Ackerman," *Terrorism and Political Violence*, Vol. 15, No. 4, Winter 2003, pp. 171–172.

Philippon, Daniel J., "Eco-Terrorism," *Gale/St. James Encyclopedia of Popular Culture*, Gale Group, 2002.

Phillipkoski, Kristen, "Eco-Terror Cited as Top Threat," *Wired News*, June 16, 2004.

Randall, Tom, "Ecoterrorism Surges: Attacks Become More Frequent and Severe as Forest Service Stands Idly By," *Environment News*, August 1999.

Schmid, Alex P., *Political Terrorism: A Research Guide to Concepts, Theories, Data Bases and Literature*, New Brunswick Transaction Books, 1983, cited in Sean P. Eagan, "From

Spikes to Bombs: The Rise of Eco-terrorism," *Studies in Conflict and Terrorism,* Vol. 19, 1996, pp. 1–18.

Schneider, Gary, "An Eco-Illogical Disaster Waiting to Happen," *American Daily,* September 9, 2003.

Schwarzen, Christopher, "Environmental Radicals Shift Targets to Streets," *Seattle Times,* June 12, 2004.

Sullivan, Robert, "The Face of Eco-terrorism," *New York Times,* December 20, 1998.

Taylor, Bron, "Religion, Violence and Radical Environmentalism: From Earth First! to the Unabomber to the Earth Liberation Front," *Terrorism and Political Violence,* Vol. 10, No. 4, Winter 1998, pp. 1–42.

___, "Threat Assessments and Radical Environmentalism," *Terrorism and Political Violence,* Vol. 15, No. 4, Winter 2003, pp. 173–182.

Part II: Theory and Application

Prologue

An understanding of how terrorist organizations change over time could make an important contribution to better characterization of the terrorist threat and to development of improved responses to the actions of these organizations. The five case studies presented in Part I provide an empirical foundation for that understanding. The case groups—chosen to cover the spectrum of terrorist and insurgent groups—vary in their characteristics, including religious, ethno-nationalist, single issue, and apocalyptic motivations. They range from large insurgencies to small clandestine groups; some are state-sponsored and some are not; some have pursued unconventional weapons. And they represent a range of organizational structures. However, each group has a reputation for specific types of innovation and learning across a number of dimensions, including weapons, tactics, intelligence, and operational security, providing a rich dataset for examining learning choices and behaviors.[1]

In Part II of this report, we develop a transferable framework for understanding terrorist learning. In doing so, we shift attention from describing specific groups' actions toward consideration of *how* learning is carried out within terrorist organizations. The framework has two primary components:

1. Concepts and models drawn from published literature on learning in organizations, which provide a new lens through which to view terrorist group learning
2. Cross-cutting observations about how the case groups carried out organizational learning processes.

---

[1] The five selected groups provide an extensive body of information on how terrorist groups learn and allow us to build a framework for assessing their learning more broadly. However, because the groups themselves are not representative of all terrorist organizations, the specific conclusions drawn from this dataset should not be broadly generalized to all such organizations.

CHAPTER SEVEN

Theory: Organizational Learning as a Four-Component Process

Horacio R. Trujillo and Brian A. Jackson

In research on the performance of organizations, significant attention has been devoted to examining the factors that make some organizations better learners than others. To better understand the factors that affect terrorist groups' ability to learn, this study draws on the conceptual and analytical resources provided by the rich body of literature on organizational learning. This chapter reviews concepts and models drawn from that literature. In Chapter Eight, those concepts and models are applied to the results of the case studies of Part I.[1]

We have defined organizational learning as a process through which members of a group acquire new knowledge or technological capabilities that can improve[2] strategic decisionmaking, tactical planning or design, and operational activities.[3] While individual members of a group must build new skills and knowledge for organizational learning to take place, learning at the organizational level is more than simply the sum of what each individual member knows or can do.

An organization is a system that structures, stores, and influences what and how its individual members learn (Fiol and Lyles, 1985; Hedberg, 1981; Shrivastava, 1983). As such, it possesses a "memory" greater than that of any individual member: "Members [of an organization] come and go, and leadership changes, but organizations' memories preserve certain behaviors, mental maps, norms and values over time" (Easterby-Smith et al., 2000). This memory enables an organization to utilize the capabilities of individual members to achieve group goals while limiting its dependence on any specific person. When knowledge is *organizational*, a group has cap-

---

[1] The material in this chapter is also discussed in Chapter Two of the companion volume, *Aptitude for Destruction, Volume 1: Organizational Learning in Terrorist Groups and Its Implications for Combating Terrorism*.

[2] However, we note that organizational processes that enable learning can teach destructive behavior if misinformed.

[3] The learning literature contains a range of definitions of organizational learning, differing in, for example, what must be demonstrated to show learning, whether the process must be intentional, and whether the knowledge gained must be relevant to an organization's actions and goals. The definition used here is roughly equivalent to the consensus definition proposed in Miller (1996).

tured new or expanded capabilities in such a way that it does not depend on particular individuals to exploit them.

Although they are significantly different from the private-sector organizations that are the focus of much of the analysis of organizational learning, terrorist groups are still organizations. To be successful, they must change, and to change effectively, they must learn. Operating in extremely volatile environments, they must capture their learning at an organizational level in order to survive. By doing so, they gain critical advantages (Romme and Dillen, 1997): They can more readily gather the information they need than any single individual could. They can interpret that information through the diverse lenses of many different members. And they can transmit information from an original learner to multiple group members, reducing the risk of losing important knowledge if one particular person is lost.[4]

To analyze the actual process of how terrorist groups learn, we have selected a model that breaks organizational learning down into four component processes that can be analyzed separately:[5,6] acquiring, interpreting, distributing, and storing information (see Figure 7.1). All four processes must occur for knowledge to become organizational—that is, clearly tied to group objectives, accessible to many different group members, and resistant to the loss of individual members.

The four processes are not sequential stages of a progression; they are interrelated and can happen in different order, depending on context. For example, when the individual group members who acquire new information are also qualified to interpret the information, there is less need to distribute it to anyone else in the group

Figure 7.1
Component Processes of an Organizational Learning Framework

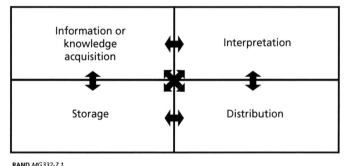

RAND MG332-7.1

---

[4] Argyris and Schön (1978, 1996) best summarize the advantages and limitations of organizational learning.

[5] Romme and Dillen (1997) present a brief but detailed treatment of organizational learning as an information process.

[6] Lutes (2001) applies a similar four-stage model, also used to examine terrorist organizations.

before interpretation. But when those members with the expertise to make sense of new information are not the ones who collected it, the information must first be transferred.

By breaking down organizational learning into component processes that can be analyzed separately, the model provides a framework for understanding organizational learning in terrorist groups and offers the opportunity to examine specific stages of the process for potential intervention in efforts to combat terrorist activities.[7] Each process is described below, along with its relevant features for examining learning in terrorist groups.

Acquisition

To assist in evaluating and improving their performance, groups must acquire information on their current activities and on potentially beneficial ways they might alter their future behavior. Groups can acquire new knowledge both from outside sources and by mining or developing it internally.

External Knowledge Sources

Small organizations seldom have all the capabilities or knowledge available among their members to meet all their needs or to enable fully internal learning processes. Therefore, they must frequently reach outside their boundaries in search of the resources they lack. They can do this through several means, described below.

Vicarious Experience. Observing the activities of other groups can be a relatively straightforward way of gathering information. However, the information gained is frequently incomplete. Although direct observation provides insights into the outputs of other groups' efforts, it frequently does not provide all the information needed to reproduce the efforts themselves.

Cooperating with Other Organizations. Groups gain access to information through interactions with other groups that already possess the necessary expertise or technology (Romme and Dillen, 1997). Linkages to other groups that are engaged in similar activities can greatly facilitate learning (Hardy et al., 2003; Mowery et al., 1996), although such linkages are not always easy to make, nor are they always effective as sources of information. Barriers to knowledge transfer, differences in group goals, or clashes in group cultures can hinder the effectiveness of this learning mode (Jones, 1991).

---

[7] This model also draws on descriptions of organizational learning such as that of Barnett (n.d., cited in Lipshitz et al., 2002), which defines organizational learning as "an experience-based process through which knowledge about action-outcome relationships develops, is encoded in routines, is embedded in organizational memory and changes collective behavior."

Outside Human Resources. External experts can provide a rich resource for organizational knowledge acquisition, provided the right individuals can be located and persuaded to help. These outside resources could be recruited into the organization or simply retained as consultants to teach group members.

Acquisition of Knowledge Sources or Technologies. Acquiring potentially useful technical systems or other knowledge sources, ranging from weapons to blueprints of desirable targets, can be a rapid way to increase group capabilities. Even this type of information acquisition is not easy, however. Depending on the characteristics of the technology, a group that acquires it may or may not have all the knowledge needed to use it effectively. As a result, acquiring information by this route alone may not be sufficient (Jones, 1991), and a group may need to draw on other information sources as well to gain the additional required information.

Internal Knowledge Sources

Groups commonly gather information from within their ranks. Internal sources of organizational knowledge can be broken into three categories: congenital knowledge, direct experience, and internal knowledge development.

Congenital Knowledge. The knowledge that an organization inherits from its original leaders and members is critical early in its development. Such knowledge provides the basis for the group's initial organizational learning efforts. As the organization matures and requires new knowledge—i.e., when congenital knowledge becomes obsolete due to changing circumstances or evolution in technologies—other forms of knowledge acquisition become more important.

Direct Experience (Learning by Doing). Groups learn as a result of their ongoing efforts. In the course of certain activities, groups can improve their skills and identify ways to obtain better outcomes from their efforts. While learning by doing may be pursued intentionally, it often occurs unintentionally and unsystematically as mistakes offer lessons on how a group can improve over time (Cyert and March, 1963). When organizations intentionally focus on learning from their ongoing activities, they may pursue specific strategies to help capture lessons from experience. Groups may also design their operations in ways that will increase the information they produce.

Internal Knowledge Development. A group may be able to develop new information internally. By devoting human and other resources to research or development activities, an organization can discover needed information, build new weapons, or hone tactics that can be applied to its ongoing operations. Internal knowledge can be developed, for example, through experimentation or testing of new concepts or working through the deployment of technologies during training activities.

Interpretation

For acquired information to be useful, a group must be able to judge its value and meaning (Huber, 1991). To learn effectively, a group must have the ability to interpret available information and make judgments about three classes of activities:[8]

- **Current activities.** Are the group's actions effective? Are they moving the group toward its overall strategic goals? How can the group alter these actions to make them more successful?
- **Possible future activities.** Would a new tactic or technology help the group? Does the group know what it needs to know to use that tactic or technology? Is the group likely to be able to use it successfully?
- **Older or invalidated knowledge and procedures.** Is older knowledge still useful? Are established routines still effective? Should they be discarded in order to adopt newer operating procedures (Hedberg, 1981; McGill and Slocum, Jr., 1993)?

For interpretation to be most effective, a group must have the knowledge needed to make sense of new information, as well as the time and opportunity to think through what it means (March and Olsen, 1975). The ability to interpret information within a useful time interval is also key in the learning process.

Factors that influence a group's ability to interpret information effectively include how commonly the information is shared within the group; the extent to which different members of groups share common assumptions (Kim, 1993); and the richness and feedback speed of the media through which the information is communicated to and within the group (Huber, 1991).[9] Bottlenecks in communications within a group can degrade interpretation and lead to discordant learning, i.e., different group members interpreting information in different, incompatible ways (Daft and Lengal, 1986). Group culture also critically influences an organization's ability to interpret new data it receives from its environment; unless the group is open-minded enough to recognize that it needs to reevaluate its circumstances or actions, the interpretation process will be stalled before it even begins.

---

[8] Much of the following discussion is framed in a language consistent with viewing terrorist groups and decisionmakers as essentially rational actors—interpreting information based on some concept of the organization's goals and making decisions on the basis of whether an activity does or does not contribute to them. Other elements of the literature on terrorist group decisionmaking (reviewed recently in McCormick, 2003) provide different "frames" through which to view the interpretation activities of terrorist groups. The analyses reported here do not depend on the specific decisionmaking model appropriate for a given terrorist organization; a group can learn, no matter what interpretive model it applies, and can make rational decisions and choices within its interpretive frame, though the specifics of its model would be a primary shaper of the aims of its learning efforts.

[9] This point emphasizes the connection between the ability of a group to interpret information and the nature of its distribution mechanisms (discussed below.)

Distribution

As we noted earlier, information acquisition is a necessary but not sufficient condition for organizational learning. Information must also be distributed, interpreted, and stored for organizational learning to occur. Distribution, in particular, plays a critical role in advancing the learning process, because the more broadly information is distributed within an organization, the more likely it is to be interpreted—and interpreted in multiple ways—which can increase the likelihood that it can be effectively utilized by the organization.[10] After information has been interpreted, distribution also plays a central role in facilitating its storage and increasing its availability for later use. Thus, effective distribution significantly lowers the risk that an organization's learning will deteriorate (Huber, 1991).

Different types of knowledge have different requirements for effective distribution within an organization. Earlier studies of learning in organizations have shown that there are two general classes of knowledge, which differ significantly in their ease of distribution. *Explicit knowledge* is knowledge that is preserved in a physical form, such as documents describing activities, blueprints or instructions, or technological systems or devices. This type of knowledge can be transferred from one individual or group to another relatively easily; its distribution may entail nothing more than handing someone a book or downloading a photograph. *Tacit knowledge*, more abstract knowledge held by individuals but still needed to learn successfully, is much more difficult to transfer than explicit knowledge.[11] The most common example of tacit knowledge is the knowledge and skill an expert builds over the course of his or her career. Tacit knowledge might be a high level of marksmanship skill with a firearm, tactical intuition about operational design, or the engineering skills that go into fabricating particular weapons. Because this type of knowledge is hard to articulate, much less codify, it often requires an individual seeking information to meet the expert face to face (reviewed in Gertler, 2001).

Few activities require explicit or tacit knowledge alone. For example, to use a firearm effectively, a person must not only have a gun and know how to shoot it—explicit knowledge that can be gained through obtaining the weapon and reading an instruction manual—but must also be a good enough marksman to hit the desired target—tacit knowledge acquired through practice and experience. A group's ability

---

[10] However, the multiple interpretations must eventually be rationalized and standardized to avoid the problem of conflicting interpretations persisting in different parts of the organization.

[11] Different groups attempting a task described in an explicit format will perform that task similarly, because explicit knowledge can be transferred uniformly among the groups (Edmonson et al., 2003). Tasks that rely on tacit knowledge are more difficult to transfer among groups because of the difficulty of transferring tacit knowledge effectively.

to bring together explicit and tacit knowledge depends on having the appropriate distribution mechanisms (Jones, 1991).[12]

Storage

Groups must store information to ensure that they can access it in the future. Newer organizations frequently rely almost exclusively on the memories of individual group members to store group knowledge. However, individual memories are highly vulnerable (Carley, 1992; Kim, 1993), and as a result, established groups tend to favor other repositories, such as the following:

- **Language, rituals, and symbols.** Group culture and language play an important role in defining the way a group thinks about its activities and carries out particular functions. Both help to standardize activities across the group and to transfer lessons to new members.
- **Organizational structure.** Because organizational structures define what and how group members interact, how specific activities or subunits within the group are managed, and responsibility relationships within the organization, they can provide a durable way to institutionalize some types of organizational knowledge.
- **Written and unwritten operating guidelines.** Manuals, recipes, and certain operations procedures specifically define the processes through which a group carries out tasks and therefore capture group knowledge in explicit form. Operating guidelines provide a repository of group knowledge that can be readily passed among group members.
- **External repositories.** Storing information outside a group—for example, on the Internet or with members of allied organizations—can provide an alternate strategy to ensure that key knowledge is preserved.

References

Argyris, C., and D. Schön, *Organizational Learning: A Theory of Action Perspective,* Reading, MA: Addison-Wesley, 1978.

___, *Organizational Learning II: Theory, Method and Practice*, Reading, MA: Addison-Wesley, 1996.

---

[12] It should also be noted that not all information sources provide both tacit and explicit knowledge. Thus, although a group might gain the explicit knowledge needed for a particular operation from a sympathetic source, it may have to seek the needed tacit knowledge elsewhere or develop it on its own.

Carley, K., "Organizational Learning and Personnel Turnover," *Organization Science,* Vol. 3, 1992, pp. 20–46.

Cyert, R. M., and J. G. March, *A Behavioral Theory of the Firm*, Englewood Cliffs, NJ: Prentice Hall, 1963.

Daft, R. L., and R. H. Lengal, "Organizational Information Requirements: Media Richness and Structural Design," *Management Science*, Vol. 32, 1986, pp. 554–571.

Dodgson, M., "Organizational Learning: A Review of Some Literature," *Organizational Studies*, Vol. 14, 1993, pp. 375–394.

Easterby-Smith, M., M. Crossan, and D. Nicolini, "Organizational Learning: Debates Past, Present and Future," *Journal of Management Studies,* Vol. 37, No. 6, September 2000.

Edmonson, Amy C., Ann B. Winslow, Richard M. J. Bohmer, and Gary P. Pisano, "Learning How and Learning What: Effects of Tacit and Codified Knowledge on Performance Improvement Following Technology Adoption," *Decision Sciences,* Vol. 34, No. 2, 2003, pp. 197–223.

Fiol, C. M., and M. A. Lyles, "Organizational Learning," *Academy of Management Review,* Vol. 10, 1985, pp. 803–813.

Garratt, R., *The Learning Organization*, London, UK: Fontana/Collins, 1987.

Gertler, Meric S., "Tacit Knowledge and the Economic Geography of Context or the Undefinable Tacitness of Being (There)," Nelson and Winter DRUID Summer Conference, Aalborg, Denmark, June 12–15, 2001.

Hardy, Cynthia, Nelson Phillips, and Thomas B. Lawrence, "Resources, Knowledge and Influence: The Organizational Effects of Interorganizational Collaboration," *Journal of Management Studies,* Vol. 40, No. 2, 2003, pp. 321–347.

Hedberg, B., "How Organizations Learn and Unlearn," in P. C. Nystrom and W. H. Starbuck (eds.), *Handbook of Organizational Design*, Oxford, UK: Oxford University Press, 1981, pp. 3–27.

Huber, G. P., "Organizational Learning: The Contributing Process and the Literatures," *Organizational Science*, Vol. 2, 1991, pp. 88–115.

Jones, K. K., "Competing to Learn in Japan," *McKinsey Quarterly*, Vol. 1, 1991, pp. 45–57.

Kim, D. H., "The Link Between Individual and Organizational Learning," *Sloan Management Review*, Fall 1993, pp. 37–50.

Lipshitz, R., M. Popper, and V. Friedman, "A Multifacet Model of Organizational Learning," *The Journal of Applied Behavioral Science*, Vol. 38, No. 1, March 2002.

Lutes, Chuck, "Al-Qaida in Action and Learning: A Systems Approach," 2001, available at http://www.au.af.mil/au/awc/awcgate/readings/al_qaida2.htm (last accessed October 21, 2004).

March, J. G., and J. P. Olsen, "The Uncertainty of the Past: Organizational Learning Under Ambiguity," *European Journal of Policy Review,* Vol. 3, No. 2, 1975, pp. 147–171.

McCormick, Gordon H., "Terrorist Decision Making," *Annual Review of Political Science,* Vol. 6, 2003, pp. 473–507.

McGill, M. E., and J. W. Slocum, Jr., "Unlearning the Organization," *Organization Dynamics*, Vol. 22, Autumn 1993, pp. 67–79.

Miller, D., "A Preliminary Topology of Organizational Learning: Synthesizing the Literature," *Journal of Management*, Vol. 22, No. 3, 1996, pp. 485–505.

Mowery, David C., Joanne B. Oxley, and Brian S. Silverman, "Strategic Alliances and Inter-firm Knowledge Transfer," *Strategic Management Journal,* Vol. 17, 1996, pp. 77–91.

Romme, G., and R. Dillen, "Mapping the Landscape of Organizational Learning," *European Management Journal*, Vol. 15, No. 1, 1997.

Shrivastava, P., "A Typology of Organizational Learning Systems," *Journal of Management Studies*, Vol. 20, 1983, pp. 7–28.